The Labrador Shooting Dog

By
Mike Gould

Copyright © 1998 by:

Clinetop Press

Post Office Box 95
Carbondale, Colorado 81623
970-963-0696 • 970-984-3801

ISBN #: 1-893740-01-3

Bill Tarrant
May 4, 1929–November 22, 1998
"He loved the dogs."

Foreword

Mike Gould is the most brilliant and innovative gun dog trainer in America today. He is sensitive, thoughtful, tireless, and humanely devoted. So in this book you'll learn successful non-stress, non-impact training. And the result? The best trained dog you'll ever have. And the happiest trainer you'll ever be.

Mike was a long time getting where he is. Which means he took in every snap-stanced, wanna-fight, dead-end-dog-disaster who ever shredded a carpet. Which further means, Mike learned how to train. For if he can train the worst, then the best is just dessert.

Mike eats a lot of dessert these days.

Join him as he tells you how he got where he is, where he came from, what happened, and, through it all, how to train your own dog to be a sure 'nuf gun dog that no field trial prospect can enter the field with.

For Mike's not into field trials nor test hunts. Nope. He's into shooting dogs. Join him now for the fun and the revelation of your life. Your dog will be mighty glad you did.

Bill Tarrant
The Dog House
Las Vegas, Nevada

Acknowledgements

A special thanks goes to Bruce Keep for his excellent black-and-white images of the training techniques illustrated in these pages. Except where otherwise noted, the black-and-white photos are his. The color portrait of Mike Gould on the back cover was taken by Bruce, also. Thanks for the good work.

We owe Ken McGraw a special thanks for his beautiful photography and for his patience in getting his images returned to him.

The design of this book was accomplished by Michael Bonds of Studio MB, Aspen, Colorado. Bland Nesbit of Nesbit Graphics was responsible for production. Thanks go to both of them for a beautiful book.

Thanks also go to Danny Watson, Jay Daniels, Jason Brown, Bob Gould, and Gary Ruppel for their loyalty and hard work.

Above all, we thank the Grand River dogs that grace these pages.

Dedication

This book is dedicated to Grand River Webster.

"Web" was, is, and will always be the greatest shooting dog I'll ever know. Throughout the pages of this book you will read of his heroics. From time to time I'll tell you of all the days in which he made the sun shine brighter. My respect for him personally is beyond description.

Training dogs is much like coaching baseball. A trainer needs to impress upon his students to be the best they can be and not worry about being the best player on the team. I love a dog who tries his best every single time out of the blocks. Every day he comes out working, hustling, eager to learn, with a smile on his face.

I can't remember a time in which Web disappointed me with a poor effort. I can't remember a poor attitude. I don't remember him failing.

He has worked with and around several thousand dogs and I've never seen him start a fight. I only remember one fight in his life and that was when he was jumped in the house by a young Chesapeake.

Web commanded respect and virtually every dog he came in contact with respected and admired him. He led by example and no one questioned his leadership.

Web was wonderfully built. I've never seen a Labrador with more grace or endurance. I never grew tired of watching him as he effortlessly flew across his ground like a thoroughbred racehorse. I would often sit on a rock or a log and watch him hunt a mountain park. I would crumble dried flowers between my fingers and drift. He took me away and allowed me to consider my life as I admired his work ethic.

Web worked in front of hundreds of wing shooters in seven states. He outshined movie stars, he outranked top military brass. He outlasted pro athletes and outguessed corporate genius. He would handle the large crowds at sports shows or dog demonstrations with the same relaxed attitude as the individual workouts we shared together.

Web led a dream life. He lived and trained on some of the most spectacular ranches in the country. He flushed in excess of a thousand game birds and retrieved a couple hundred before he was five months old. He could handle ice flows and 100-degree heat. He cruised the 14,000-ft. peaks of the Continental Divide and the thick mud of lowland swamps.

Web learned to handle most all of the upland game bird species and was always stellar on any kind of waterfowl. He loved all birds, but there was one species that stole his heart, and in the process, took mine, too.

It's really too bad that most bird hunters don't get a chance to appreciate blue grouse. They take you to the mountaintop during the most glamorous season of the year. They naturally draw you into the quakie forests and the seeping bottoms. They are, in my mind, the most misunderstood of all upland game bird species.

Web was a blue grouse master. I truly believe he found and flushed over five thousand. If ever there was a dog who knew more about blue grouse, my hat's off to him because I know how hard he had to work to get there.

The mountain ridges and parks are Web's kingdom and I don't know anyone who has seen him there who doubts it.

During times when I grew faint and wondered about my future, Web carried me and gave me the vision of success. When the vision seemed fleeting and unachievable, he would search for it while I rested and then lay it at my feet to provide inspiration when I awoke.

Web wasn't a field champion. Oh, we did a few trials and some hunt testing, but he always hated that stuff. He hated trickery and deception. He hated setups and unreal situations. He enjoyed a plane well above that of a field trial dog.

Follow me into this book and I'll tell you the way I see it. I'll give you cause to dream of the vision. I'll show you how to develop your own dog as you explore the natural world.

Field trial champion, ha! Let's do something really great. Let's build a Labrador shooting dog, and Web can lead the way. I hope someday you can say, as you look back upon your journey, "I have seen the vision of greatness. It was fashioned in the likeness of the legendary Grand River Webster."

Introduction

The purpose of this book is not to prepare you or your dog for tests or trials. There are many books that can help you greatly if you aspire to put a title or championship on your dog.

The AKC licensed trials, the AKC hunt tests, the HRC hunts, and the NAHRA hunting tests represent the standards by which most working Labradors are judged in America today. These trials and tests have contributed much to the development of the Labrador as the premier retrieving breed in the world. Most serious breeders look to these dogs for their foundation stock, and rightfully so, but only a very small percentage of the working Labs in this country ever compete in these tests. The Labrador breed is so popular that each year they are among the top in AKC registrations. The huge majority of the Labs in America are either pets or personal hunting dogs or both.

This book is designed to stir Lab owners to wonder. I hope bird hunters of all types will gain an understanding about their dogs that they might never have believed possible.

It's really too bad that Labs have been stuck with the "Retriever" moniker because they are capable of much more. They may be the most used and loved of all shooting dogs in the U.S.

It is my intention to enlighten the sporting public as to the true working qualities of this great breed.

I have no ax to grind with certain trainers, methodology, or breeds. I simply want to express a view that has become increasingly harder to suppress.

This book is written from my personal experiences while breeding, training, and handling Labradors over half my lifetime. I've worked with dogs for thousands of clients over the years, training all kinds of dogs, including many breeds of pointers, spaniels, and retrievers. In addition, I have done formal obedience on non-sporting breeds for the general public for over 15 years.

I have learned that all breeds can add to your overall knowledge of dogs. Tendencies, temperaments, and conformations of non-sporting breeds have helped a great deal in my effort to understand the criteria necessary in breeding quality working dogs.

In the pages in this book, I am going to ask you to move away from conventional wisdom for a time and to dream about your ideal shooting dog.

I will emphasize natural controls that all animals have to respond to as they learn to interface with each other. In the end I hope you will gain a new appreciation for the dogs, the birds, and the world they live in.

Table of Contents

Chapter One:

What the Heck is a Shooting Dog, Anyway?   21
Shooting dogs are pros
What we want

Chapter Two:

Birds   27
Birds hold all the secrets
To the mountains to learn
The sheep dogs
Catch and release hunting
Respect the birds
The lesson of the birds
Protect the privileges, Preserve the resources

Chapter Three

Habitat   37
Nature moves us
Search and rescue
What is habitat?
Judges are tricksters
Too much habitat?

continued on next page

Chapter Four

The World Above the Trial Ground 41

The big picture
Keeping score
Grouse from above
Educating judges
Straight is stupid
Digging 'em out and running 'em down
Splitting up
Field trials are the imitation
The games people play
The tail points the way...Up

Chapter Five

Breeding and Conformation 59

Winning ugly
Running smart
Movement/Locomotion
Thanks, Mr. Wehle
Running wild
Running is swimming
Balance—static and kinetic
Where's the center
The front assembly
Kinetics
Some builds will sink you
Lateral displacement
Elbows out, elbows in, built like that you'll never win
Cats and hares
Wide receivers
Croup
What coat to wear
Eyes
Ears
What we did

Chapter 6

Chapter Seven

Chapter Eight

Chapter Nine

Chapter Ten

continued on next page

Escape responses
Heel and sit
Stay and here
In transition
Sharing the good news
A look at the table

Chapter Eleven

Marking and Field Work

Steadiness and dependability
Dummies
Extra large-problems
Control first!
Don't turn your back
Sending rhythm
On the wind
Meander
Suction
Singles in chains
Walking singles
Doubles
The John Wayne syndrome
Relax with it
No
Water
Watch for fatigue

Chapter Twelve

Using Cover to Enhance Your Field Work

The bird isn't always there
Rocks are cover too
Terrain
The silver miner
Triples and quads
Use what's working
It's not hay until it's in the barn

Rambo
Make sure you're finished

Chapter Thirteen

Chapter Fourteen

Chapter Fifteen

continued on next page

Chapter Sixteen

Chapter Seventeen

Chapter One:

What the Heck is a Shooting Dog, Anyway?

W hat the heck is a shooting dog, anyway? If you asked a couple thousand bird hunters this question you would probably get at least several hundred different answers.

Each of us has our own vision of the perfect shooting dog. Hunters in different parts of the country require specific qualities in their respective dogs.

The term "shooting dog" has always been synonymous with pointing dogs and they certainly deserve it. Even though there has been an uprising of sorts about "pointing Labradors," there is much ground to gain before Lab enthusiasts can lay claim to equal rights with pointers.

Pointers are special in so many ways. Lab folks should stay with working Labs instead of worrying about comparison and competition. There are plenty of problems with the Lab breed that need to be hammered out without automatically assuming the "pointing instinct" is the absolute answer.

Besides that, Labs have been pointing forever, this is no new development. I know many trainers who have 50-year-old stories of Labs that pointed and I've had plenty who showed the pointing instinct.

If your Lab points, great. If he doesn't, great. If you want your Lab trained to point, this is no major feat. Most any good trainer can accomplish that for you.

I personally believe the pointing trait is irrelevant when considering Labradors.

The bottom line is "PRODUCTION." The dog that goes out and hits a lick every time out of the blocks is an inspiring student to work with. If he can find birds consistently, he is a true treasure.

Not all dogs can make it happen when birds are scarce. When you run a large string, say 15 or 20 dogs, you will see a new star emerge daily. There are some who produce so regularly they can become your hole card.

A dog like this can pull the fat out of the fire, he can save the day, and just like some athletes, he can make the rest of the team play harder.

One might think this is the best-bred, best-trained dog responding perfectly to his handler during the hunt, but I've never seen that. Many times the dog who brings the crowds to their feet is out there flying. He's running, hunting, searching, and checking every likely cover. A dog like this is relentless in his desire to find birds.

Lots of times he will seem out of control, but when the action gets heavy, he's in there helping out. It's a shame to handle a dog like this a lot. Give him the slack he needs and you won't be sorry.

A dog can never get to this level without tons of bird contact throughout his life, especially when he is young. Exposure to birds has to be the absolute priority in the early stages.

A dog who lays around the house or yard most of the year will never stand a chance in a bird finding contest with a true producer.

It doesn't matter if he's your dog or mine, it doesn't matter if he's good looking, it doesn't matter if he minds flawlessly, it doesn't matter if he's bred in the purple, he doesn't stand a ghost of a chance if you haven't shown him the birds.

There is no substitute for experience with birds. None.

On a guided hunt, where sportsmen pay the big bucks to hunt game birds, they are only impressed with the dog who produces.

These guys could care less how great the trainer or handler is. They are only temporarily impressed with the dog's pedigree or field trial accomplishments. They want to see the dog who can make it happen.

Some dogs acquire super handling skills and are capable of adjusting to their handler's slightest whim, but if they can't find birds on their own they are just about worthless as a shooting dog. About the only thing a dog like that can do is pick up after the shooting's over.

A dog who is controlled back and forth, in and out throughout his hunt spends much of his time worrying about his performance. He knows if he screws up there will be hell to pay. This is terribly fatiguing to a dog; it will adversely effect his endurance as well as his efficiency.

Just think about it. If your boss is leaning over your shoulder all day, looking for a mistake, you couldn't possibly be a happy, productive worker. This type of approach robs personal confidence from people, and, likewise, from working dogs.

A worker who is under scrutiny day in and day out will be afraid to be innovative and bold. A dog under scrutiny will be likewise affected. That's right, great shooting dogs are extremely innovative. If one thing's not working, they go to another until they get the job done.

A shooting dog must be in shape to run. If he is too fat or unhealthy, he will get the blame for quitting early, even if both of these problems are the fault of the handler.

A shooting dog must have endurance; he must be able to sustain his race over the course of the hunt. He must be a confident adventurer, willing to try something new. He might have to work on a dozen different species of upland game birds and all kinds of waterfowl during his lifetime.

He has to have intelligence and a smooth temperament, even though his owner doesn't. He will often have to travel great distances and share his quarters with other dogs or people.

I never liked dogs who were fighters, biters or run-off artists. Who needs them?

A shooting dog has to be content to curl up in his kennel and wait patiently for food or water while his owner is toasting his friends and making excuses.

He must fit into the family. Most Labs are an integral part of the family. The old saying, "A hunting dog has to be separated from the house and kept in his kennel as a working dog," has long been dispelled as ridiculous. The closer you become to your dog, the better your relationship gets. He will work much harder for someone he loves and knows intimately.

He has to learn to pull stickers and thorns himself, and sometimes play hurt. I've always admired a dog who will give you the effort even though he doesn't feel like it. A dog like this knows you are depending on him and he will come through if he can.

A shooting dog is a pro athlete. He works for a living and he'll stay late every day just for the fun of it. I've only known a few men in my life who showed the work ethic of a shooting dog. I've not known one you could trust more.

Bird hunting is a team sport. A good shooting dog must be a team player. There is always at least one dog and one hunter on the team, but most of the time there are other dogs and a steadily changing group of shooters.

Sometimes the dog will be carrying the ball out there, making things come together. Other times he will be playing back-up, working off his handler's side. He has to be willing to play where he's needed.

The same dog who needs to acquire the stamina and skills necessary to handle chukar along a canyon rim in September heat must learn about ice flows and river current. He must learn to lay under a magnum goose decoy or sit in a pit or blind.

While most pointers are resting up during the late winter and spring, Labradors are working on marks and blinds. The Labrador shooting dog is the consummate utility infielder. He can play any position on the field, and when he gets it together, will always be the MVP.

If you're the kind of guy who is basically lazy and out of shape, your dog will probably be also. He will be at a serious disadvantage when the season starts and so will you. Don't despair, you can effectively run your dog off horseback, with a vehicle, or by your side to get in shape. I'm not talking about hunting here. I'm talking about conditioning.

Go ahead and laugh when I talk about hunting Labs off

horseback, but it's an easy transition to make and it's extremely productive in big country.

If you don't like this kind of talk, then build a fire. But before you throw the book in, remember, we're not talking retrievers anymore. We're talking shooting dogs.

We want a dog who is smart and trainable, a good athlete with a nice attitude. A cattle rancher likes a horse with good "cow sense." We want a dog who is naturally "birdy." We like toughness tempered with reason, boldness without dominance.

We're looking for a dog we can develop into a top-notch shooting dog, a dog who can hunt any bird anywhere. Take him out day or night, on land or water and he'll hit the ground hunting, trying to produce birds.

If you're interested in this type of dog, then follow me. It's going to get fun. I must warn you, however, it's going to be awfully hard to look at the Labs with the same old eye. You will be wanting more, and more is what they have to offer.

If you didn't throw the book in the fire, why don't you poke it a few times and pour yourself a cup, because on the next page we will start a discussion about the birds. It can be no other way.

Chapter Two:
Birds

Shooting dogs, bird dogs, hunting dogs, gun dogs, retrievers, pointers, setters, spaniels, wing shooting, and sporting clay shooting all owe their very existence to game birds. Shotgun and shotshell manufactures and dealers are in business for one reason: to make shooting products available to bird hunters.

Sportsmen routinely travel abroad and cover virtually every inch of America searching for one kind of bird or another.

Millions of dollars are expended each year toward wing shooting, dogs, and clays. Bird hunting appeals to every class of humanity. Some have to save up for the hunting season, and others fly their private jets to destination resorts that cater to their every wish. Some camp out and tell their stories around campfires while others stay in lavishly decorated rooms with their names printed on the door. Some shoot their grandfather's old pump gun and some shoot "fowling pieces" that will burn up most of a hundred thousand dollars.

Wealthy sportsmen seem to gravitate toward wing shooting, like horse racing, as an extension of their affluence and of their overall understanding.

People who ordinarily wouldn't consider inviting me to dinner often treat me and other dog handlers like celebrities so we will handle special hunts for them. Most hunts are graded by how many birds are killed and to a lesser degree by the quality of the company and dog work.

An experienced handler can make things go pretty smooth for the shooters without them knowing about it. Some are very skillful at camouflaging problems as they occur within the hunt.

Although the various upland and waterfowl birds differ greatly in their respective needs, they have one common goal each and every day. They must find something to eat, find something to drink, and stay alive until tomorrow. Sounds relatively simple, doesn't it? All animals, even humans, face the same challenge but the humans take most of it for granted. Seldom will anyone list survival as one of his most pressing concerns.

When I first started training bird dogs, I soon learned the birds held all the secrets. If you want to get educated about the dogs, you have to start with the birds.

You can spend your entire life working dogs, you can read every dog training book ever written, and still, you will fall miserably short unless you expend as least an equal effort toward understanding the birds.

I have attended retriever training seminars where birds were scarcely even mentioned, much less the incredibly important factors of scenting and wind conditions.

In my opinion, the focus should be placed on the enormous value the birds represent rather than the number that are harvested. If sportsmen would place the highest value on the pursuit of game and the talent of the shooting dog, and a lesser value on birds taken, they would greatly enhance the quality of their hunts.

Every August, I take my training dogs to the grouse woods to learn. I used to think that I took them up there each year to expand their knowledge and to prepare them for things to come. Now I realize they take me up there every year to expand my knowledge and prepare me for things to come.

I have watched hundreds of young dogs go from clumsy puppies, playing with flowers and mormon crickets, to full-blown bird dogs slashing the parks to ribbons. I always take my string but many of my clients have asked me to start their dogs on birds because the dove, partridge and grouse seasons are due to start in September.

From time to time one of them would ask to accompany me for a day or two. The Colorado high country is really something at that time of year and just being up there is worth the ride.

A couple of large sheep ranchers share this range with us throughout the fall and sometimes we are treated to dog work provided by the sheepherders. I remember one time we were camped at the top of a mountain, along the edge of a slender meandering park. Gary Ruppel, a professional dog trainer and long-time friend, had his string up there and all together there were about 40 dogs staked out on our chain gangs. Through one end of the park we saw a Basque sheepherder bringing about a thousand head of sheep toward us. He had two border collies keeping things lined out but there were four kuvasz taking up positions at the perimeter for entirely different reasons. These dogs were there for protection only. One of them seemed to be in charge. He heard our dogs start to bark so he came to the front to check things out.

The kuvasz are legendary for their ferocity and they certainly look the part. They live with the sheep for their entire life and they don't have the luxury of grooming or primping. They are dirty white and sport long, shaggy hair. An adult will weigh in excess of 100 pounds and they are built to run. I know herders who have seen their kuvasz take half-grown deer in stride.

There we were, with 40 fired-up bird dogs, right in the path of a thousand sheep that were guarded by dogs that could take out a pack of coyotes without breaking a sweat. The herder was occasionally whistling softly, and if he was the slightest bit worried, he didn't show it. The park was only about 100 yards wide, and as they came nearer, the guard dogs set up a formation: one in front of the herd, one on our side, a third of the way back, the boss dog on our side, about in the middle, and the last one was bringing up the rear between the herd and us.

Now, we had some high-dollar dogs with us, so we decided to get a shotgun ready. We didn't want to mix it up with those dogs for sure, but we didn't know what to expect.

If that sheepherder looked our way, I didn't notice. He was

thinking about supper or whatever a sheepherder thinks about. Those dogs brought the herd right past us without a single move in our direction. As the border collies moved the last of the sheep past us, we looked at each other. "That was some dog work," Gary said. And so it was. Pretty darned impressive and no hollering or hand signals, just a few soft whistles that could have been some old Spanish ballad, for all we knew.

You can learn a lot from other dog men if you keep your eyes open. Later, the owner of those sheep told us that one of his collies brought 3,500 sheep across that mesa all by himself one day in a blinding snowstorm.

At first light the grouse are in the parks feeding, and because of that we try to be there also. We are not there to shoot birds, we're there to learn. Gradually, more and more of the training clientele made the effort to get up extra early so they could share a morning with their dog and others. I have never seen anyone come up there for even a single day that didn't include this experience among the finest things they had ever done in the outdoors.

On an average morning, we flush between 35 and 55 grouse over the dogs, and our guests can be back in town having breakfast by 10:30. This is some of the finest training you could imagine, and nothing gets shot. It's training like this that brings you to admire the birds and their environment.

It's a great training opportunity wrapped in spectacular scenery and nothing gets killed. We call it "catch and release hunting."

The birds deserve more respect than they get from hunters, and certainly more than they get from the dog game folks. As I have said, I sometimes provide the grounds for retriever trials. The tests are set up, the dogs run, the awards are given out, and, after it's all over, someone throws 250 dead birds in the dumpster and everyone leaves, satisfied that something good has been accomplished. I wonder?

I am ashamed to admit that in the past we have held driven

shoots and live pigeon shoots under the auspices of providing quality wing shooting for our members and guests. After the driven shoots, the shooters drive away, all with big smiles, leaving a small mountain of birds for us to process. I can't remember even one of them ever asking for a few birds to take home for supper. We would give away what we could, eat what we could, and the rest were thrown away.

Live pigeon shoots are best described as carnage, pure and simple. The concept is so publicly sensitive that the shooters who attend these shoots regularly are notified in an almost underground fashion. Huge wagers are placed during the pigeon shoots and thousands of dollars sometimes rest on a single shot or race. Dead pigeons are conveniently stashed to avoid offending the participants or onlookers, but wounded birds are soon forgotten as they are no longer in judgment.

After pigeon shoots, I have picked up wounded, suffering birds for days from an area maybe a half mile in circumference. Some of these birds finally succumb to their wounds and are found dead a great distance from where the competition was held. Again the birds are disposed of after the shoot en masse via the dumpster.

This type of competition is sport for the wealthy, but much damage is done to ethical hunters who wouldn't consider shooting in an event like this.

We, as hunters, are increasingly going to find ourselves in circumstances where we must define and defend our position. The possession of firearms is a right, but hunting is a privilege. Anti-hunters are fanatics for sure, but they are well funded and well-represented. We need to be smarter these days. We need to be more respectful toward the game we hunt.

I held those bird shoots to promote my sportsmen club business. I was caught up in the drive to be successful. Five minutes into a driven shoot, when you look to the sky and see beautiful rooster pheasants folding up by the dozen, you know you have made a dreadful mistake.

Live pigeon shoots should be outlawed and retriever trial committees should come up with a better plan for the disposal of their birds. Let's think about it together. The birds deserve more respect.

Anyone who has ever trained dogs for bird hunting knows that you must shoot birds to get where you need to be. A trainer who goes about his trade while remaining sensitive to the treatment he gives birds is generally a guy who has been around a lot of birds, and has developed a plan to be conservative.

I have listened as some retriever trainers brag about shooting live marks for the dogs every day. This might well be an advantage in training, but, in my opinion, it's a senseless waste of birds. This is sacrificing birds for the sport of trialing and usually has nothing to do with hunting.

I believe it is a very wise approach to show your dog birds every day, or as often as you can. This can be a tremendous aid in the development of your dog and the completion of the training process, but there is no real need in shooting birds every day.

Some trainers break wings or toes to get a bird to act a certain way. This is caused from a lack of knowledge as far as handling birds is concerned.

As I learned about game birds, I developed a great appreciation for them. Even pigeons are remarkable animals who are very interesting to study.

I have been involved with game bird incubation, brooding, breeding, and flight conditioning during the past 15 years. I have released over 100,000 birds on many different ranches and wildlife projects. While training, hunting, or guiding, I enjoy several thousand wild bird contacts each year. While each game bird species is unique, many lessons we learn from one may transfer easily to another.

I've found it worthwhile to study soil composition, annual precipitation, and the combinations of habitat in the area I'm going to hunt. These factors tell us much about what species of birds we could expect to see there and where they are.

It is definitely worth your time to study the normal wind patterns and directions before you get to your hunt location. Check the weather forecast and note the temperature in the early morning, at noontime, and especially for the last five hours of daylight.

Learn the birds' roosting habits and what they prefer for food. Some birds don't require a live water source, but most do. Where is it? Find out when they feed and when they go for water.

I am convinced most game birds have a pre-arranged escape plan they favor when danger presents itself. Learn about the specific flight patterns of the different species.

For example, some grouse and most partridge love the downhill escape. They have a convex flight pattern that makes shooters follow through in a downward motion if they are to connect. This is an extremely unnatural movement for most shooters. Chukar and huns will taunt you as they leave and they will almost beg you to come after them as they chuckle from their escape cover. After the covey rise, a close inspection will sometimes find a bird or two holding tight. These are unlucky souls who are in charge of calling back or relocating the covey.

Pheasant are basically flat flyers once they get above the cover. Their frequent escapes are aided by their shape. Pheasant are a streamlined bird that comes to a sharp point at the tip of the tail feathers. They sometimes resemble an arrow in reverse. If a shooter is not careful, he will let his eyes slip along the body of the bird and he will shoot at the tail. The shape of the bird causes us to look at the tail. This is the main reason that many roosters are hit in the butt, and many more are missed completely. It takes lots of practice during the heat of battle before a shooter can swing out to the head and not be fooled by this beautiful bird's tail.

Some birds rely on quick course adjustments to keep shooters guessing. Dove, snipe, woodcock and teal are among this group. When dove are on a brisk wind, they don't need much help in the form of darting moves. Their speed alone can be frightening.

Waterfowl, especially geese, also have a built-in defense mechanism. When a goose flies within shotgun range, the shooter's eye is drawn to that big chest. This is the spot on a goose where he has the most protection. Many geese are saved by the thick down and overlapping chest feathers when shot patterns center them there. If a wing doesn't get broken, the bird may escape unharmed. Unfortunately, what happens in a lot of cases is that the goose takes a few pellets into the breast and abdomen. This goose may die miles away from where it was shot with the possibility of recovery by the hunter almost nil. The nationwide requirement to shoot only steel shot for waterfowl has greatly increased the incidence of this tragedy.

The goose gives us a good target in the form of his outstretched neck and head, but again, it takes some thought to swing out in front of the bird. If you hit him in the neck or head, you will probably kill him, but the real value of taking this shot is in the reduction of wounded birds. If you miss his head, he stands a lot better chance of escaping unwounded.

Quail use the surprise of the covey rise to confuse hunters. The sound of the covey breaking into flight will cause shooters to choose poorly on the first barrel and a sense of urgency will empty the second barrel as the hunter watches the covey swarm and disappear.

Some species of quail will use sheer numbers to keep hunters out of their shooting rhythm. If a hundred quail are buzzing and crossing and leaving in every direction, it's hard to decide which one you like. On many occasions I've watched and waited for the shots as the covey escaped, and as I glanced back to the shooters, I realized they were handcuffed by indecision.

Many species of upland birds are adept at putting brush and trees between you and them soon after the flush. It is a wise plan to get where you can see and swing, if you can, before the flush.

Most upland birds are good runners. Usually they won't hesitate in putting distance between themselves and danger.

Pheasant are the undisputed king of all runners, especially late in the season. Chukar can outrun a mediocre dog uphill and often prefer running to flying.

Several species of quail come with good running gear, and in favorable ground conditions they can really stretch it out.

Running birds are the hardest to handle for the bird dog. If the birds are moving, a smart handler will change tactics and try to run them into holding cover or pinch them between natural barriers. Don't be fooled into chasing running birds without some plan to stop them. They will run clear out of the country.

Each feather on the bird's body is unique. There are the same number of feathers on one side of the bird as there are on the other. Both wings carry the same feathers for the same reasons. Careful study of the body style, feather configuration, wing shape, and tail can really help a person understand more about how the bird flies.

I've found this knowledge to be particularly helpful in correcting shooting problems that sometimes occur. The more you know about the birds you intend to hunt, the easier it is to answer questions about gauges, chokes, shot sizes, and shotshell loads.

If you go into the hunting field hollering, whistling, and causing commotion, you're not going to surprise anybody out there. Instead, think about the birds you are hunting and what their tendencies are. Don't be handling your dog all the time, trying to tell him where to hunt. Try to relax and always have a plan B.

Your dog is a master conservation tool. He will find, then help you to recover most of the birds that you shoot. Remember, you are a team. You can bet that he is putting data in his bank every time he goes out, so you do the same. Make a priority of educating yourself regarding game birds. Learn to respect and admire them. Make every effort to find wounded birds. Try to resist the temptation to take those shots that hold little chance of bringing the bird to bag. Never stop asking questions, never stop learning, never stop caring, and never stop thinking of ways to preserve this sport.

PROTECT THE PRIVILEGE
PRESERVE THE RESOURCE.

Chapter Three:
Habitat

*I*n all of the training books and videos that I have seen, seldom is the word "habitat" used, much less explained. Habitat is a general term meaning the natural environment of an organism. Because all of the animals represent different organisms, the habitat requirements of each are unique to that animal.

If you are interested in learning about shooting dogs, you must pass through a cycle where you learn as much as you can about habitat and natural controls.

There are many natural controls and rules that we must play by when we go afield, whether we like it or not. The sooner a person recognizes the effects these things have on us and our dogs, the sooner he will understand the finer points of handling a shooting dog.

There are many factors in play as a dog goes bounding across a field or when he enters water. Obstacles and natural forces tend to move him and push him one way or another. Some pull, some push, some beckon, and some repel. Various scents cause some of it, specific water characteristics cause some of it, soils cause some of it, habitat causes some of it, lateral displacement and fatigue cause some of it, and even predators cause some of it.

When a trainer tries to enforce his will on the dog when he really doesn't grasp the situation himself, he is putting his dog at an angle to the rest of the world. The trainer must be alert and sensitive to all that is going on around him, not just what the dog happens to be doing at the time. The trainer needs to try to understand what the dog is doing, why he is doing it, and what he did immediately preceding it.

If a trainer sees behavior that he doesn't like, he should first question himself, "What did I do to cause that?" You won't believe how many times human handling errors cause the unwanted behavior.

I truly believe that the dogs are our "window into this natural world." When we study the dog and the way he interfaces with the rest of the natural world, we can greatly enhance our ability to understand our environment.

Why is it that many times the birds seem to disappear about 11 a.m., and then suddenly reappear after 3:30 p.m.? Why is it so hard to find birds in an east wind? Fishermen have a saying, "When the wind is from the east, fishing is least." The same holds true with bird hunting. An east wind is mysterious.

One time I asked a member of the SARDOC (Search and Rescue Dogs of Colorado) team to come to our ranch and give a seminar to all of our trainers. It was so fascinating to hear about the properties of scent and how the rescue dogs worked to figure it all out. She taught us that as we move, we are shedding thousands of scent cells.

These particles of scent fall toward the ground but are subject to wind currents as they swirl and eddy just like water does as it moves. The scent falls on foliage, rocks, and soil. Some of it catches high in the air on branches or leaves of shrubs, and some of it catches on grass.

When the scent hits the ground, it is alive. For a time the scent intensifies, and is actually stronger a few minutes after it falls than it is immediately.

Much can be learned about dog handling from the trainers who work with search dogs. We tested the dogs with tracks over rough terrain, water, and heavy cover. The experienced search dogs that were brought to the seminar worked these trails with little or no difficulty.

An important factor that goes overlooked by everyone is temperature. When the air temperature is 80 degrees at waist level, the temperature on the ground is way over 100.

This translates to problems with our bird dogs because it is much hotter down where the dog is breathing than it is where we are breathing. I have seen dogs get rubber legs and collapse because I didn't fully understand the conditions under which they were working. This situation is magnified when the dog is working in dense green vegetation. I believe this type of cover robs the dog of oxygen, and when the temperature is high, he gets lightheaded and dizzy. In addition, dense green cover is usually synonymous with poor scenting conditions.

A bird's body scent usually originates on or near the ground and moves away from the bird in a cone shape. This scent is also susceptible to changes in wind direction, strength, and current. The scent cone is affected by relative humidity and air temperature. I have heard many hunters exclaim, "I want my dog's nose right down on the ground where it can do some good!"

That's OK if we are talking about foot scent or trail scent, but a dog who keeps his nose down on the ground during his hunting pattern is working at a distinct disadvantage. I have always liked a dog who hunts with a high head so he can contact the scent cone farther away from the birds. Once he gets a nose full of bird scent, he then can manipulate the scent any way he wants to find the bird.

A study of bird dogs as they come in contact with scent will tell the handler which direction the bird is and how far away it is.

When the bird is flushed, it will fly to escape cover and many times stick like glue. After a bird flies for a time and then lands, it is "air washed" and if it holds still, it will provide very little scent for the dog to work with. It is often extremely hard to find singles after a long flight, even if you see exactly where they landed.

Where the birds feed, where they nest, where they roost, and where they escape danger depend on principles of habitat. The more we work with bird dogs, the more we understand about the type of habitat certain game birds prefer. We learn colors and shapes of cover that the birds choose to abide in. Roosting and nesting cover is much denser than feeding habitat, for instance. The escape cover is usually higher profile brushy areas, like windbreaks, fencerows, or creek bottoms. Partridge-like birds love to use topography to conceal their escape and sometimes land on benches or the back side of ridges. A lot of the upland game bird species love to catch that early morning sun so it is a good plan to try and determine where that is going to be.

Quail actually need about 40 percent open ground (or bare ground) in areas where they feed. This, combined with their tendency to use the edges of woody cover for feeding, give us good clues as to where to drop the dogs in the morning.

Row crops are favorite feeding grounds for many game birds and the weedy areas adjacent to these various crops are prime roosting locations. Shortly after daylight, the birds will move out into the row crops to feed. Some row crops will hold birds, some will not. It's worth your time to find out which is which.

Roosting cover will reveal definite roosting sites. Concentrations of bird droppings will tell you how many birds are using this cover, and how long they have been doing so. Game birds are very gregarious and habitual by nature, so use this to your benefit.

The more trips to the hunting field, the more you will absorb about the habitat scenario. Each trip will add data to your evolving bank of statistics. The same thing is happening to your dog. He will remember certain places that he has hunted before and, more importantly, he will remember where he was successful in finding birds. Dogs have great memories concerning these things and they are capable of selecting the birdy areas of a given hunting field. The dog starts hunting where he thinks birds may be, instead of quartering mindlessly back and forth in front of the handler. This is called "hunting objectives" and every decent shooting dog must acquire these skills.

Chapter Four:

The World Above the Trial Ground

We have to remember, finding the birds is our goal out there and learning to read the habitat is one of the most important disciplines that we will study in the development of a shooting dog.

Retriever field trial judges developed an art form of tricking the competing dogs by using particular habitat conditions to entice them into making mistakes. This is most often seen in open or amateur all-age stakes. They will deliberately scent points of land so when the working dogs swim past the point, they will be drawn to that point. They use diversions and wind direction to confuse the dog and in order for the dog to complete a complicated test, he has to close his eyes to his natural tendencies. Basically, the licensed retriever trials are a training contest, not a field trial to test a dog's talents.

A few years back I allowed an AKC retriever club to use my training facility to hold a licensed field trial. I was training up in the high country at the time, but decided I had better come back down to the ranch to keep my dogs quiet and be available if they needed me. It wasn't likely that they would need me as most of them considered me just about totally ignorant regarding quality dog work. Oh, they were nice, but in a condescending sort of way.

I had been working on the water and riparian development on this ranch for about four years and the training conditions for retrievers were fantastic. That's actually the only reason the trial committee wanted to hold the trial there. The lakes were specially built to train retrievers while they also served as a wonderful trout fishery.

The lakes were situated in an oxbow of the Roaring Fork River and the riparian habitat was designed to attract and hold many types of wildlife, both game and non-game.

I was working back in the White River National Forest a couple of hours from home, so I had to get going early that day in order to load up the dogs and break camp. I was already tired when I arrived at the ranch, and I must admit, I was feeling out of place as I rolled by all of those expensive dog trucks. I came into the ranch from the back entrance so I could check the bird pen and see where they were setting up the tests. As I arrived at the lower lakes, I saw one of the judges clearing an area for the "line," or the place where the dogs would start from. He held a buck saw in one hand and a six-inch aspen tree in the other. He had just removed the tree from the shoreline—I guess it was in his way. If you had to buy that tree, it would cost more than two hundred dollars.

He was a big guy. I recognized him from other trials I had attended. His shirt was drenched with sweat and he reached for his handkerchief to daub his forehead and face. "Hi, Mike," he hollered. "Man, it's hot this morning!" I waved back at him and drove on, though I couldn't believe what I had just seen. What the heck, the tree was already cut down. What could I say that would make any difference? When the field trial committee came out to the ranch the week prior to the trial, they had cut down about half an acre of cattails and some red willows. I didn't feel too bad about that, but losing the tree really torqued me.

I put my dogs away and went into the house to check in and clean up some. The trial was underway, so I grabbed a big glass of iced tea and a lawn chair and headed over to the area they had selected for the gallery. I found a place to put my chair where I could watch the dogs run and mind my own business. Shortly afterward, a lady came up and sat next to me. She was an amateur handler but had put several titles on her dogs. "Boy, this is a beautiful place, a dog trainer's paradise," she said. "You know, there is only one problem—there are too many rocks around the lakes."

"This is a river bottom, ma'am," I replied, "not much here but a little top soil and a lot of rocks. You couldn't haul them all out of here if you tried." She looked at me kind of funny and went about her way. Not five minutes later, another of the trialers stopped by and extended his hand.

"Great location you have here, really pretty water, but you need to get rid of some of the vegetation around the lakes. The handlers can't see the dogs work on those long blinds."

"It's taken four years to establish that riparian habitat," I told him, while I was still shaking his hand. I know he figured I was hopelessly lost and probably didn't understand what he meant. Just after he walked away, guess who showed up to take his seat? The judge who had cut down the aspen tree.

"I'm judging the amateur all-age," he said.

"That's what I heard, how's it going for you?"

"Oh, all right, I think, but I just thought I would come over and talk to you about your place here. I have never seen a finer facility, Mike, but there are far too many trees in this river bottom. They really interfere with the visuals."

"I noticed there is one fewer over there," I said, as I pointed toward the spot on the bank where the aspen used to be.

"That one was right in the way, so I got rid of the damn thing for you," he laughed. I took a big drink of tea and looked out toward the mountains.

Let's see now; get rid of the rocks, get rid of the vegetation, and get rid of the trees. All we have to do then is get rid of the water and we could park cars. We could build houses; we could add pavement or concrete. I folded up my chair and walked to the kennel. I couldn't stop shaking my head. My point is this: Quality habitat is worth studying. Don't take it out if you don't understand it. Learn about it. You might be able to run a field trial in an area void of natural habitat, but you will never do any good for your shooting dog out there.

As you and your dog go through the training process together, you must continually try to educate yourself regarding habitat. If you are genuinely interested in the species of grasses, forbs, legumes, shrubs, and trees that the birds call home, you will dramatically improve your understanding of your environment as well.

Please, consider this: the earth is a living, breathing thing. A river or lake is a living, breathing thing. The land has a heartbeat —look for it. Each species of animal plays a role in this great puzzle. Find out what it is. Your dog can teach you much of this if you give him the chance. The more you study the natural controls that all animals work under, including you, the more you will embrace the team concept of bird hunting. You and your dog are a team and practice will make you win—together.

The world above the trial ground

I'm not going to spend a whole lot of time pounding field trials or tests. We have more important things to cover. I do, however, have some ideas and observations I would like to express.

Field trials are supposed to be designed to simulate a day in the hunting field. Retriever trials have taken this concept and warped it into an unrecognizable, unconventional, and unrealistic form.

The trial is based on retrieving skills alone. Anyone who has ever taken a dog to the hunting field knows retrieving is only necessary if you find birds and then only if you're successful with your shooting.

The trial assumes you have already located the birds, flushed them, and in many instances, already shot them. Picking up the birds is the tail end of the sequence. A whole lot has to happen before any of this is possible.

How can we honestly call a field trial retriever a "Field Champion," if his only duty is to pick up dead birds?

Retrieving skills are vital to a Labrador for sure, but they're only part of the whole, some of the picture. I'm trying to separate retrievers from shooting dogs. I've seen brilliant pieces of dog work put down by dogs without any formal schooling regarding retrieving.

When we spend the morning in a duck blind, there are many moving parts. A seasoned waterfowl dog has to keep track of people moving, talking, calling, and shooting. He has to be aware of the heron crossing in front of the blind as well as the numerous non-game birds who love the early morning. He must realize that every bird who gets shot at doesn't get hit. As a matter of fact, many more are not hit than those who are.

When waterfowl are shot in front of a retriever, often the birds fall from a flight of birds. Some are falling, some are cutting and swerving, some are pulling up with all they've got. The sky is alive with birds trying desperately to escape.

Wounded birds catch their balance and try to stay aloft as long as they can. This takes them beyond the field of vision and sorely tests the marking ability of the dog and the hunter.

This is a very exciting, noisy, busy scene. Anything can happen and usually does.

This same situation is depicted at a retriever trial with one bird being presented at a time with no distractions if possible. If a person even coughs, or laughs loudly in the gallery, it will bring a scowl from the judges and competitors.

Trial marks are thrown into the air by a bird boy wearing a white jacket, and as the bird barely clears the thrower's hand, it is pulverized by two gunners who are also wearing white jackets. Sometimes the bird is blown apart or driven through the air twisting and spinning from two high-powered duck loads discharged at close range.

In the hunting field, this is a situation all hunters would like to avoid. The only reason the judges have the bird shot in that fashion is to make sure it doesn't move when it hits the ground. Blasting a bird like that does no one any good. Not the hunter, not the dog—no one.

In the real world of bird hunting, crippled birds that sail out of sight before falling present those tough blind retrieves. In the case of waterfowl or pheasant, some of these retrieves can be extreme. More importantly, though, these birds are thinking about one thing: "Stay alive."

They swim, run, dive and fight to get to a place where they think it is safe to hide. Some pheasant feel the only safety is running for it. I have seen wounded birds travel amazing distances in an effort to survive.

An experienced dog learns to track and trail. He must be willing to check under every bush, if he must, to find that bird. This work is solo once the dog gets on the scent trail of a cripple. He doesn't need any more hand signals or whistles from his handler. All he needs now is patience and trust.

When the dog does find the bird his problems may not be over. While a field trial retriever casually heads for home after picking up the fall, a shooting dog still may have work to do and challenges to sort out.

A goose or a rooster pheasant can be formidable when wounded. Sometimes the dog will encounter other birds along the way, before or after the pickup. What about other animals? The variables are many and there is no pre-set way of handling them.

In a field trial, a blind retrieve is carried to a certain location, again by the bird boy, and placed where every other blind for that test will be put. They use one of the birds that was previously shot for the marks so it is not only dead, it's been shot twice and retrieved once. A piece of survey ribbon is tied to a nearby branch or weed so the handler knows exactly where the bird is laying.

Licensed trials are the granddaddy of all retriever trials in this country. In order to get separation, the tests got harder and harder. To complete the tests, the training methodology got tougher and tougher. That is why I say, "Today, a licensed retriever trial is more of a training contest than it is a field trial for dogs." These trials are supposed to replicate hunting situations, but do they, really?

If you're going to try to put FC or AFC titles on your dog, then you must face some facts.

You will have to spend about 85 percent of your training time running ultra-long marks and blinds. This will go on throughout the dog's trialing life. Almost all of the birds your dog has the opportunity to see will either be thrown in the air by someone or planted in a blind location by someone.

You will have to dedicate thousands of hours preparing your dog to handle trick tests. You will demand absolute compliance with every command. You will expose yourself and your dog to political situations that you won't believe.

Let's see now, if you spend all that time training for 350-yard marks and 400-yard blinds, that ought to really pay off in the hunting field, right? If you spend all that time trying to anticipate some judge's ideas of a "meaty test," you should be in fat city in bird season, right?

I've guided more than 950 hunts in seven states. I figure the average number of shooters to be around three per hunt. This translates to more than 2850 bird hunters I have personally guided.

We have hunted chukar, Hungarian partridge, three different species of quail, pheasant, grouse of all types, snipe, dove, and various waterfowl birds.

I have seen shooters who range all the way from Olympic champions down to young boys and girls on their first bird hunt.

Get this! It is rare, I mean very rare, that you see a wounded bird give you a 400-yard retrieve. It sometimes does happen, and occasionally you will have to pick up a blind in excess of a quarter mile.

How about trick tests? In nature and on actual bird hunts, there are no trick tests. None. For sure there are tricky situations that require special skills for the hunter and the dog, but nature is not nearly as hard to deal with as a judge with an attitude.

My questions are these: If a field trial is supposed to duplicate a normal day in the field, then why do the trainers have to spend nearly all of their training time preparing for tests that almost never happen in the field?

Why are the only birds used in trials birds that are presented by people? This is another example of something that never occurs naturally.

During a field trial, the working dog is seldom out of his handler's sight. The dog is not permitted to work on his own.

The field trial dog must be under constant supervision.

In the hunting field, the dog has to know he may work out of sight of his handler if need be. He needs to relax with it and go about his business without worrying about getting disciplined. Lots of times the handler will need to let the dog work things out on his own, because for one reason or another, he can't.

Last grouse season I got a break in the action here at the kennel so I decided to take Web hunting...just the two of us. He spends most of his time helping me train young dogs and working for hunters on paid trips. We seldom get a chance to get out by ourselves, and when we do it's special.

I train grouse dogs in the high country of Colorado, up near the Flattops Wilderness area. Most of this country is made up of huge parks filled with fescue grass and various forbs. The parks sprawl for miles across the Flattops until they drop suddenly into almost vertical canyons. The footing is terrific for the dogs and you can fully appreciate most of the alpine flower species Colorado has to offer.

Blue grouse spend their entire summer in or near the parks and up until the onset of cold weather they feed out there all day long. It's an unbelievable place to work dogs and you can see five mountain ranges at the same time.

The reason I brought you here is to give you an example of a Labrador shooting dog plying his trade in the most unorthodox fashion. This dog is so experienced with grouse it would be absurd to boss him around and tell him where to hunt.

I have spent many years training on those mountains so I have a good idea where the birds go for escape cover, and I try to be there.

I was walking out across a park that is shaped like a giant bowl. I was crossing the center of the bowl and Web was working far above me, out of sight. I had my shotgun broken open and was carrying it over my shoulder as I glanced up the hill from time to time.

I noticed a man walking across the park. He seemed to be walking toward me so I decided to wait for him. I wondered what he wanted. I think he was one of the cave explorers from the canyons of Deep Creek.

They found an 8,000-year-old human skeleton in there last year. They figure he was an Indian. His remains were turned over to the Southern Ute tribe for burial.

The man walked up to me and said, "Hi, my name is Jim. What are you doing out here anyway?" I introduced myself and told him that I was grouse hunting.

"Grouse hunting? I used to hunt grouse back home in Michigan, but we always used a bird dog."

"I am using a bird dog," I replied.

He looked at me then looked around for a minute. "Where?"

"He's above us, working on that bench up there. He knows where there is a covey of blues just out from that little patch of quakies. By the way, how's the cave hunting going for you guys?"

"How'd you know I was headin' to the cave?"

"You don't see many people walking around out here with a headlight on their forehead, at least in broad daylight."

We both laughed.

About that time a brace of blue grouse appeared on the horizon. We watched them beat then sail, beat then sail, and when they came over us, you could have nearly killed them with a tennis racquet. Thirty seconds later, three more came into view and sailed over our heads.

"See, I told you," I grinned. Just about then Web showed on the hill above us. He stopped and sat down. He hadn't heard any shots, so I know he thought I had screwed up the plan.

"Get back in there," I told him, and he disappeared again up the hill. "Those grouse have been doing that as long as I can remember, Jim."

"Well, I'll be damned."

"My dog is going to get mad if I don't get involved here, Jim. Good to meet you." We shook hands and off I went. Jim walked away and I never saw him again, but I'm sure his idea of grouse hunting was changed forever. I've never known anyone who has seen it who didn't try to do it.

There's not a field trial Lab in the world who can manipulate birds like that. Web's been doing it routinely for years.

You will never see field trial judges set up on a fast-moving river, especially if it is cold and flowing ice. You will never see a setup where the dogs have to handle large tracts of cattails or standing corn. If you run your retriever in field trials of any kind, you will never encounter deep ravines or draws filled with every kind of thorns you can imagine. You won't have to handle mesquite thickets or jumping cactus or entire pastures of dense prickly pear. You won't be required to send your dog off of rockslides, avalanche chutes or lava beds. You won't have to worry about the whereabouts of your dog because if you can't see him for any length of time, you are probably out of judgment. At a field trial you most likely will not run into wild hogs or javelina. You won't generally be concerned about rattlesnakes. Your chances of jumping deer, elk, coyotes, rabbits and any other animals are minimal. During a field trial the competing dogs work for short periods—usually less than half an hour—rest up, and wait for their turn to run again.

If you hunt waterfowl, you sooner or later have to work your dog in icy conditions and extreme winter weather. You will not have the luxury of conveniently placed marks and blinds. You have to take 'em as you get 'em.

If you hunt the Midwest for pheasant or quail you have to learn to handle large grain fields and cattail draws if you want to find the birds. In mountain country deep gorges and ravines are part of the deal. If you want to find the birds you have to hunt the tough country. Ptarmigan and blue grouse are going to be on top, I don't care which state you hunt in, and if you've ever wondered where the Rocky Mountains got their name, one ptarmigan hunt will give you the answer.

Valley and Gambel's quail take you into dry, harsh terrain, always brushy and sometimes a good ways from the water. There are millions of bobwhites in south Texas and they are easy to find if you have a dog who won't shrink as he faces that spiny wilderness.

As the Continental Divide strings out through Colorado it leaves behind more peaks that exceed 14,000 feet than any other state or province in the world. If you plan to hunt ptarmigan, you need to be prepared to witness some of the most spectacular and hair-raising retrieves you could imagine. I always found it odd that people have great difficulty walking at that elevation but the dogs seem to run as efficiently as they do down below. Why doesn't the thin air affect them as it does us? Why can they sustain their race while our legs fail us in short order?

We were working dogs above Lincoln Lake one morning when a friend of mine shot a ptarmigan who fell just over the cornice and skidded to a stop 60 yards below in the middle of an avalanche chute. He had an old golden retriever whose best years were behind her and I had a gassed-up Lab who was running in master stakes.

When we got over to the edge, we saw what looked like a fairly routine 60-yard blind with the only problem being the very steep slope and loose rocky footing. I decided to send my dog for the retrieve. I lined him up and sent him with the usual "back." He didn't move. I carouseled him about and lined him up again and this time I barked, "BACK." Twice more I tried to send my dog with the only reaction from him being a dart sideways on my last attempt. My friend George was sitting on a rock enjoying the morning, waiting for me to pick the bird up so we could go on. His dog, Dandy, was leaning against his leg, her head on his lap and her eyes closed to the glaring sun.

"Let me see if Dandy will get it," George said as he creaked to his feet.

"Go ahead," I was already trying to figure out how I was going to get that bird once Dandy failed. Dandy wasn't a trial dog, she was a hunting dog. She didn't understand formal lining and handling; all she understood was hunting and retrieving. George called her over to the edge, waved his hand to her and said, "fetch it up, girl!" Dandy scooted up to see where she was going and mince footed over to the right about 20 feet, traversed to the left 20 feet, back to the right and once again to the left, snatched up the limp ptarmigan and came back the same way. My souped-up sport model was totally frustrated and embarrassed by the whole affair. Dogs are smart! Sometimes a lot smarter than we are. It was downright dangerous to try the middle of that chute and the dog knew it from the get-go. He hated to disappoint me, but he hated the idea of dying more.

Long, clean lines are impressive, and straight lines to blinds are always the goal. But, on some occasions, straight is stupid.

In a field trial, my dog would have been laughed off the line because he refused to go. He would have undergone tremendous pressure in training the next week to avoid a recurring problem. In the hunting field, the old golden fetched the bird, saved the day and maybe my life.

When a guy's pride gets injured like that he can do crazy things. I might have tried the chute myself and found out too late why the dog wouldn't go. Your dog can't learn these skills running long marks and blinds every day. You cannot train your dog to be a superior shooting dog. Only the laws of nature can do that.

One of Web's daughters is the best dog I've ever known at finding wounded or dead birds. She works on quail hunts down south for Danny Duff.

Field trials demand steadiness, and there is some merit to this, but there are many instances where a steady dog is a lost bird.

One year Danny and I worked together for a couple of months in south Texas. We saw over 11,500 quail in covey rises and another 2,500 or so as singles or fragments of coveys. Our pointers had over 3,000 points and 2,000 backs. The hunters shot 1,182 quail.

We were both working Labradors off our side to pick up and dig birds out of the thick stuff. Danny's dog, Colie, picked up more than 450 birds on those hunts. She would regularly trail wounded quail for unbelievable distances and on many occasions she would dig them out from the maze of rodent tunnels that are beneath the large prickly pear.

I have seen her dig and scratch until her entire body was in the hole before she made one final lunge and came out with the bird.

One day, on the King Ranch, Colie made a retrieve on a single wing-tipped quail that I still can't believe.

The pasture we were hunting in was almost totally covered with prickly pear. We couldn't even walk without jogging and meandering in and out of the pear. It was about impossible to maintain a straight line of travel no matter how hard you tried. I think it's safe to say there is not a denser stand of pear in all of south Texas. We were trying to get to the other side so we could hunt some grass along the edge of the pasture when a single bobwhite flushed and flew about five or six feet off the ground in a beeline for the brush. We saw a leg come down at the shot but the quail kept on for over two hundred yards before he settled into the pear. Colie was there at the flush and gave chase after the wounded bird. She ran at full speed, winding her way through a jungle of stickers, and somehow kept an eye on that bird. She reached the fall moments after the quail landed and scooped him up like it was no big deal. Just to run through that pear was a major feat in itself, but to keep track of a wounded bird and actually mark the fall while navigating and adjusting to the terrain was miraculous. In a field trial, Colie would have been disqualified for breaking. We gave her a standing ovation.

Sometimes splitting up works best. I remember one time while grouse hunting on the Flattops we were just about finished for the day and only needed a couple more birds to fill up.

I thought of a covey of blues that liked to hang out around a small seeping spring just over the hill from where we were hunting. I mentioned it to the hunters but none really looked interested in walking up and over another hill. I decided to check it out myself and I promised to meet up with them in a short while. I knew this covey pretty well and I figured I could find them if they were home.

Soon after Web and I reached the spring he started getting birdy. He and I both realized the covey was definitely there, so I blew my whistle for him to sit. He sat down and looked at me but kept glancing back over his shoulder toward the breaks of Deep Creek. I said "Stay," and took off back toward the hunters.

I walked about a half mile before I caught up with them to tell them of what we had found. One of the hunters found the energy to come along, so we hustled back up the hill to where Web was waiting. When we came over the top, we saw Web still sitting where I had left him but he was starting to get pretty antsy.

I hollered "Stay!" again while the hunter and I caught our breath. We walked up to Web and I told him to "Get in there." Web jumped into a patch of sagebrush and seven grouse blasted out of there, hooking it for the rim. The hunter knocked one down with the first barrel but was just behind the second. Two more grouse lifted from the cover as he quickly reloaded and a pretty down-and-away shot collected one more bird. We were both excited about our successful plan. We chuckled together as we headed back toward the other hunters.

The significant thing about this story is this: Web sat within 15 yards of a covey of grouse, that he knew was there, for at least thirty minutes while I went to get a shooter and returned. He could not see me for most of that time but he knew what I wanted. Your dog cannot learn those skills at a field trial. You develop that kind of rapport by working together and depending on each other. This is teamwork, and this, folks, is a Labrador shooting dog.

This is very important: in the United States it is common to consider field trial dogs superior to shooting dogs. Many dogs are washed out of trial camps and given gun dog status.

"He will never make it as a trial dog, but he will be OK for a gun dog." That's so ridiculous, it isn't even funny. A quality shooting dog can do anything a field trial dog can do and much more.

There is a world above those trial grounds and you can find out about it if you stay with me.

Remember, field trials are the imitation. It's not the other way around. The HRC and the NAHRA were formed in an effort to bring some sort of reality to the game of retriever trials. The concept was noble and needed, but in my opinion the good was short-lived. The testing started out with the best intentions but soon got tangled up in the usual politics and trickery. Some of the tests you will see at these hunts are so bizarre you won't believe them.

I have never seen a meaningful "bird finding test" in a retriever trial or test. I used to run dogs in some of the hunt tests and we had local clubs for a while. I also ran dogs in the AKC hunt tests every now and then. The only reason the AKC started doing hunting retriever testing was because of all the pressure brought on by the other two bodies. The AKC tests are the best of the three, I think, but usually turn into watered-down field trials.

I always enjoyed the people I met at those hunting retriever tests. A lot more single dog owners are involved and you don't see that many pros running numerous dogs. I really like dog people of all types and I especially like hanging around back where I can see dogs loosening up. I can check out the type of dog that other people prefer.

After reading the last few pages on the trials, you might get the idea I don't like the people. Not true. I have made some great friends while attending trials and tests. I have a lot of respect for the professionals who train dogs for testing clientele. If you want to see someone work for a living, just catch a pro retriever trainer working each day. Those guys and girls earn every dime they make. If you think it's glamorous hauling a team of dogs around the country, then you should try it sometime.

Their clientele is the hardest to please and they are always away from home and family. I couldn't go out and set up training tests every day and work each dog, one by one, on these time-consuming drills. It's more of a waste of time to me but I certainly understand why they do it. They do it to win the game, for that's all trials are. If you want to win, you have to play the game.

I decided a long time ago I didn't enjoy the game or training for them. I do truly enjoy training shooting dogs and working them every chance I get.

An all-age shooting dog still has to learn complicated handling skills and must be able to do difficult marks and blinds on land and water. I work on these things about 25 percent of the time and spend the other 75 percent on the field and bird work.

I don't like to work on trick tests or deception. I like to train for confidence and I believe the more deception you throw at your dog, the more you undermine confidence.

The guy who owns a Lab for personal enjoyment and for hunting owes a heck of a lot to the field trial game because they have developed the bloodlines that work. If Labrador breeding was left up to the show breeders, the breed would be just about useless, to my way of thinking. A good show specimen is nice to look at but the athletic ability is inferior.

I remember one day a training friend of mine and I were working a dog on the force table while an AKC hunting test was going on over on the other side of the ranch.

A lady drove up, got out and walked over to us. She looked so nice. She's a pretty girl to start with and she had just returned from a dog show upvalley. She said she was curious about force breaking and wondered if she could watch for a while. She also competed in hunting tests and was quite good at it. Her husband and she are about as dedicated as anyone you will meet and they are always friendly. I'll bet they judge or compete nearly every weekend during the trial season.

We talked about the table method of force retrieving and I was carefully outlining what I considered to be the important aspects of it.

She said a friend of hers had just bought Bill Tarrant's new book, *"Training the Hunting Retriever."* In that book, Bill described in detail what he considered to be ideal functional conformation. On the same page with his description, there was a picture of a Labrador being posed to illustrate what Bill was talking about.

She said, "Isn't that ridiculous. That dog's tail is sticking almost straight up in the air. He wouldn't stand a chance in a dog show."

Because I liked her so much, I didn't say too much, but I did take the time to tell her it was my dog in the picture and I was standing behind him to show his conformation.

I went on to tell her, "That dog has the best functional conformation I've ever seen on a Labrador. He has superb movement and I've never seen a Lab with more endurance."

Bill Tarrant knows what he's talking about when he's talking dogs and I hope someday he gets the credit he deserves for the contribution he has made. You see, Bill not only studies Labs, he loves all dogs—big, little, short or tall. He knows how a dog is supposed to be built, he knows when he sees it, and he's been trying to tell the sporting dog public about quality working conformation for as long as I've known him.

In this book, we are talking about the Labrador shooting dog. Although there is a lot we may glean from the field trial breeders, I believe they have overlooked many critical items of criteria. If we are to explore the values of functional conformation and bird-finding ability, we must be willing to look to other breeds and even other species for our answers.

Let's move on. Let's study breeding for a time so we can decide what our dog should look like and how he should move.

Chapter Five:
Breeding and Conformation

*B*reeding dogs is not a mathematical or scientific endeavor. You simply can't use some theory of "a plus b" or "b plus c." That's not to say one can't get significant benefit from study of other breeding programs and other breeds.

We have already established some critical criteria that we want to see in our ideal Labrador shooting dog. The single most important factor is intelligence.

I believe the best bird finders are the smartest dogs, everything else being equal. I have seen some

Two examples of great conformation

pitiful specimens who turned out to be great bird dogs because they were very smart. A dog like this is like a street-wise kid. He learns every trick, every back alley. He learns how to get away with murder and seldom gets caught.

One such dog I remember was a pointer who was working on a string in south Texas. He had very little training and what he had didn't show. He was one of about 20 pointers who several handlers were using and sharing on the vast expanse of the King Ranch and several other ranches. If you lined up 500 pointers and started picking from best to worst, you would probably pick him about last. He wasn't much to look at and had several bad traits that made him special to handle. He wouldn't come to you at all. The only reason he ever came in to the truck was to get a drink. If you could grab him then, you could go ahead and load him up. He wouldn't back another pointer, and he tried to steal any point he could. He wouldn't retrieve, and when he did pick up a dead bird, you would have to tell the hunters, "Watch that dog, watch that dog!"

After he carried the bird for a while, he would spit it out and go about his business. At that time you would have to send the pickup dog to retrieve the second-hand bird.

I couldn't say he had horrible pointing style, but it was best described as ugly. He would lay down with his tail kind of curled to one side and sometimes he would scoot around the covey like a cornerback trying to cover a wide receiver one-on-one. Sometimes he would slam into the covey, and if they didn't flush, he would quickly spin and retreat a few yards where he would establish one of his prettier points. Every now and then he could be seen, off in the distance, standing tall as if to show us he could if he really wanted to.

Each day he would spend a substantial portion of his hunt AWOL. I can remember looking for him forever out in that thick brush country. I remember thinking of leaving him out there, that the frustration just wasn't worth it.

He didn't ride well with other dogs. He was a little surly, especially around males. He didn't like to eat with other dogs and he was a messy fellow. You know, some dogs are real clean. They always keep their kennel spotless except for maybe one corner where you can scoop each days' leavings. Some dogs love to walk or even roll in their own fecal matter. He was one of those. Some days it would take him a half an hour of running to finally scrape off the last of the crust.

If all that wasn't enough, he had a little kink in his tail, about four inches from the end. I always wondered if someone did that on purpose after one of his stunts. I know I felt like it on several occasions. I'm glad he wasn't mine, because if he was, I would have shelled him out long before I realized his tremendous talent.

OK, for all intents and purposes, this dog was worthless, a waste of dog food. By all standard of measurement he had no redeeming qualities, right?

Now, now, now, not so fast there, folks. As Paul Harvey says, "This is the rest of the story."

In south Texas, a dog has to develop a running gait that will take him where he wants to go, but not to the grave. Lots of young pointers will tear into that country with all they've got until they realize air can get scarce even that close to sea level. On a fairly warm day, say 60 degrees, with a high percentage of relative humidity, a dog can outrun his legs and lungs in less than 20 minutes. I know a handler who has lost several nice dogs to heat, only because he couldn't shut them down.

When you see a dog go down because of a combination of heat and humidity, you have to act fast to save his life. When you first get to him his throat is opening so wide, it seems like you could throw a softball through it on each breath. Dogs who have run down there for a while learn to pace themselves to keep from overdoing it.

This dog was one of those. He could stay out there and hunt for as long as he wanted, even on a warm day. He had a long stride that came and went in an easy rhythm. He both ate up ground and conserved energy. These are qualities that we want to see in our dog, remember?

Because he was such a rebel, he spent long stints on his own. He wasn't bothered by the handler's whistle, or honking horns, or even attempts to fake him out by firing shots. He did, however, know that water was on the truck, and if he wanted to get it when he needed it, he had to keep within some proximity of the hunting vehicle.

I honestly believe that if there was more live water out there, he would have gone out one day and never come back until he had found every quail on the over 800,000 acres of the King Ranch.

This dog was smart. He was a born hunter, a natural bird dog. Because of all his faults, he had the time and the opportunity to learn everything possible about finding quail. In this part of the country there are literally millions of bobwhite quail. I'm sure he saw most of them from time to time. He learned to be a quail specialist. This dog could make it happen. This dog was a bona fide bird finder. Again, this is an important factor in the overall make-up of our shooting dog.

Even though he had other limiting habits, this guy would handle his birds, and when the action got heavy, he would come in to help. When the shooting started, all of the sudden you wouldn't have to look for him anymore. He was right in there showing his stuff.

He would stay handy, even in tight country, and seemed to know when things were pretty much in control. He then left his bracemate to pick up the pieces as he struck out for greener pastures and another covey.

I have always tried to keep a running record of the hunts that I guide. Even in training, I like to know which dog is finding the birds and how many birds each dog finds. I keep track of covey finds, single finds, backs and retrieves. I estimate the number of birds per covey and record the number of coveys found each day.

Over a stretch of trips to the field, it's an easy thing to see which dogs are erratic and undependable, and which ones are the true producers.

One winter in Texas, I had the opportunity to work more than 40 hunts with this specific string of dogs. This maniac we have been cussing and discussing was by far the most productive over the long haul. This incorrigible cur found the most birds on a full 75 percent of the hunts.

This means he found them in the heat, in the rain, in the morning, and in the evening. He found them when cover was plentiful and he went out and found them when the cover was overgrazed and sparse. In short, this wild man was a bird dog and he earned my undying respect and admiration.

Each morning we were to meet our hunters at the gate of the specific pasture that we intended to hunt that day. Unfortunately, too many hunters measure the quality of the hunt by how many birds are actually killed.

No matter what kind of weather or how good the bird population is in this pasture, these guys want to shoot birds.

I can't tell you how good it feels to have a dog along who can save the day. If you can put up with him, he will make you look like a star. We would always brace him with a dog who was easy to control, so we only had to worry about keeping track of him instead of two.

I remember one lady's comment as she walked up behind a malformed, scrunched-up point, "That's the ugliest dog on point I've ever seen."

To that a grinning dog handler said, "Yeah, but do you recall how many times that dog's been ugly today?"

That dog handler was Bud Daniels of Monticello, Arkansas. He has seen plenty of dogs come and go in his life and he has guided hundreds of quail hunts. Bud knows the value of a bone-headed bird dog who knows where quail live.

OK, so we're looking for a smart dog to fit into our plans, but I think we need one a heck of a lot more trainable. We need a dog who wants to please and wants to work with us. Trainability won't hamper his birdiness or his ability to make the "A" team, so let's go for one who's honest and willing to handle.

The old pointer proves that looks aren't everything, but I can assure you, endurance is. No matter how smart your dog is, if he is burned out after 15 minutes, he just won't make the show.

A large percentage of Labradors are hardly capable of sustaining a race over half an hour in good conditions, much less when things get tough.

Many hunters are satisfied with a plodding, panting Lab who shuffles back and forth in front and couldn't care less what was over the hill. Most Lab owners shouldn't worry about how big their dog runs first thing in the morning cause his build probably won't allow him to keep it up long. For the most part, these dogs aren't coming in because they want to. It's just that they aren't built to run.

In my opinion, this problem is intensified by the old myth that a Lab should always stay within gun range. I don't think breeders ever thought about a dog that could go out there and run with his head up, covering a maximum area, hunting objectives and working on his own.

Stay with me on this. After it's all over, if you want you can still throw the book in the fire, but I'll bet you won't.

There are lots of factors that have to work together to achieve endurance for our dog and for a while we will explore them. This is a study of movement and locomotion.

Let's load up 25 Labs and go to the field. It really doesn't matter where we go. All of the dogs will be running over the same ground, but let's pick an area with sparse cover and no fences.

I like to do this in wide open country where I can see the dogs no matter how far and wide they go.

OK, let's cut them loose and let them fly, no whistles, no hollering, no arm waving. For this experiment, we don't care which way they go or how fast they run. At first they will wrestle and play, spin and growl. Gradually, they will line out and start running. All we're going to do is walk along behind them and take notes.

There is no need in bringing a dog along who is fat or unhealthy. He would just take up space and still not shed any light on the situation.

All of the dogs seem to have speed and power from the get-go, but soon we will start to see signs of fatigue. When a dog is noticeably tiring, we will pick him up, give him a drink, and put him away. One by one they will succumb because of the energy they are exerting, both mental and physical. One by one we give them a drink and put them up.

After a time we will be down to the last two or three dogs. As they run, it's a good idea to visually study their conformation and their movement.

Now we load all of the dogs up and drive down the road to the nearest working water. Again, let them all out to swim and cool off. This is just to relax them for the ride home.

If we do this several times, we can gain an appreciation for the dogs who show the best endurance of the group. If we do this with the top three of our first group running with an entirely different group, then we can compare. If the same dogs consistently show to be at the top regardless of the rest of the group, then it is smart to take a good look at their build. How are they put together? How does their height compare to the length of their bodies? How long is their neck? What shape are their feet? What kind of angulation is in the front shoulder assembly, and in the back assembly? In short, how are these dogs put together?

I have always been interested in the pointing breeds and because of that I have a string of pointers around all the time. I did the same kind of experiment with the pointers and what I

Classroom study of conformation

65

saw was informative, to say the least.

I found my interest in the pointing breeds moving toward the English pointers because of their legendary endurance and bird-finding ability. I read about famous pointer strains and breeding programs. This is where I stumbled onto the best dog breeder in the world.

Robert Wehle's pointer program is celebrating its 60th anniversary this year. Elhew pointers are the absolute epitome of the term "shooting dog."

I will work on my Lab program for as long as I live, I suppose, but I will never be without a few Elhew pointers in my string. I have 10 of them at this time. Bob Wehle told me one time, "If a guy works on a breeding program long enough, the dogs will start to resemble the man." Sound weird?

Not if you've ever met him. He is one of the most distinctive men I have ever met in my life. He talks in low tones and carries himself with class and dignity. He loves his dogs so much and each time he addresses one or touches it, the dog just melts into his hands. His shooting dogs are covered in nearly every book or magazine you pick up.

I think he is a fierce competitor, but he shows the long-range insight and courage to keep at his task, to fulfill his criteria. His dogs are so graceful and wonderful to work with. They look at you with eyes that care about you and how you're feeling. They make great friends.

Elhew pointers are built to run and are easy to handle. These are true bird dogs.

I'd like to see some of those pointing Lab advocates run in this kind of company. They would spend most of the time looking at their feet. They would realize that just because an animal shows a tendency to stop before it pounces on a bird, it still doesn't have the right to lay equal claim to this hallowed ground.

Within the Elhew program I found the qualities that I needed to bring to my program. I'm not talking about breeding black pointers here, folks. I'm talking about decent conformation, solid temperament and bird-finding ability.

I found myself watching wild animals to learn more about efficiency in movement. Evolution has preserved the best builds of the various species, so I was eager to learn about the specific factors that give animals, like elk, the ability to move across unbelievably rough terrain for 30 miles in one night. Time and time again, I watched the elk glide in that effortless lope of theirs.

I studied coyotes running across an open park through a couple of inches of snow and then went out and measured the tracks and saw the straight line of travel.

I was raised in mule deer country. The bouncing gait of mule deer provides much information about angulation and balance. The shock that is absorbed by the bounding deer on each jump is astounding.

I learned that some animals depend on a burst of speed but lack endurance. I learned that it's all a tradeoff—give here, take there. If you want endurance, you have to sacrifice some speed out of the hole. If you want sprinters' speed, you have to give up some endurance. You can't have it all.

The same rules of physics apply equally to the thoroughbred racehorse and the ground squirrel.

I've already established some of the most important criteria in our ideal shooting dog, but what about swimming? Some Lab breeders have told me, "OK, so your dogs are showing more endurance, but it takes a wider body and bigger feet to do the best job in the water."

Well, I tested this, too. I found out the dog who was built best to run was also built best to swim. If wide bodies were more efficient in the water, they would build racing boats shaped like rowboats instead of splinters. The wider body style displaces more water than a leaner dog. This uses up more energy and causes fatigue. Big feet require more energy per stroke in the water and I can think of no advantage whatsoever they bring to our ideal dog.

I know a hunting club operator back in the Midwest who loved to hold what he called "duck races." He would wing clip a duck and set him free on a large pond. He would challenge his hunting dog clientele to catch the duck if they could.

The competitors were a mix of pointers, retrievers, and spaniels. At the starting signal, the dogs were all released to chase the duck out across the water.

When one of the dogs got too close, the duck would flap wildly and skim well out in front with the canine pack working like mad to close the gap. After a certain time limit had expired, the dog closest to the duck was declared the winner.

One might think the retrievers had the definite advantage, but he told me the German shorthaired pointers were the fastest swimmers overall. That makes a lot of sense to me now, but it had me shaking my head back then.

During an amateur all-age stake at a retriever trial, I was taken by the smooth speed of a young flatcoat retriever in the water. He didn't win but certainly got me out of my seat to follow him and his handler back to their truck. He was fairly tall, lean and muscular. To this day, I have not seen a flatcoat that remotely resembled him.

Water aptitude is very important to our shooting dog. We want a dog who loves the water. Everyone likes that bold entry, but it's not critical as long as we have good water in our dog. I favor dogs who are crazy about water because I feel they take to the difficult water training situations more easily. This type of dog is less likely to be intimidated by strong currents of ice. Long water work demands patience and perseverance, so it's to our advantage if our dog is relaxed out there.

OK, what difference does it make if our dog is balanced or not? Many trainers I have talked to don't really care if their Labs are balanced. They like a good marker with a trainable temperament.

If we were just using our Labs for retrieving, then I can see the point—who cares how they are built? Well, I think it makes a major difference, because we are using them for every duty that a shooting dog can come across. Why settle for a dog who is built poorly? Why not aspire to the athlete who carries all of the great marking and retrieving talents with him as he takes us where

Labs have never been allowed.

I believe a proper front assembly is critical to our success so let's start with the part of our dog that can come apart the easiest.

As we look to our criterion, we need to realize most Labs are "weight forward." Because of a short neck, a heavy head, and large front shoulders, the front ends on these dogs take a tremendous beating.

The shoulder blade assembly and the pastern act as the shock absorbers on our dog. The front is also responsible for lifting the front weight of the dog prior to each stride. If the dog is heavy out front, this causes a great deal of energy to be used, especially during the fast gaits. It's like the wild animals we talked about–if you go for speed, you sacrifice stamina.

The center of gravity on most Labs is such that it puts weight forward and increases speed. Many of the Labs that we hunt over have a good burst of speed, and when they flatten out in a full-blown sprint, they get low to the ground. Short, powerful legs contribute to this situation. We also see many of these dogs with a modified hare foot. Again, this aids in getting that early speed.

What's wrong with this? Nothing, really, if all you want is a retriever, but if we want our dogs to run in extended workouts, we must look to making them more comfortable with it.

We are seeking balance, so let's try to identify what that is. Balance comes in two types: "static," or standing, and "kinetic," or moving. We can achieve static balance in our dogs by tending to things like proper leg structure and angulation. It's like a kitchen table: if one of the legs is leaning even slightly, the table is unsteady. If one of the legs is shorter than the other three, the table is hopelessly rickety.

Let's start from the shoulder blades. These blades should be laid back, say somewhere between 60 and 45 degrees. This gives the dog a nice cushion to soften each jolt that comes up through his front legs on each stride, whether walking or running.

When viewing the dog standing, from the side, you should be able to drop a line perpendicular to the ground, that will pass through the center of the shoulder blade on down to the center of the pad. Ideally, the carpal, or knee, joint should be slightly behind this line so the angle from the carpal to the center of the pad will again aid in shock absorption and a smooth ride.

We can't put up with a leg that drops straight from the center of the shoulder blade and down through the pad without offering these cushions at the blade and the pastern. A leg of this type is called a "post leg," or a "straight leg," and affords no shock-absorbing qualities at all.

Now, let's look at the leg from the front. Again, you should be able to draw a straight line from the center of the shoulder blade on down to the center of the pad. This line gives you the chance to see any problems like bowed legs or feet turning in or out.

Our dog is much like a bicycle. You know how hard it is to ride a bike very slowly; you have to keep turning the front wheel back and forth to maintain your balance. It's hard to keep your feet up on the pedals without touching the ground for stability. As you gain speed, this presents less and less of a problem until finally you can sail along, pumping away, with your hands off of the handlebars completely.

This is kinetic balance at work. When the dog increases speed, his feet move closer and closer toward the center until he is single tracking, just like the bike. This is when the dog is in kinetic balance.

Remember the coyote running through the snow? The tracks are nearly in a straight line. A fox is so balanced, you could snap a chalk line along his tracks and it would touch them all.

Because we are looking to get those feet to the center at speed, we have to look at lengthening the leg some. We hope that will occur above the carpal joint along the forearm.

It's important that we keep our sloping pastern, so we don't want any additional length below it.

If you really want to check your dog's kinetic balance, you can do that easiest as you watch him swim. First, you have to find some clear water to work him in. Around my place, the lakes, creeks, and rivers are clear most of the year with the exception of run-off season. I have always felt sorry for trainers who have to work in muddy ponds or rivers. Water is water, but I think it's much prettier when it's clear.

Remember when we loaded up all the Labs and took them to the field to evaluate their running style and endurance? You can do the same in the water. Actually, it's a little easier to determine your dog's balance while he's swimming. I like to take a large group of Labs to the water so they stay fired up while I measure their natural balance.

When a dog is swimming at full speed, his feet should converge to the centerline just like when he is running. As you throw marks out into the water for the dogs to retrieve, you can move up and down the bank to position yourself directly in front of each dog individually. As the dog swims to you, you can see his feet and legs beneath the water's surface.

I once read an article written by a well-known dog columnist and was astonished by his complete ignorance concerning the swimming mechanics of a dog. He declared, "Dogs only swim with their front legs. The rear legs drag along without offering any support to the swimming effort, thus the term 'dog paddling.'"

Some dogs swim with only their front feet, but most dogs swim with all fours. Dogs who swim with only the front assembly are slow swimmers and are not very mobile when it comes to turning in the water or changing directions.

When the dog is swimming directly toward you his front feet should naturally "cup" to the centerline of his body. If the front feet are pulled to outside on the power stroke, the dog's head and body will wiggle from side to side corresponding with each stroke. This dog will look like he is hinged in the middle as he swims, especially if he is competing with other dogs and is trying to swim as fast as he can. The poor guy will be far behind when the other dogs reach the marks. Again, not because he didn't have enough heart or desire, he was stuck with an inferior build.

I remember a Lab who came in for training early one summer. He belonged to one of the best clients I ever had. I trained several dogs for this fellow and sold him three. I considered him a friend and I really thought the feeling was mutual. He bought this new dog from a breeder I knew in Iowa. He was about a year old, sired by a field champion and had great breeding top and bottom. This client of mine was a big bird hunter for sure, but lived for waterfowl. He bought all the right equipment, leased private land, maintained a duck hunting club, and regularly drove in excess of three hours to be in his blind at dawn.

I was very disappointed in this dog from the get-go because he had a terrible temperament for a dog bred like he was. He had a sorry attitude towards training and honestly wasn't all that bright.

We got through our obedience after a time, but it was on our fun walks together where I first noticed his undoing.

I routinely took the working dogs around the lakes to let them swim and tear around with each other. It's not all that unusual to see young Labs break the water with their front feet for a time while they are getting the bugs worked out of their swimming technique. Sometimes this problem hangs on until they finally learn to plane out and put their heads down. It's hard for a dog to lower his head while his front feet are splashing water in his face. He tries to hold his head as high as he can to get out of the splash and all he ends up doing is making the dilemma worse. As he lifts his head, his feet come further out of the water and his body becomes vertical, like a half-filled pop bottle floating around.

To make matters more hopeless, there is no way the dog can either motivate or navigate. A dog in this situation becomes frightened and can be permanently scarred emotionally if it drags on.

I like to keep a watchful eye on the dog. I prefer him to work it out on his own if possible. I throw a large rubber dummy within easy reach. If he will just try to pick it up he will unconsciously lean toward it, and as he lowers his head to grab it, his butt comes up. The extra weight in his mouth will help to keep his head down and he will start making progress toward the shore.

If the dog won't pick up the dummy, I like to wade out into the water and support his body until he relaxes enough to swim on his own. It's not much different than teaching a young kid to swim.

Understand he is afraid, let him relax, then support him until he feels comfortable in the water.

Take your time. There is lots of water work ahead and how you handle his water introduction is critical. Some folks think all Labs swim naturally, but I assure you, many of them need assistance when they first get started.

Back to my point—as I took this training dog around the lake he seemed confident and bold. He dashed along the bank and leaped off the dike to retrieve a dummy I had tossed out. I have seen thousands of Labs swim, but never had I seen a dog with swimming style like him. His front legs were frantically working but they seemed to be working for separate dogs. One would go one way and the other would go the opposite. He wouldn't quit. He kept trying to get that dummy. The dummy was only about 20 feet off shore, but I'm reasonably certain a full 10 minutes elapsed before he snatched up the dummy and unbelievably hauled it to land. He was exhausted, but not smart enough to realize he had nearly died out there. He grabbed the dummy and chewed and growled as he sprinted up and down the bank.

I wanted to confirm what I had just witnessed, but wasn't about to throw another dummy in the lake for him. I took him to the river where I knew he could get out if he got into trouble. I threw a dummy out in a back eddy, and, just like the last time, he flew into the air on a mission to bring it back. Unfortunately, just like last time, he nearly drowned.

After I put the dog in his kennel, I walked to the house and thought a long time before I dialed the owner's number. He heard what I said but he didn't believe me. Even after he came to the ranch and saw for himself, he doubted whether or not we should take him out of training. He instructed me to go ahead with his force breaking and his formal marks. I reluctantly agreed.

Throughout the following few months, I would occasionally take the dog to the water hoping for the problem to dissipate. I saw no progress. I again asked the owner to reconsider and I told him I would help him with a replacement dog. He told me to start him on lining and casting. After another couple of months I was able to send him out into the water for a blind only as long as I kept them within 50 yards. He would beat and thrash and struggle out and back every time.

Hunting season thankfully came around and he was sent home. I didn't hear a word for some time but was not surprised when the call came in late December. The owner called me every name in the book and accused me of taking his money without working his dog. He told me I had never prepared his dog for water work even though I kept him apprised of the dog's progress during the training.

He described an incident which had happened that morning on the Colorado River. Five degrees above zero, flowing ice, 50 yards of open water to a small island, and the raging Colorado beyond. A duck was shot and landed somewhere in the vicinity of the island but the dog didn't mark it. The owner tried to send the dog numerous times without success.

This owner is not a bonehead, he's a good guy, he's a good hunter and he loves his dogs. He tried to look past a physical problem that totally compromised his dog's balance. He tried to look the other way and hoped I could fix it through training. He blamed me and the breeder and hasn't spoken a word to me since.

Please take a long look at your dog's balance when running and swimming. Please understand, this factor alone can nullify a super training program. We need to know how far he can swim. If he's in shape, he can swim as far as he can jog—no kidding.

Many of the water drills we will do later in training will exceed 1000 yards. A dog who is built right can do them without showing fatigue or fear. When the dog is struggling with his swimming style, sooner or later, fear will become an obstacle.

Lateral displacement

Lateral displacement is a force that inflicts itself equally upon all of us. As we study the dynamics of locomotion we have to examine this very real issue. I have continually emphasized the body style that we prefer in our shooting dog, and I do that because of the physically limiting effects of lateral displacement.

As all animals move, they have to respond to the force of

gravity. All animals move from side to side laterally as they travel forward. If we are looking to efficiency, we must understand, the more the animal moves from side to side, the more energy it burns in the effort to maintain the gait.

We have established the need for our dog to move in the straightest, flattest line to get optimum endurance, so here is where we will bury, once and for all, the old blocky Lab build.

For example, if our Lab has a wide, short body he will experience more "roll" as he moves and he will continually have to combat extreme lateral displacement during all gaits.

I once read of an experiment you should try. Pick up a five-pound sack of sugar or something similar. You can hold anything of weight in your hands and gain a real appreciation for lateral displacement.

If you hold the weight against your chest firmly, you can run across the lawn or downtown for that matter without tiring much. Now hold the same weight with your arms outstretched and run.

That little five-pound sack of sugar has you weaving all over the place, doesn't it? It's hard to run very far that way without falling down.

The force you are feeling is lateral displacement. Now you see why we want to keep it limited so our dog can stay out there and run for extended periods. It's hard for a dog to cover as much ground as possible while he's expending most of his energy just to keep his body going straight. Incidentally, the same holds true in the water. Straight, level and smooth. That's the rule whether you're wet or dry.

One of the greatest Labradors I've ever known was a prime example of the limiting effects of excessive lateral displacement. He belonged to Kenny McGraw, a friend of mine who had trained with me for several years. Together we picked him out of a super litter to work as a professional guiding dog. I have never seen a Lab with more spring and his speed out of the hole was frightening.

I remember hunting with him in an apple orchard one day. The orchard was fenced with woven wire about eight feet tall to keep the deer out. Maybe he winded a bird or heard one or whatever, but anyway, for some reason he tried to jump that fence. He didn't make it, but the notion he thought he could was unbelievable. Besides that, he didn't miss by much.

This dog was beautiful and had a warm temperament. He was tenacious at this game and trained with the best. "Then what's the problem?" you might ask, "He sounds like the perfect dog." Well, he came pretty close and I would take them all like him, with one exception.

He was what I call a "wiggler." At any gait, he would sort of bend in the middle, like he was hinged. You see this problem in a lot of dogs.

This particular dog was such a great athlete, he was able to conceal the effect of this wiggling motion for the most part.

His drive and determination held you spellbound although he was burning gas like a fuel dragster.

This spectacular Labrador possessed the best spring of any Lab I've seen. I'm convinced he could've jumped over the bed of a full-size pickup. He achieved not only height, but good distance with each bound.

He would bounce straight in the air and look you in the eye before landing equally on all fours. He spent so much energy going from side to side and up and down it was hard to keep the whole thing going for long.

Kenny trained with me for years and had been around enough dogs to know of the problem. In the field this Lab was "all world" for about 20 minutes, but when fatigue came calling he was frustrated.

Please understand, I'm not complaining. Just having the opportunity to train with that dog was an honor, to say the least. What I'm saying is, lateral displacement is a severely limiting force and you must learn to deal with it.

Gravity and lateral displacement are dark forces that vow to rob our dog of his speed, agility, and endurance. Learn to recognize the effects. Keep your eyes open. It will help immensely in your training program.

If a dog moves out in the elbow, he will likely turn his front feet in to achieve balance. If he moves in at the elbow, he will have the tendency to turn his feet out. Nature always compensates one thing for another.

If a dog has a structural problem in the rear, there is equal compensation in the front assembly.

A good example of this is the basset hound or the dachshund. The front legs are bowed dramatically, so the feet compensate by turning out equally to accomplish static balance.

Basic principles of physics teach us that for every action, there is an equal and opposite reaction. It's not only true with dogs, it's true throughout our environment.

One of the most successful yellow field trial Labs in the history of the breed is also one who was bred numerous times in an attempt to perpetuate his fine qualities. I'm not going to name him because I would get so much criticism for what I'm about to say.

This dog achieved just about every goal you could possibly set for a trial dog and for several years you couldn't pick up a *"Retriever Field Trial News"* without seeing several breedings sired by this dog. I was interested in him because I had no access to a truly fine yellow breeder and I subsequently acquired a number of his offspring, both male and female. I trained about a dozen young dogs who were owned by others who were also sired by the same dog.

I didn't see one single good front on any of these dogs and when I had the chance to watch him run on my grounds, the answers were obvious. He threw a "pinched front" in all of his puppies. This caused the elbows to hold tight to the rib cage and the front legs were thrown out on each step. Kinetic balance suffered and none of these dogs had beans for endurance. A half an hour in the field would bring them walking at heel, not because they wanted to, but because they had to.

This dog not only possessed this terrible fault, he threw it in the majority of his get. Because he was so successful in the trial game, most breeders overlooked this. I can just imagine the pressure that was put on by trainers when these pups started lagging. Now this was a great marking dog with a trainable temperament.

I have one fine young Lab in the kennel now who is super in nearly every regard. He is extremely birdy and is wonderful to handle. He comes from the middle of our breeding program here and we had high hopes for him as a breeder, but he is decidedly out at the elbows. Because of this problem, his feet turn in to provide balance, and his elbows get very sore after a long hunt. Again, this is an extremely good marker with a good temperament.

Close, but no cigar.

How can the shape of a dog's foot affect his endurance?

Basically, there are two types of feet on our dogs: the hare foot and the cat foot. The hare foot is a special tool to give the dog quick speed, and the cat foot is designed to reduce fatigue over the long haul. The only real difference is the length of the third digit.

Make a fist. Now, look at the bones between your row of knuckles and the first joint of the fingers. This is the bone we're talking about. Transfer it to the dog's foot. In the hare foot, that bone is some longer than the cat foot.

I like a modified cat foot and here's why: first and foremost, the additional endurance. Secondly, this foot is not as prone to injury because it is tighter. I also believe the dog with a cat-type foot is more likely to stand up on his toes rather than back on the heel of his pad. This is important to agility or quickness. The last quality of a cat foot is the toenail. I think the toenail of a cat foot is less likely to break or tear.

By striving for a modified cat foot we are giving up some speed out of the hole, but we are putting running gear on our dog that will sustain him. I have not seen any depreciation of swimming efficiency with this type of foot.

Our shooting dog should have well laid-back shoulder blades, a little longer leg, a nice slope to the pastern, a modified cat foot, and a leg that provides support in a straight line from the center of the shoulder blade on down to the center of the pad.

We have to remember, the same holds true with horses and dogs. The front assembly is critical to endurance. The chance of

Bob Gould with a beautifully built Labrador

the animal breaking down in front is far greater than the rear. The front has to lift the center of gravity, and then prepare itself to absorb the concussion of the stride with each and every step. The problems with the front are particularity magnified when you run the dog in mountainous country. The downhill grades are murder on a dog's front quarters.

Think about it, remember the last time you were hunting or hiking? Isn't it harder on your legs, and especially your knees and ankles, when you go downhill?

I've often watched hunters as they walk along the Continental Divide searching for ptarmigan. The hump up the hill is tough on them, but the trail usually favors a direct approach.

After a time walking around at 14,000 feet, the descent is quite different. They start down the trail and quickly change to a traversing route because it's easier on the legs.

Now, let's go to the rear assembly: this is our dog's motor, the power plant, the drive. The rear legs propel the animal forward and the front steers it, just like most cars. In many of the Labs, the rear legs are not equal supporters of the weight. We talked about the problem with weight forward and how it has a limiting

79

effect. We can help things drastically by moving the center of gravity slightly backward.

Some other things are going to happen as a result of what we are trying to achieve with balance. When you lengthen the legs, the wheelbase has to correspond. When this happens, you will see a longer tail and neck and the head will narrow some. The neck is a little longer and the dog has more of a tendency to carry it higher.

If you lengthen the neck and head without a higher carriage, you will actually worsen the weight forward problem instead of helping it. We want our dog to carry his head high because that's where he is going to encounter scent first. Also, a high head is more stylish and keeps the dog in focus with his surroundings better.

We are talking about an athlete who resembles a wide receiver more than a linebacker or lineman. The old style Labs were linemen for sure, and they suffered from the same cruel tricks that Mother Nature saves for the stocky, blocky builds.

I remember in the superstar competition one year, they had to save a heavyweight boxing champion from the pool. He was a terrific athlete but not suited to that competition.

Did you ever notice what type of athlete excelled in the superstar games? That's right. The wide receivers of football, and the track men, namely the pole vaulters. These games were testing overall athletic ability, speed, stamina, endurance and power. It's not a coincidence that our shooting dog has to be representative of these same qualities.

At the top of the rear legs, where the head of the femur tucks into a hopefully deep socket, the pelvis bone acts as a stabilizer to hold the contraption together. This is called the croup. The Labrador retriever normally sported a fairly steep croup. In other words, the croup slanted downward from the front to the back. In the horse world, you see the same croup on quarter horses.

The thoroughbreds, or distance horses, tend to have a flatter croup. A flatter croup made for longer drive muscles. The rear leg is also capable of a greater arc and enhances endurance. The longer, leaner muscle is not stronger than the shorter, more coupled muscle of the quarter horse; it is capable of more endurance. A flatter croup will bring the tail higher on the rump. I learned from the pointers, high tail means more endurance. We're looking for a flatter croup in our shooting dog. We're not giving up power; we're just changing the structure of it.

Again, we want to look at the dog from the side to study the rear assembly. As we position the dog to show the rear angulation, a line dropped from the point of the buttock should graze the inside edge of the hock joint. The line should parallel the bones from the hock down to the pad. This position gives us the opportunity to measure the angulation of croup and the stifle.

From the rear, a nice, straight back leg should be located exactly under the pelvis joint on each side. If the back legs are "wide at the hocks," then the dog will sore up near the stifle after workouts. If he is "cow hocked," or in at the hocks, his pads will not converge to the centerline at fast gaits.

I like a dog to measure nearly the same from the ground to the top of his withers as he does from his withers to the tips of his pelvis.

If our dog is built according to the rules that we have been discussing, he will be a little taller and some leaner than Labs of old.

When he heats up, he will not be able to get additional heart and lung room from a wide-sprung chest, so he will have to get it from depth. The chest on our dog should be deep with ribs shaped more like quarter-moons than circular.

I think there are at least five different coat types on our Labradors. They range from short and slick to thick and curly. I favor the short, slick coat because it doesn't heat up so much in hot weather, and it slips burrs a lot easier. Remember, we are going to put this dog down in some hot climates in our search for upland birds. I know some breeders like the thicker coats for cold weather, but I have not seen the advantage.

I have worked short-coated Labs at 26 degrees below zero. When the air temperature is that cold, the dog isn't wet, the hair is frozen, much like your pant legs do as you walk through snow on a cold day. Your legs aren't cold while the pants are stiff, it's when they start to thaw out that you have to be careful.

I think it's colder for a dog at 15 degrees above zero than it is when it dips below. Just a little preparation toward the dog's comfort will keep him happy and working until after the hunters are folding it up. On a warm day, I think a simple brushing prior to the hunt will extend a thick-coated Lab's endurance up to 15 percent.

I like dark-brown eyes and avoid very light or yellow eyes like the plague. I think there are other undesirable traits linked to yellow eyes, mainly dealing with temperament. OK, it sounds crazy, but it's just something I've noticed. Anyway, I wouldn't breed a yellow-eyed dog for love nor money.

As long as we're talking crazy here, I also favor a dog who looks right at me. I like dogs who raise their heads and look up along their nose at me when I'm talking to them. A dog who tilts his head down and looks up like he's looking over his glasses has always bugged me. That tilt also brings along some physical traits that are hard to warm up to.

Mid-size pendant ears make the most sense to me. Long ears are prone to injury and offer no advantage. Short ears usually wrinkle and tend to stack up. Mid-size ears frame a Lab's head when he's alert and are important to his overall good looks.

There are lots of experts on dog conformation that can give you specifics of what we have been talking about, but from my experience, this kind of dog can get the job done. Some folks can get into the muscles and finer points of structure and can answer even the hardest questions.

Here's the way I look at it: the dog that moves his center of gravity along the flattest, straightest line is the most efficient.

We needed to move the center of gravity back slightly to achieve endurance, and we did that. We needed well laid-back shoulders and sloping pasterns, and we did that. We needed a flatter croup and longer thigh muscles, and we did that. We needed tight feet and we did that. We needed a high head carriage and we did that. We started with intelligence, because without that we had nothing.

We wanted boldness in water and a good water aptitude. We wanted good temperament and trainablity and we accomplished that.

OK, what's left? The nose, oh, yeah, the nose.

I have a good friend who has been training dogs for more than 40 years and he claims that you only buy the first inch and a half of a bird dog anyway. The quality of the nose is important for sure, but I think most dogs have good enough equipment if they are smart enough to work it.

We only select for good bird-finding ability, so we hope to select for nose, but if you get your dog into enough birds I'll bet his nose will be sufficient.

I know many Lab owners feel without a doubt the dog I'm describing is laying at their feet or pacing just outside in the kennel. It's just normal to believe our own dog is the ultimate working Lab. I call this the "My Dog Syndrome." We all suffer from it at one time or the other.

We have one dog for 15 years and we consider him to be the best ever. We replace him with one who doesn't share any of old what's-his-name's attributes, and automatically the new guy is the best. That's what is great about providing puppies and dogs for people. Each dog is going to be the sure-fire best.

The problem is the same for our kids. We think our kids are tops and even in public most people will nicely agree. When the same people get away by themselves, they openly declare what a bunch of heathens our kids are, and if they were theirs things would be different.

Truthfully, though, how many Labs can fulfill the criteria that we have laid out here? Not very many. I have been breeding Labs for 25 years now, and I've seen a handful.

I'm trying to challenge Lab breeders and owners to aspire to their ideal dog. It doesn't matter how your present dog stacks up, don't run him off the place. Don't send him packing if he comes up short. Thank God we don't have to stand for that kind of culling. We're looking for a team player, right? He doesn't have to be the best player on the team. We just want him to be the best player he can be.

I think by studying the functional conformation of our dogs we can learn more about their capabilities and how our training program can be adjusted to each dog individually. When training a Lab to handle, we use an incremental system of drills. Some of these drills include several thousand yards of running or swimming. If we know the physical and mental limitations of the dog in training, we can bend the program to suit him.

When you do see a special dog run, he is a beauty to behold. He is so graceful and stylish. He seems confident, sure of himself, and proud. This dog barely touches the ground. Everything is so well-proportioned, he just "wrists his way" effortlessly. This is called "class," a word normally reserved for pointers.

It's no wonder he has the stamina we desire. He is stingy with his energy, only burning what is on demand. Confidence keeps him from using too much mental energy. A thoughtful handler is mindful of waste, both mental and physical.

This is our Labrador shooting dog, smooth and easy to handle. We can take him anywhere and be happy with his effort. This is the dog I hold up to the light every time I attempt breeding. This is the vision, the quest, so to speak. This is what I strive for, knowing that most will fall short.

If you want to know how to pick the best puppy, you'll have to ask someone else. I have never known anyone who could do it. Oh, I know about all the tests and how you can rate the puppies along those guidelines, but I also know some great late-bloomers and overlooked puppies, who, in the end, blow their littermates away.

Spend your time looking for a breeder who has a plan. Stay away from the first or second time breeders who have "My Dog Syndrome." A good breeder will tell you the good about breeding, and he will also tell you of his fears.

I read an article in a popular gun dog magazine where the gun dog editor claimed, "Any breeder who guarantees his stock is either a fool or a charlatan."

Nevertheless, if there is no guarantee, don't buy the dog. I might be a fool, all right; however, I'm not a charlatan. I have guaranteed every dog I've ever sold.

Avoid a breeder who has a dog he thinks is special and has bred him to every female whose owner can cough up the stud fee. This fellow doesn't have a clue what he's doing. A quick study of the offspring will reveal massive inconsistencies.

A breeder should be able to provide a pedigree and direct you to his probable goals. He should have some intimate knowledge of at least the first 14 dogs on the pedigree.

Forget about the price tag! If you're looking for something shiny, you're going to have to go to the hip for it. There's no easy way out. Keeping a dog is expensive, but no more expensive for a good one than a bad one.

If you go for the bargain, you need to know some certain rules of nature. This bargain dog will live at least 15 years and he won't have a sick day. You could tie him up in the middle of a four-lane highway and he wouldn't get run over, not a scratch. He will have an appetite that will scare you and will even thrive on the cheap stuff you will finally resort to. He will fight with at least half of all your neighbor's dogs, and he will breed the other half. In spite of his faults, you will love him like no other and when the question is asked, you will reply, "He's the best dog in the county." You'll probably end up with at least one of his pups.

When looking for a litter, be picky, be smart and make your choice based on sound criteria. Once you have decided on a litter, pick a puppy whose temperament you like. Pick one who is friendly and precocious. You might not have snagged the best athlete of the litter, but at least you have a dog who will be nice to get along with, a good bet for the family.

OK, grab your pup and let's go. Let's help him to become a Labrador shooting dog. We want him to be somebody—a productive individual who enjoys pride in accomplishment. He's going to be a team player on a team where everyone shares in the successes and the failures. He can live a dream life, a life a field trial Lab would sell his soul for.

Come on! Let's take to the fields, and keep our eyes open, for there's glory out there, and only a dog can show us where it is.

Chapter Six:
Starting Your Puppy

There is no way I'm going to let you have all the fun. I'm grabbing a pup of my own so we can go through this together.

We have no way of knowing how well either of us picked, but there are some things we should take care of before we get too far along.

Let's take the pups to the vet and have him go through them with a fine-tooth comb. No need in taking it any further if we have some glaring congenital problems. You see, we still have our guarantee, so if something comes up, we can make the switch now.

Even out of good breeding programs there are sometimes recessive traits that come out of the blue to haunt us. The first thing out of most new owners' mouths is "Are the hips OFA certifiable?" You can't tell right away, but there are many things you can do as an owner to ensure that hip damage does not occur after you purchase your puppy.

I think most veterinarians these days can do a decent job of reading radiographs. I don't send any of the shots of my dogs' hips to the OFA anymore. By the way, OFA stands for "the Orthopedic Foundation for Animals." One of the main reasons this foundation was formed was to monitor hip problems in dogs.

I have seen a few veterinarians who are good at palpating the hips on a puppy to get an early jump on noticeable problems. If we bought from a good breeder who attends to these things, we are most likely going to be in good shape regarding the hips. The OFA will only certify dogs two years old or older.

How can you help to prevent structural problems? Let's see. First thing, be careful of slick floors like hardwood or vinyl. Puppies have soft bones and we don't need them sliding all over the floor chasing balls or children. I try to limit the time a puppy spends on any slick surface, because much permanent damage can be done without even knowing it. If you're going to play fetch or wrestle with him, do it on the ground. Carpet works OK, too. Just be watchful of situations where the puppy is sent sprawling across the floor.

You know how it is when a couple has a new baby. They have to baby-proof the house, especially when the baby starts getting around. Our puppy will be getting around, to say the least, when he first arrives, so take some time to pick things up that the puppy could get interested in. Watch out for things he could put in his mouth because anything he can get in his mouth, he will.

Stuff like D-Con or antifreeze will kill a dog in a heartbeat and there's virtually nothing you can do about it.

Some people will buy an assortment of squeaky toys and chew toys for the puppy to string around the house. I don't think this is a particularly good idea. We have a goal in mind here, so I like to start with an object, like a puppy dummy, to get him thinking "retrieve" right off the bat.

Your puppy will want to seriously chew when he starts teething, but that's generally down the road a couple of months. Then I provide chewing objects like "Nylabones" for him to work on. I don't like rawhide chews because they are easily chewed up and can cause digestion and stool problems.

Do not let him chew on his throwing dummy. When you get done playing with him, put the dummy up where he can't get to it. Only bring the dummy into play when you can work with his retrieving, and stash it afterward.

Several dog supply outfits sell special dummies sized for puppies, but an old pair of gym socks works well, also. Roll one sock in a tight ball and push it down into the toe of the other sock. Tie a knot or two to hold the ball down there and leave a tail. Pups love this kind of a dummy but one caution: He can't tell the difference between his sock dummy and a brand new pair.

Do not get into a pulling game with a puppy! Don't let him latch onto the sock and then drag him about the house. This can literally rip every tooth out of his head at this age. Don't let him get into a habit of shaking his head and pulling on his dummy. This habit will stick with him and we definitely do not want him shaking his birds. Scenting your dummy is not a bad idea. Any one of the game-bird scents will do. Most companies carry it.

I always get a kick out of clients who give their dog an old tennis shoe to chew on when he is little. They actually think he will be able to recognize a $150 pair of running shoes as off-limits.

Some people will bring old shoes, chew toys, old T-shirts, and a special blanket when they bring their dog in for training. Ha! As soon as they drive away, the blanket gets drug out and ripped up. The shirt gets you-know-what on it, and the neighboring dogs in the kennel find a way to scoot the toys over to the fence so they can either pull them through and devour them or simply urinate on them from the other side.

Soft rubber toys can pose a problem for dogs who are going to be asked to retrieve with a nice tender mouth. Just think of how fun it was, when you were in school, to chew on art gum erasers or the little ones on the ends of pencils. I used to love to chew on rubber bands and anything soft and pliable, especially the ones I could get to squeak.

I have trained for a couple of tennis pros and their dogs were always in for touchup on their mouths. Dogs love to squeeze tennis balls just like I used to do with erasers. This almost always causes a hard mouth problem. Don't throw tennis balls or soft rubber balls for your puppy or you will likely pay the price later.

Roly-poly puppies are cute, aren't they? They are so fat and lovable. The kids feed him, the wife feeds him, he gets snacks of all kinds and he sucks up every bit of it.

Nowadays, American parents are worried about their young children because, overall, kids are a lot fatter than kids of the past. Adolescent obesity is a real problem, both mentally and physically. Many structural worries lie down the road for these kids because of a faulty diet and bad eating habits.

Fat puppies are cute, just like fat children, but they're walking a dangerous line. Nothing good can come from being too fat. We already talked about how hard it is to get a shooting dog with all of the physical attributes we desire. Let's not compromise what our puppy has by breaking him down as an infant.

We're going to talk about his diet, and what to feed him, but the main thing is, keep him fit. Ask your vet about this. I've found they usually favor a little more flesh than I do.

Puppies are growing so fast, you don't dare rob them of important nutrition, but keep an eye out for obesity. What do we feed our pups anyway? We are going to be asking a lot from our pups when they're grown, so what's the best policy?

Well, you and I both are in luck. Many dog food companies have addressed the premium diet market for puppies and dogs. I can remember when there were only a couple of companies that provided for the needs of a hard-working dog and breeders routinely supplemented diets with various foods.

From one time to another, I have fed literally tons of different brands of dog foods. Sometimes, in a dog trainer's life, he would like to feed what he considers to be the best, but he can only afford lesser quality. I can recall a time when my main concern daily was to figure out some way to make enough money to buy dog food for that day. There were a few occasions when I unfortunately did not get it done and the dogs went hungry until the next day. On those occasions, I found it necessary to fast myself so I was particularly motivated to get dog food for the next day, by hook or by crook.

I have cooked venison and potatoes for the dogs a time or two, mainly because that's what I was eating. If you're too broke to buy dog food, chances are you're not living too high on the hog yourself.

I'm a mountain kid. I never considered living on "buckskin and spuds" much of a hardship, but my wife turns her nose up at the thought of it to this day. I was about 14 years old before I learned people ate beef. I can still remember how shocked I was. Why would anyone eat their cattle? You eat deer, you milk cows.

One time my dad brought a new cook into hunting camp, he about got run off the mountain for bringing a bunch of beefsteak. Pretty ignorant, huh?

It seems the depth of our ignorance was not limited, even though this part of Colorado is famous for record-book mule deer. We seldom brought the antlers home. It didn't make much sense to haul the lower legs and the head out, especially if you're packing on horses. I would like to get another look at some of the huge racks we left in the high country for the porcupines to eat.

One time some hunters from California were visiting our house, trying to talk my dad into taking them deer hunting. We were all standing in our backyard when one of them cried out, "Where in the world did you get those?" and he pointed to my mom's flower garden. "Get what?" my dad questioned.

"Those deer antlers," and he frantically waved toward the flowers again. It just so happened my mom used to turn deer antlers over onto their tips in the flowers to keep the dogs out. "Would you consider selling those to me?" he whimpered.

My dad was a big laugher. He loved to laugh for any reason and this was reason enough. "You want to buy those deer antlers?"

The guy asked if we had any idea what a rack like that was worth, and, of course, we didn't. We didn't sell him the antlers, but Dad offered them for the taking. He might have been ignorant, but he wasn't unfriendly.

After that, we always brought our big game heads home and collecting shed antlers is a favorite pastime of mine now. Just think of it. We actually thought the meat was the primary reason for hunting.

Oh, well, back to the dog food.

Like I was saying, there are lots of good dog food brands out there today. Ask your vet which one he prefers, and why. Have you noticed we are starting to depend on the advice of our veterinarian? That's why it's important to use one you can trust.

That's the way it's supposed to be. He's the one who went to school to learn about animal health and welfare, so ask him instead of your neighbor or mother-in-law.

...and is moderately active, feed him	1/3-3/4 cup	3/4-1 1/3 cups	1 1/3-1 3/4 cups	1 3/4-2 1/4 cups	2 1/4-2 3/4 cups	2 3/4-3 1/2 cup
...and is highly active, feed him	1/2-1 cup	1-1 2/3 cups	1 2/3-2 1/4 cups	2 1/4-2 2/3 cups	2 2/3-3 1/2 cups	3 1/2-4 1/4 cups

Remember to have fresh water available at all times for your dog.
Because Eukanuba The Original Premium is completely balanced, you do not need to add vitamins or supplies

Portions are based on the use of a standard 8 oz. measuring cup.

Eukanuba The Original Premium Ingredients
Chicken By-Product Meal, Ground Corn, Chicken, Rice Flour, Chicken Fat (preserved with BHA), Dried Beet Pulp, Chicken Digest, Dried Whole Egg, Fish Oil (preserved with ethoxyquin), Brewers Dried Yeast, Monosodium Phosphate, Flax, DL-Methionine, Potassium Chloride, Choline Chloride, Vitamin E Supplement, Ascorbic Acid (Vitamin C), Copper Sulfate, Ethoxyquin (a preservative), Zinc Oxide, Ferrous Sulfate, Manganese Sulfate, Manganous Oxide, Biotin Supplement, Vitamin A Acetate, Calcium Pantothenate, Vitamin B12 Supplement, Niacin, Thiamine Mononitrate, Riboflavin Supplement, Inositol, Pyridoxine Hydrochloride (Vitamin B6), Vitamin D3 Supplement, Potassium Iodide, Folic Acid, Cobalt Carbonate, Sodium Selenite.

Guaranteed Analysis

Crude Protein not less than	30.00%
Crude Fat not less than	20.00%
Crude Fiber not more than	4.00%
Moisture not more than	10.00%
Omega-6 Fatty Acids not less than	3.19%
Omega-3 Fatty Acids not less than	0.58%

There is an excellent Eukanuba product for every dog's age and activity level:

Eukanuba Puppy in small and large bites	Eukanuba Adult a maintenance formula for adult dogs	Eukanuba The Original Premium for more active adult dogs	Eukanuba Natural Lamb & Rice adult and puppy formulas

Look for quality ingredients in your dog food.

If you feed a premium dog food, you should not supplement with additional vitamins or people food. This food is nutritionally correct and supplementation could cause more problems than help.

I took the time to learn about dog foods and found that quality control is the key. If you're talking protein, for instance, look for the source of protein in your food. Chicken or eggs are great sources of protein. Soybean meal is not.

Dog food suffers from the same types of fads that people foods go through. For a time everyone was looking for the highest protein available without equal concern for the fat, carbohydrate, or fiber content.

By law, the dog food company must provide a list of ingredients on each bag that lists in descending order the ingredients used in producing that food. In my opinion, most of the commercial brands that you normally see in supermarkets fall short of our puppy's nutritional needs.

A good rule of thumb is the end result, if you know what I mean. I can tell a lot about the quality of the dog food by the volume of the stools. If stools are firm and consistent, you're in pretty good shape, but if you're seeing loose pancake-shaped stools, chances are you could do better with your dog food.

I don't care how many kids you have or if you live in a neighborhood full of young folks, do yourself a favor and "scoop your own kennel." If your puppy has a health problem, the scooper will be the first to notice if he's paying attention.

OK, use a puppy diet that suits your vet and don't squeak about the price. If you honestly compare, you will find you're getting a deal.

Puppies need to be fed small amounts frequently. I like to break a day's ration into four feedings: one in the morning, one at noon, one in mid-afternoon and then one in the evening.

At about four months of age, I go to three feedings daily and then at six months, I go to two. I keep puppies on puppy rations until they are 15 months old.

Again, ask your vet what schedule he likes. He will enjoy helping you out and he will feel more involved with the dog long term.

Vets have different preferences regarding your puppy's vaccination program, also. Each vet has a schedule he likes and I think it is a good idea to follow his particular favorite.

Your puppy probably was started on his protection while he was still at the breeder's, and hopefully he was wormed at least twice. Your breeder should provide you with this information so you can take it to your vet. Just take the health record with you when you get his first checkup. That way your vet can see what shots were given and what product was administered.

I know you can buy all of these shots from vaccine companies at a greatly reduced price, and it's an easy task to give a proper shot but it's just not that simple. When you take your puppy in for his shots and worming, the vet will routinely give him a physical exam. Sure, all of this costs money, but so does a health problem that you didn't catch.

Give him the protection he deserves, and at the same time start a relationship with your vet that will endure. I think a vet has a right to be more than a little peeved with a client who gives all of his own vaccinations and spews out medical advice to all of his friends then calls the emergency number at 3 a.m. to be bailed out of troubling circumstances.

As you get to know your vet, ask him to help you put together a complete first aid kit. The ones who are advertised in supply magazines are pretty hokey, I think. You are getting ready to develop a topnotch shooting dog here. I can guarantee he will get hurt, and he will get sick.

Put together a good kit and learn how to use it. The best first aid kit in the world is useless if you have no idea what's in it or how to apply first aid. As your dog grows, you will cannibalize the kit, and if you're not careful, an emergency will arise and you will tear open the kit to find it pretty much empty.

Believe me, I have seen the time where quick action saved a dog's life. I also have administered first aid to my dogs and saved the hunt. If you're not prepared, and you're hunting a good ways from the nearest town, a fairly minor first aid emergency can blow a whole day or more. If you're hunting in snake country or javelina and hog country, you better have a plan.

One day in south Texas, a family of javelina tore into one of my pointer bitches. I was guiding a quail hunt on the Rio Paisano Ranch near Riviera. It happened just as we were heading in for lunch. A beautiful, hard-working bird dog was in critical condition in a matter of seconds.

We bailed off the truck when we heard the melee. Raoul the ranch manager and I

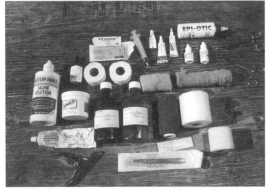

Protective boots (top) and first-aid kit

94

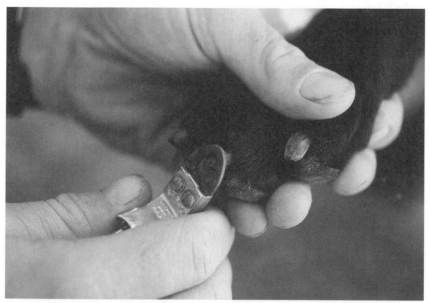

Trim your dog's nails and they won't splinter in the field

got to her as quickly as we could and first aid saved her life.

She had been bitten in the lower rear leg, the mouth, the underside of her chest, and her left front leg was nearly severed. She was in tremendous shock and was losing blood like nothing I've ever seen. We stopped the bleeding and treated her for shock while she lay on top of the hunt truck on the way back to the ranch headquarters.

Most of those hunt trucks have some kind of radio or telephone equipment on board. This one had both. Raoul called ahead to the ranch house and the owner called his veterinarian in Falfurrias on his emergency number.

While the guest hunters had lunch and rested, I hustled my dog to the clinic. The veterinarian on duty assured me he would do his best, but I had my doubts as I drove back to the ranch. I realized I had to trust a doctor I'd never met before, and tried to prepare my attitude for the afternoon hunt.

I was there in time to cast a brace of pointers into a coastal grass and mesquite mot pasture, but I was less than enthused as I handled the dogs from the tailgate of the hunt truck. Thanks to Raoul and his staff, we salvaged the rest of the day and a nervous call to the clinic confirmed I was the recipient of a minor miracle.

Several hundred stitches and $350 later, I thanked the doc for a job well done. "I gave you a break where I could," he apologized. "She was a mess."

Today she still has that beautiful, graceful style and if you didn't know where to look, you couldn't find evidence of her struggle.

Take the time to learn about first aid for your dog. Keep your first aid kit handy and have a plan for unexpected emergencies. You won't be sorry.

Where are we going to keep this new puppy of ours? Where should he sleep and where do we put him when we are away? Is a kennel best, is the back-yard best, or is the house the best? What is the safest and most practical arrangement?

One at a time— where should he sleep initially? When you first bring a puppy home, I think it is smart to spend as much time as you can with him. I like to introduce him to a portable or airline kennel right off the bat. I locate the kennel as near my bed as is possible. The first few

Portable kennels are best to start puppies

nights, he will be a little restless and may whine or howl some. When he mouths off, I reach out and tap the top of the kennel and tell him to shut up. Barking or whining is behavior that we don't want to get started so the best time to deal with it is the first time it happens. I usually turn a radio on low during the night.

The music seems to have a calming effect.

Most puppies are hesitant to foul their own quarters so the kennel is the perfect tool to start house-training as well.

Take the puppy outside right after he eats or drinks and then first thing in the morning. After a few days, he will get into a pattern. He will understand you want him to go outside to relieve himself and, with the exception of a few mishaps, he will want to also.

I get a kick out of people who say, "The puppy had an accident in the house." It wasn't an accident and he will do it again if you don't deal with it. Don't rub his nose in his bad news. Instead, take advantage of the opportunity to introduce him to a word that will mean much to him for the rest of his life: "No."

I like to pick him up and tell him "No" firmly while I gently shake him. I go directly to the door and put him in the place I want him to associate with success.

I never could see the point in encouraging him to use papers inside the house. First of all, the papers are a huge mess to deal with, and secondly, I don't want him to think it's OK to foul my house, either.

Keep your eyes open and housebreaking will go pretty smoothly. Use your portable kennel. It will save you a lot of grief.

I think it is a poor idea to give your puppy the backyard to play in while you are at work or away from home. This arrangement always leads to trouble. Most people (usually wives) spend a lot of time and money to make the backyard as pretty as possible. That's where you barbecue, that's where the family plays, that's where the lawn is, that's where mom has her flowers and the vegetable garden. No matter how much the family loves the new puppy, there is trouble brewing if you give him free rein over the backyard.

You will find the flowers dug up and strung all over what used to be the lawn, you will find your watering hose chewed into 18-inch pieces, you will find little pieces of treasure everywhere the kids want to play, the shrubs will not leaf out because they will be void of bark above the ground, a musty odor will keep the back door closed, and the barbecue will be moved to the front.

Some people believe kennels are cruel and they want to give their little puppy freedom. They don't like to be restricted and they won't tolerate restriction for their pet. They want to give him the run of the backyard, for exercise. After all, how can he get enough exercise enclosed in a kennel?

Get this—the laziest dog you will ever see is the dog who has unlimited space to run around in. He will yawn and stretch before he digs a hole in the flower bed so he can get down to cool ground.

Do yourself a huge favor, build a kennel for your puppy to stay in. He'll thank you for it. A dog needs a place he can call home sweet home, his turf, his pad. It doesn't have to be ornate, it just has to be his.

Ten years ago I managed a world-class hunting club for a rich guy. He wanted the best kennel money could buy so I built him one. It wasn't the biggest kennel in the country—it could comfortably house about 85 dogs—but it was decadent.

This kennel had every convenience known to man: heated concrete floors, a complete one-bedroom apartment, whelping and puppy-care units, offices, and a veterinary facility where my vet could do anything from fecal samples to major surgery. We disinfected at least once a day and had special water pumps to make cleaning easier. We had a state-of-the-art septic system and had a big enough furnace to heat the entire Colorado outdoors. From the outside it looked like a custom house complete with manicured lawn and patio furniture. You could sit on the deck and look out over many mountains and valleys. We had a complete staff of trainers and helpers and the whole thing cost more than three hundred thousand dollars.

People came from all over the world to shoot at this ranch and without exception were impressed by this great kennel. The only real problem was, the dogs weren't nearly so impressed. We had built a near-perfect dog kennel, but we built it so it was comfortable and convenient for us.

The dogs never did like that place. I made a promise to myself when I left there never to build a kennel to suit people again. Dogs don't like concrete and dogs don't like heated floors. Some disinfectant can be helpful, but too much can be harmful.

I'm quite certain that a dog would rather dig a hole in the flower garden and cover himself up with dirt than try to make concrete comfortable. Digging is good for dog feet. Walking on concrete is not. Dogs aren't impressed with the financial statement of the people peering through the wire.

Dogs are wonderful creatures and if you want to build a kennel in your yard for your puppy, build it to suit him. Build it to keep him warm and safe. Give him the security he needs, but be thoughtful in construction. You will find yourself saving money and providing a superior kennel at the same time.

Here's my idea of a great kennel, you do what you want.

For one dog, I think a kennel six feet wide and 12 feet long is perfect. Dig a rectangular hole about a foot deep that measures eight feet wide by 14 feet long. Lay 2x4 welded wire or remesh across the entire bottom of the hole. Place railroad ties around the perimeter on all four sides. Make sure the wire is under the ties. Fill the hole with pea gravel, or coarse sand, to the top of the railroad ties. You can buy a six-foot gate panel from any kennel fabrication outlet.

All of these panels should be six feet high. You end up with a kennel six feet by 12 feet by six feet high. You can build the house

A great kennel—clean and sheltered with room to exercise and dig.

outside any of the panels except the gate panel. Don't build the house inside the kennel because it takes up valuable run space. I think it is a good idea to build a low platform up off the gravel and cover it with indoor/outdoor carpet, like Astroturf, for lounging.

Elevate the door of the house to at least 20 inches so the dog has to jump in and out. When your dog is young, place some kind of blocks in front of the door so he can climb into the door. As soon as he is big enough to jump into the door hole, take the blocks away.

Cover the entire top with a kennel shade product. Several companies make a tight-woven shade that lets the disinfecting rays of the sun in, but shades the kennel. A top of this shade material stretched tight and secured will also provide protection from other dogs jumping in or your dog trying to jump out.

Don't build a great big house! Four feet long by 30 inches wide by 30 inches high is fine. Make the door hole no bigger than 11 inches by 18 inches. I like wood houses but dogs chew wood and there are some great heavy-duty plastic houses available these days. If you do use wood, protect the corners with metal edging to guard against chewing.

This is a kennel you can easily scoop and wash clean with the hose. The dog can dig and work his toes to his heart's content, but he can't dig out. He has shade and a lounging area to rest. He has room enough to exercise but not enough to get too bored. He has a house of his own where he can sleep free of the wind and he can stay warm even in severe low temperatures. This whole outfit is cheap and nice looking. You need to replace the gravel about twice a year to keep it loose and draining free.

With a kennel like this, and a portable kennel, you can provide your puppy with all the comforts of home. He will soon be proud of your effort on his behalf and will always prefer this system to lying around the yard, making enemies.

We have selected your puppy, we have worked out our health care program with our vet, we have decided on proper nutrition. We have given him a comfortable, safe home, we have constructed a quality kennel that he can call his own, and now we will embark on a development program that will take us toward our ultimate goal, "a Labrador shooting dog."

Right now we have a puppy who is only a couple of months old. Let's not buy into problems that may occur down the road. Let's enjoy him for what he is.

Give him a name you can be proud of. Think about it and come up with a fitting name that is easy to say and will carry well. Think about how accomplished he will be later. He needs a name that will reflect a good feeling when you say it. This dog is going to be somebody, so name him accordingly.

Initially in his training process, the puppy will be controlled by an encouraging voice and kind gestures. He will learn to respond positively to routine feeding and watering. He will learn the word "No" during his house training and incidents concerning chewing, and he will learn praise from doing what we enjoy.

We need to pick out a collar for him so we can gradually introduce him to lead pressure and restraint. Forget about chain choke collars. Don't ask why, just don't even consider them. No sense buying an expensive collar at this time because he is growing so fast he will go through several before his first birthday.

Pick out a nylon web collar with a stout buckle. Even an eight-week-old puppy can break the plastic fasteners on cheap collars. Leather works OK for older dogs, but I think nylon is a better deal for young puppies.

Put the collar on your puppy and adjust it to where you think it fits. Now take it in at least one notch (most people leave the collars too loose; this is dangerous). If you can slip two fingers between the puppy's neck and the collar, you are in good shape. Remember, the puppy is growing fast so you will have to adjust it frequently.

Any kind of a short lead is all right at this time. We will introduce the puppy to a waist cord when we start with his formal obedience, but for now we just need something to keep track of him.

Any time I take a puppy into a crowded area or along a road or someplace where he could get hurt easily, I place him on his lead. All other times, I like to let him run loose so he can start to form habits of staying with me and responding to my movements. This will be very important later on. I will often even remove his collar while we are exploring together to keep from accidental entanglements.

From the get-go let's bring our puppy dummy along with us and practice with our retrieving at every opportunity. Don't get caught up in formal retrieving skills, don't even worry if he doesn't pick up his dummy right away, and don't demand a prompt return. Throw his dummy once or twice, then tuck it under your arm or in your pocket as you walk along.

I like to take a puppy into many different environments— some fields, some light cover, some medium cover, some shallow water, some deeper water, some still water, and some moving water. Keep a watchful eye on him so he doesn't get hurt but don't get in the habit of helping him through obstacles. Make him figure out ways to handle fences and creeks and ditches and brush.

When you see the puppy starting to tire, head back. Don't let him play out if you can help it, but only pick him up if you feel you have to. Don't let him get in the habit of looking to be picked up at the first feelings of fatigue.

At the end of your walks, when you return home, I think it is a very good idea to hold the puppy on your lap and praise him as you let him relax. As he grows older and bigger, you can call him to the side of your chair and give him the same attention without letting him crawl up on you. This will greatly improve the bond between the two of you and he will look forward to your praise and soft touch at the end of your workouts together.

Talk to him directly, look at him and touch him softly as you talk to him. Let him study your face and your voice as you say his name and praise him. Make him feel special.

If your attempts at retrieving aren't going well outdoors, work on it in the house while there aren't so many distractions. Again once or twice is plenty at first. Don't try to make him stay before you let him retrieve.

Every time you notice him coming to you, call him. He thinks it's his idea and it will help to form positive habits of obedience. Do not call him while he is moving the opposite direction or looking away from you. From the very start we are working to develop confidence, not compliance.

If you train for total confidence, your program will be successful.

If you train for total compliance, your program will ultimately fail.

There will be plenty of time for formal obedience and advanced skills later on. Right now let's concentrate on giving him a happy, well-adjusted puppyhood. Nothing is sadder than a person or a dog who is forced to duty before he has experienced the dreams of a child.

The happiest times of this dog's life will have something to do with feathers so you might as well get started right now. If you're lucky enough to live where you can keep pigeons or game birds, then get them into the picture pronto. If you know someone who has birds, make a deal with him to buy or rent his birds for training.

Sounds kind of funny, "renting birds," but it's not as crazy as it seems. You can get a lot of high-quality bird work done with someone's homing pigeons without harming a feather on their bodies. You can set them in cover and let the puppy flush and chase while the birds wing for home.

Wing-clipped birds are intoxicating to young dogs and can be used with care over and over again.

If live birds aren't readily available, use wings from last year's game birds to get your puppy cranked up. We need to introduce our puppy to the gun, but, for now, the birds are plenty to keep him interested. If there is a place nearby where you can show your puppy live game birds, then by all means do it. You don't have to shoot them, just let him have some success with the game.

Birds are the common denominator throughout his entire pyramid. He can't get off the ground without them. As we establish our goal, we identified this great need. Find a way to show him birds on a regular basis, I don't care where you live or what the circumstances are, you can do it if you want to.

If you are using live birds, the puppy will sometimes get carried away and either injure or kill the training bird. Remember, we are also trying to show respect for the birds. If the bird is not going to live, dispatch it quickly. Don't let it suffer while you try to extend the training session.

Be smart as you handle your training birds. Any birds that are killed in training should be disposed of properly. Don't leave them scattered around the training field or kennel area. You can use birds repeatedly if you keep them in plastic bags in the freezer.

These first few months in a puppy's life are extremely important to our end result, so let's not rush it. This phase might last four months or it might last six months. Each puppy is unique.

If we keep things fun as we learn together, there will come a time where the puppy starts to change. He will get cocky, he won't come any more like he used to, and he will start getting mischievous and sneaky. He is more than likely chewing on everything now and can dig like a badger.

The puppy is showing us his transition to adolescence and his need for obedience. You never start a dog on formal obedience until he shows you he is ready. That's why you can't follow a program without regard to the puppy's individual temperament.

So, if you were about to ask, "When do we start formal obedience?" there's your answer: "You start it when the dog is ready, not when you are."

As I have tried to emphasize the importance of the gradual development of our puppy during the past few months, I can't go on without bringing to light the significance of this time for ourselves.

We have taken the puppy on walks through woods and along streams. We have watched him wrestle with cattails until he rolled into the lake. We have seen him intimidated by other dogs and people. We have seen him bold up with the prospect of catching a bird. We have seen him scared and worried, happy and sad. Our puppy has grown literally by leaps and bounds. He is three times the size he was when we first saw him. We have washed thick, black mud off him so he could continue to mingle with us in the house. He has shivered on the veterinarian's table a few times while we reassured him all was well. He has accepted our love and stood our wrath.

Remember back when I was talking about birds and habitat? Remember when I stressed the importance of the team attitude? Remember when I asked you to be more observant as to the world around you as we go about this endeavor?

Do not think we are bringing our puppy to these places for his good alone. This puppy will give you reason to reflect on your life and this bundle of trouble can offer support you have never felt.

As he tumbles and chews while you sit on the riverbank, consider the natural world about you. Allow yourself to be drawn into his adolescent dream world. Think about your desires and your hopes, think about the air, and the water he just shook on you.

Have you given up on personal goals you set for yourself years ago? Are you so caught up in the struggle of life that you have betrayed your deepest need of self-respect and integrity?

Are you gazing upon sedge grass or reeds? What kind of seeds are you crumbling between your fingers as you drift and dream? What is the composition of the soil?

What is the habitat that you continually see while you and your puppy think about tomorrow? Breathe deep and smell what you can, pledge to yourself to learn about it all.

If you doubt these values, let me tell you of a time when I was starting the greatest Labrador I've ever seen.

I have already introduced you to Web and have told of some of his heroics, but the most powerful moments we have shared together had nothing to do with birds or hunting.

Web is, without a doubt, the most talented Labrador I have

ever worked with, but he is also one of the luckiest. He has lived a dream life of glamour and glory. I have never known anyone who didn't like him. Dogs have always respected him and I have never seen him in a fight. He has an air of worthiness that is visible and unforgettable. He has lived his life on some of the finest hunting ranches in America and has seen thousands of birds of all types. Before he was six months old he had flushed a couple thousand pheasants and retrieved a hundred or so.

Web didn't start out with all this knowledge. He acquired it brick by brick, just like your puppy will. He didn't start out great; he was just a talented puppy who needed someone to give him the opportunities of learning.

When Web was a puppy, I was going through the most troubling hardship of my life. I was working under tremendous stress and gradually I felt the numbing fatigue that continued stress brings on. I think it was Vince Lombardi who said, "Fatigue makes cowards of us all." This fatigue can spawn depression, lack of self-respect, and loss of hope.

When a person is physically tired he can rest up for a spell and renew his energy, but it's much harder to recover from prolonged emotional stress and pressure.

The fatigue becomes an unbelievable weight that he must shoulder even upon waking in the morning. The heaviness doesn't dissipate as the day goes on and sleepless nights contribute to an already tense situation.

I once read of a man who finally sank to the ground under the weight of his troubles and said, "Alas, my burdens have encompassed me." This is the state of mind I was trying to shake off while I fought desperately to give Web the start he deserved.

One day, as Web and I walked along a mountain creek, I was frightened by the realization that I could no longer stand. My strength had left me. First, I knelt down on one knee and tried to relax. I was in my thirties, in good physical shape. It had to be a passing condition.

I found myself wanting to sit down, but when I tried to, I was unable to keep myself from lying on my back. I laid there for a long time, first closing my eyes to rest, then staring at a clear, blue sky.

Each time I opened my eyes, I saw Web. He was worried, too. He had never seen anything like this and he knew something was wrong. Web lay down right beside me and put his head on my waist. I put my hand on his neck and we remained that way for quite some time. He was no longer interested with swimming and running. He couldn't care less about what was going on around him.

Slowly I rubbed his neck until I felt the need to get up. I raised up on one elbow, then back to my knees, then on to my feet. We walked back towards the car together. He never left my side.

He didn't get over it for several days. He wouldn't leave me alone and turned into pretty much of a pest with his nosing affection.

In some strange way, Web gave me the lift I needed. He inspired me to keep going through my hardship. Every time I felt the urge to quit, I thought of Web's trust and devotion and the load got some lighter.

Throughout that summer and fall he kept me moving steadily ahead. He wouldn't let my problems take me down. In retrospect, I honestly believe Web saved my life that year and to some degree he is still doing it today.

Now, can you take a dog like that and force him into a program designed for absolute compliance? Could you shock and intimidate this dog into performance? I don't think so!

Web developed into the most magnificent Labrador shooting dog I've ever known because I recognized his natural ability, I supported and inspired him, I gave him reason to stay in there and acquire the skills he needed to climb to the top of the pyramid. I helped him by teaching and being patient, by being smart instead of demanding.

I trained him to be the best he could be and sometimes I wonder if I ever really knew how good he was.

Web is my hero because he gave me the strength to try again. He is the finest quality individual I've ever met, man or beast. My life is forever enriched because Web taught me to aspire to my best, always.

Take that puppy of yours with you and show him what you can, but don't overlook the value he brings to your life. Today, while you hold him on your lap and tell him how great he will be, thank him, also, for giving you the spirit of success.

Chapter Seven:
The Pyramid

I generally go by the theory "Castles, cathedrals, cities, and shooting dogs are built brick by brick." All of these have lasting value only if they are built properly by skilled craftsmen of patience.

If you pile up a bunch of stones and call it a castle, the storms of life will topple it. If you build a cathedral on a foundation of sandstone, it will wither and sag. If a city is built without consideration for the destructive potential of bad weather, rising rivers, landslides, or avalanche, sooner or later the city will be a statistic on the evening news. If you go about developing your shooting dog without the benefit of a solid building structure you will eventually have to accept the responsibility of his being less than he could have been.

Don't try to build this dog all in one day. Instead, choose to place one thoughtful brick each day. Brick by brick you can be ultimately successful. It's going to take somewhere around three years for you and your dog to be standing on the balcony of your castle. That's about 1100 bricks, day by day.

I've always thought this structure to resemble a pyramid. It starts with a wide, strong, base and it ends up at a pinnacle. The very top means success to me, we made it, we did this together. The pyramid is three-dimensional so it reflects depth as well as height. The pyramid is commonly accepted as a work of art, an engineering marvel, a masterpiece that transcends the ages.

The most important thing to remember at this time is to be

patient. Do not try to build an entire house in a single day. Instead, choose to place a well-designed brick and make sure it's secure. Brick by brick you can build a whole city, and brick by brick you can build a fine shooting dog.

The foundation of a pyramid is the widest part as well as the deepest. As we lay the bricks of the foundation, we will take special care to fill every crack so as we advance to the top, our project will not wobble and fall.

Think about this—Larry Bird turned out to be one of the best basketball players in history even though he wasn't very fast, he was white, and he wasn't a great jumper. He was simply dedicated to the fundamentals of basketball.

In any sport it's proper fundamentals that can take you to the top. Great athletic ability is wonderful but athleticism alone cannot get you where you need to be unless you are schooled in solid fundamentals of your chosen sport.

These same truths are just as valuable as we look towards the goals we have set for our new dog. Attention to detail and good fundamental structure will bring every ounce of potential to the top.

When a pro athlete slides into a slump of any kind, he doesn't get fancier, he doesn't use gimmicks, he doesn't make excuses, and he goes back to basics. He goes back to the fundamental that deals with his particular problem and he works to fix it there.

An all-age retriever championship is usually decided within a five-yard circle around the handler. If the dog isn't working well in that circle, his chances of working better at extreme distances are not good.

Throughout the development of our shooting dog, we will continually work to fill the cracks of our fundamental structure. We need to always be willing to back up, if need be, to make things right before we go on. How long will this take? When can we expect our dog to stand at the top of the pyramid?

Many programs will have you working on advanced training while the puppy is still a baby; some programs will promote speed in training instead of lasting quality. Some popular methods will strive for steadiness before the puppy even learns about birds.

We are going to shoot for a nice-handling, competent dog, but we are not going to sacrifice his puppyhood to gain it. We will focus on advanced training and steadiness when the time is right for him, not for us.

The whole process will take in excess of three years. Take it or leave it. There is no viable shortcut that I am aware of.

If you get in your car in southern California with plans to drive all the way to Bangor, Maine, you have many different roads and routes you may choose from but you still have to steer the car across the entire United States. If you buy into shortcuts and gimmicks to make you believe the trip can be made without crossing certain sections of the country, you may very well end up discouraged and dismayed with your progress and settle where you run out of gas.

Many hunters settle for a dog who is not as proficient as they had hoped for simply because the training program was sidetracked or the road map was misplaced. I often hear hunters say, "He's not as good as he could be, but he's OK for me." This is a concession that was not necessary had he stayed the course, kept his eye on the goal, and not lost faith.

You might very well find yourself satisfied with your dog at a certain level of the pyramid, but this is a decision you will make, not your dog. Search high for your answers for they are within your reach. We're working on something special here. Stay in there. Don't give up. There isn't one dog in a thousand who comes anywhere near the top of that pyramid. Choose for your dog to be one of those.

This is a good model for our shooting dog program, don't you think? By the time we get to the top, you will be so proud of what you have accomplished, you will be glad we picked a pyramid to fashion our program after.

We've discussed the raw materials we need to start with to eventually reach our goal, so hopefully we have placed a brick or two already by attending to quality breeding and early socialization and humanization. Maybe our pup has some bird contact under his belt.

What tools are we going to need?

Well, get out all of your dog training stuff and look through it. If you don't have any, all the better. Dog trainers have lots of stuff. Have you ever looked into one of their dog rigs? There are ropes and dummies and collars and crates and pistols and shotguns painted orange and shells and bowls and jugs and boats and waders and chains and leads and decoys and whistles and lanyards and gloves and electric devices and whips and prods and bird boxes and dead birds and scent and chaps and worm medicine and first-aid kits and vests and jackets and on and on.

All you will need right now is the whistle on a lanyard and a waist cord.

There are several different whistles popular among dog trainers. I will tell you which ones I prefer, but all of them will work OK. Take your pick. I like Roy Gonia whistles the best. There are three different types: the special, the commander and the competition.

I have used all three extensively and my favorites are the competition and the special. The commander is plenty good, also, but for some reason I like the others best. All of them will reach

Whistles and lanyard

far enough for you to do any kind of training and I believe they are kinder to your ears than the Acme Thunder or the Fox 40. The Fox whistle is very hard on your ears and anyone who is standing near you. You might not think this is important, but if it wasn't I wouldn't have brought it up. You will be blowing that thing thousands of times, sometimes as loud as you can. It will definitely harm your hearing, believe me.

I like to keep two whistles on my lanyard because first of all they are plastic and they break easily, and secondly, if something goes wrong with your whistle, you have a spare with you. I also keep several extras at home in my secret drawer (that I never can find when I need one.)

The waist cord is basically a lead, but it is unlike any lead you will see advertised in dog supply catalogs. I call it a waist cord for lack of a better term, but I use if for just about everything while training dogs. This cord is very important. I have tried many different weaves and diameters and lengths and materials over the years. I have tried lariats, piggin' strings, check cords, climbing rope, hemp, nylon, polypropylene, whatever I could find.

Check cord, waist cord, and "hondo" knot

I personally like the rope that is sold in Dunn's catalog. It is a tightly woven 3/8-in. diameter nylon check cord and it comes in either 25- or 50-foot lengths. It comes with a brass spring clip and a bright clamp to hold the loop in place.

I always take that clamp off because it really isn't helpful in training and it only serves to keep the clip on until you receive your cord.

If you get a 25-ft. cord, cut it into two 12-ft. pieces. Burn the ends thoroughly to prevent fraying and press them down flat against a piece of cold metal or concrete until they set. On one end of the cord, tie a simple overhand knot or a grapevine knot and pull it tight against the burned end. On the other end of the cord tie a "hondo" knot like the one on the end of a lariat. This knot will not come undone and the longer it stays there, the tougher it is to get undone. Make an overhand knot about 7½ inches from the end of the cord so it measures about seven inches from the center of the overhand knot to the end of the cord. Loop the burned end back and tuck it into the overhand knot to complete the hondo. Pull the whole thing down tight and make sure the knot is right so it won't slip. Now soak the knot in water or throw it in a puddle, or if you're lucky it's raining out today and you can just sling it out in the front yard. Once the knot is good and wet, I hook it over something substantial like a hook on a bumper or a spike in a post and I stretch it as tight as I can until all the slack is out of the knot. Now we have a length of rope with a lariat-like loop in one end and a nice, tight knot in the other. The more you use it the stiffer it gets, but it will take several months before your waist cord will have the "body" we're looking for.

I'll warn you now, once your training friends see the value of the waist cord, one of them is going to steal it or cheat you out of it. You might just as well make a couple to start with because you're going to need an extra.

Stick the knotted end through the loop at the other end and pull about half of your slack, now tuck the knot in the loop and pull the cord tight. I carry my waist cord around my shoulder where it is handy when I'm not using it and I can grab it in a second to help with my dog work. I carry it with me over my shooting vest or jacket when I'm hunting, so I always have a quality lead when I need it. There are many uses of the waist cord and you will hear me refer to it countless times as we train together. We start with it; it helps us through transitions in the formal obedience. It helps with force breaking, it helps with field transition, and many other situations that we encounter. Keep it with you always and don't loan it to anyone. Later on we will use a longer one for check cording if we need to, but for now this one will be our constant companion.

Waist cord and check cord

OK, let's get checked out. You got your puppy? You got your whistle? You got your waist cord?

Now, all you have to do is fix your eyes on the horizon and look to your future. We have mountains to climb and pyramids to build.

The farmer keeps the smokestack of his tractor lined up with a tree or a post far in the distance to keep his furrow straight. He isn't that worried about what is right in front of him. He looks to the end of his row. When a sailor is confronted with stormy seas, he points his bow into the wind and keeps it there if he wants to see the sunrise tomorrow.

Let's do the same. Let's not fret about whether the puppy is doing what he should be according to the experts. Let's not get excited if our puppy isn't doing blind retrieves by the time he's 10 months old. Don't measure your success or your failures day by day.

I think it's a good idea to keep a running record of your training. You can keep your training diary in a spiral notebook or a fancy shooting record book. I just suggest you keep track of your progress so you can stay on track. Day by day, month by month you inscribe your training sessions. It becomes fun to look back, especially if you're struggling with some problem, to compare where you started with where you are now.

When your new puppy becomes an old friend, it's so wonderful to smell wood smoke, sip a cup of coffee, and read of your campaign to victory.

There's an easy breeze out this morning. A couple of pheasant are walking through the horse pasture. You don't mind if I take a pup for a walk, do you? I still have to decide on which puppy I will take with me through these pages. Dang, there's a covey of valley quail out there, too. I'll see you this evening.

Chapter Eight:
Camas

Normally I'm partial to males, but I've taken a particular shine to a female puppy I've decided to name Camas. I like to name pups after things or places I appreciate. I learned to be careful about naming puppies after great friends or family members who have passed away. You know, that old high school buddy or your favorite uncle, maybe your grandpa who started you out hunting, who knows. Just be mindful of the fact that when the dog dies, you might find yourself reminded of how bad you felt when that special person passed on.

Anyway, I named her Camas after the Camas Prairie in northern Idaho. There are at least eight different species of upland game birds indigenous to that region and quite a number of waterfowl trade along the Snake, Salmon and upper Clearwater River drainages. There are a lot of wild turkeys, too, so all in all I can't think of a better place to name a bird dog after.

Did I catch you off guard when I mentioned wild turkeys? Surely you don't think I'd hunt wild turkeys with a Labrador, do you? No one would be crazy enough to expect to kill a turkey over a gun dog. Well, call me crazy or a fruitcake or anything else you prefer, but I've done it several times. I even shot a big old tom over a pointing dog in North Dakota a few years back. I shot two over the same Lab one year with the only real problem coming when the dog tried to retrieve them. A mature turkey is quite a load, even for a good-sized dog. A friend of mine actually shot a double on turkeys over his Lab on

Thanksgiving morning, 1985.

From snipe to turkey, who cares! Come on, let's get our pup into birds!

Keep in mind, I'm going to cheat a little while we're training our pups together. That's just the kind of guy I am. I got so excited thinking about all the birds in Idaho, I decided to train my pup there.

I like to take my pups with me everywhere I go while they're getting used to me and I'm getting used to them. I haul them around in the truck or a dog trailer every day so I can do something with them when the mood strikes. I'm not suggesting you can do as much as I do, but believe me, you will be money ahead if you make every effort to stay hooked up.

I'm taking Camas to the river today, maybe the fields tomorrow. Maybe I'll slip a lead on her for a walk down the road or along the creek. It really doesn't matter, just keep working on it. Keep showing your puppy new and exciting things. Be wary of extra loud noises or dangerous situations, but other than that, let 'er rip!

Do yourself another favor and resist the temptation to start formal obedience as soon as you get your pup. I know all about the accepted training programs that preach to start formal work right away, but please, look the other way for the time being and give me a chance to show you another way, and to my way of thinking, a much better way.

I like to take long walks with Camas without talking much except to tell her how I enjoy her company or how nice she looks today. I like her to put her front feet up on me no matter how dirty she is. When Camas runs far out in front, I stop walking and without saying a word I stand and wait until she starts back my way. As she comes bounding toward me, I say "here" one time and kneel to catch her as she jumps into my arms. If she runs to the left, I move to the right, if she runs to the right, I move to the left. If she is staying underfoot, I walk faster, if she is running way out, I walk slower. I always do the opposite of what the pup is doing. From this point on the pup learns that I get to decide where we walk, how fast we walk, and where I want the pup to be in relation to me, the handler.

As Camas gets older and bolder, she is growing and developing her athletic ability. She is faster and more graceful, but still I pull her from side to side, in and out, simply by letting her initiate a direction and then by moving in the opposite one. If she takes a major spin out in front and I stop but she doesn't turn back, I turn completely around without saying a word and walk directly away from her. This will put dramatic pressure on her to catch up with me and zoom to the front once more.

This kind of field work is called "influence handling." From here on out, we will talk a lot about influence and the power and control of it.

Handling by influence is the most powerful means of controlling your dog, and I can prove it. It's more powerful than electricity, it's more powerful than intimidation, and it's more permanent to boot. The idea is to influence your dog into doing what you want instead of correcting him for doing what you don't want. The dog thinks it's his idea and he responds gladly and promptly.

If a dog is conditioned to respond to the handler's influence, he can be turned, called in, cast, or driven back without a whistle, a hand signal, or a single word from his handler. I have routinely handled pointers from incredible distances while using this technique and it works just as well with the Labs. Incidentally, the dog will handle just as efficiently with his handler on horseback, driving a truck, or walking.

Think about this: The influence handling system works regardless if the dog can see his handler or not. It also works even if the handler cannot see his dog. It works if the dog is over the hill or across a body of water. It works while the dog is walking, running, swimming or sleeping. It works on hot days or cold days, in the morning or afternoon. Influence handling is the most powerful and consistently useful training technique I know of, and there is no downside whatsoever.

Remember, while working your puppy, stay quiet as much as

you can. Don't keep up a banter of "good boys" and "here's" and "stay's" and "come in's" and "hunt 'em up's" and "that's the way's." Let your puppy discover all he can on his own.

Also stay off your whistle other than an occasional come-in whistle when the puppy is running to you.

How often and how long should you work your puppy like this? Every time you get a chance, as long as the puppy doesn't tire out. Make it easy on yourself. You will probably want to call it a day before the pup does. If the pup does get too tired, take a break and sit on a log and dream together until you both can once again bounce off toward the future.

OK, back to Camas. We are learning so much right now. We are learning about light cover, heavy cover, running water, swimming water, smooth water, rough water, rocks, roads, and most importantly, friendship and devotion.

It's time for the most important factor in her equation for success: the big B, the reason for living, the salvation of a shooting dog, the equipment and the know-how to scale the heights, the soul food, the drive, the glory. It's time for birds, it's time for birds, it's time for birds.

Every day I am constantly looking for birds. When I see a covey of valley quail cross the road, I turn Camas out and tell her to "get in there." When I see that dark head of a rooster pheasant in a weed patch, "get in there." Ducks are on the creek, "get in there." If you see them, get them up. If you don't have permission to go on the land where you saw the birds, get it. If you have to get up earlier or drive farther, do it. This is a quest.

If it is illegal or out of season to jump game birds, find some pigeons. Buy some, rent some, I don't care if you steal some, just get your pup into birds. Give some guy a few bucks to let your pup flush his homing pigeons. It doesn't matter, just get the dog birdy!

Keep in mind here we're not hunting or shooting. We're just trying to get a pup started right. No commands or screaming or whistling, just teaching and waiting.

I told you I was going to cheat. You see, I live on a hunting preserve, and putting Camas into birds is no problem for me. So you say, "That isn't fair, how can we keep up with him when he has all the makings of a bird dog right at his fingertips?"

Well, let me tell you, I have paid the price. When you separate yourself from the norm, you go away from the proper ways of society. When you dedicate your life to dogs, birds and wildlife habitat, you also sentence yourself to life without visible substance. Unfortunately, your family is bound to the same fate—right, wrong or indifferent.

When it comes to acquiring the trappings of life, most people have an advantage over me, but when it comes to understanding the ways of nature and providing for the needs of a young bird dog, I breath rarified air.

I'm trying to help you here. Get some birds by hook or crook and put the fire in your puppy. You won't regret it.

If you are going to get to the top of the heap, the next few months are paramount in your puppy's life. Lots of field work, lots of birds, and remember, stay away from formal obedience and handling. It's OK to work a little on sit or stay within the structure of your workouts, and always reinforce your pup's desire to come to you by calling "here" one time, but avoid getting caught up in the control mode.

If you slip your waist cord on the pup for a short time occasionally during the workout, the pup never learns to resent control. It becomes more of an extension of your friendship for the dog. You're not mad at the pup and you're not demanding or commanding anything. You just want the pup to walk with you for a short time.

The pup learns to appreciate the close contact and he doesn't even notice the control device. Sometimes when you first put the waist cord on the pup, he will flip and flop around and pull back as hard as he can. Don't say anything to him, just walk slowly along, giving him short tugs on the cord. Be careful not to hurt him or choke him; just urge him to come with you. After a few minutes on the cord, take the lead off and pet him as you cut him loose to run.

He might be intimidated some by what just happened, but

don't worry about it. Walk along and enjoy what you're doing, and pretty soon the pup will be doing the same.

I like to put the waist cord on the pup at the first of the session and then somewhere in the middle, if possible, then again at the end as you near your vehicle or kennel.

I don't want to go past this section without bringing up another diversion from the popular development program for Labs.

Most hunters and trainers are looking to hold their dog in so they never hunt beyond acceptable shooting range. They start this practice at a very young age. I have never seen an advantage in this line of thought. I have, however, seen some serious drawbacks when it comes to developing a pup's bird-finding ability.

Please remember this very valuable tip: If you limit your pup by closing down his field, you are making a terrible mistake. You are only doing this for your own good and not his. We are not talking about hunting birds here, we are talking about training, and remember, we set about to end up with a quality shooting dog and I've never seen a good one yet that worried about range.

Let's see how this applies to birds. We have already established the need for lots of bird contact and that is your primary concern at this stage, but how do you actually handle the flushes?

Unless the dog is in some kind of danger by chasing the birds, don't try to call or restrict him from chasing as far as he wants. If your pup gets up a bird and takes off after it, great. If he gets up a bird and stands there with his head high with weeds hanging from his face, great. If he barks with excitement and spins to the ground to see where the bird came from, great. If he seems disinterested and removed, still, no real problem. Find him another one to flush.

Some puppies don't fire right up around birds, but that doesn't mean they won't be bird dogs. Give 'em a chance to come around.

We will talk about wing-clipped pigeons later on. That's when we'll push him over the top.

If the pup is frightened by the bird, be careful. Go to smaller birds or pigeons. Don't let the pup get scared of birds. Stay away from rooster pheasants or geese. Even ducks can intimidate young puppies. Get him birdy, then let a duck try to bully him.

I like a puppy who will chase after the bird, then stop to look out to the distance searching for where it had gone. When the puppy stops, that is the perfect time to influence him back. Before he starts thinking about something else, I move back a few steps and the pup spins and heads for me. As he gets closer to me, I say, "That's the way to go, good boy," and I take him right back to where the bird was. I do this for several reasons: one, often there is another bird there; two, there is definitely fresh scent there; and three, the pup relates the excitement of the bird and the flush with you. This will help to keep the dog working for you when he gets older.

If your pup chases the bird out of sight, wait for a minute, and if you don't see him, turn around and head away from him for 50 yards. This will put the pressure on him to hook back up with you. If he still doesn't come around, find out what's keeping him. Go and see.

What has your dog learned so far? Well, I can tell you what Camas has learned. She has learned her name. She has learned that I am great fun to be with. She has learned the waist cord is no big deal. She has been introduced to all kinds of cover and water.

She is frantic to learn whatever she can about these birds we are always finding.

She already knows she cannot catch them when they fly but she tries her best every time. Camas is always on the way back to me at a dead run when I say "here," so she loves to hear it and do it. She has learned what the "come in" whistle sounds like. She has learned to turn left, right, and to cast over, back, and in. She knows I care about her but I won't come get her if she is stuck in mud or across a fence unless she absolutely can't make it or is in danger of being hurt.

She has to find a hole in the fence, find an easy place to cross, look for a way to stay up with me. This is dog training, folks, I promise you.

My pup doesn't know much formal obedience and I don't care. I already know the end of her story. If she doesn't suffer an accident or if something doesn't happen to shorten her career, she will be a terrific shooting dog. I can't wait.

Oh, by the way, she is ten weeks old.

Chapter Nine:
Introduction to the Gun

W e have come too far to make a mistake here, so let's look at this from top to bottom before we jump right in. A few years back I had some Lab pups that were about six or seven weeks old and the new owners were coming out to the ranch to make their picks. One fellow from Utah was particularly interested in a nice, bold male. He asked me if I would put the others away so he could focus on the one he liked.

I was gathering up all of the other puppies to take them back to the puppy pen when I heard a shot. Ka-boom, again. I dropped what I was doing and rushed over behind the guy's truck to find out what the hell was going on where I saw him getting ready to

Guns—go easy when you're starting your puppy

shoot again. I said, "Hey, what the hell are you doing?"

"I didn't drive for eight hours to buy a gun-shy dog," he replied.

"If you shoot that gun one more time, you're not going to buy this dog or any other dog from me, you got that straight?" I said.

Some people are unbelievably ignorant when it comes to introducing gunfire to puppies. The puppy was less than 10 feet in front of someone he had never seen before who was shooting heavy duck loads through a 12-gauge right over his head. That puppy had been shot around for a week or two with caps, then .22 blanks and finally light shotgun loads, but, still, he hit the ground like a whistle pig with a redtail overhead.

"Goddammit, look at what you just did to that pup. Wait a minute and I will see how much damage is done." I finished putting the other puppies away and grabbed a pigeon out of the flight pen. "Let's take him over to the training field and give him the chance to settle down." We really dodged a bullet. The old bird saved the day. In five minutes of chasing a wing clip, the puppy came back to his old, bold self. I fired my blank pistol when he was in the process of chasing after the pigeon and he didn't blink. He picked up the bird and hustled back to us.

"I guess he'll do," the guy said.

"Well, I guess so."

In almost all cases, gun-shy dogs are made that way by people. Right now, at our kennel here in Idaho, we are working with two young pointers who were shot over by six hunters in one uninformed handler's idea of introducing pups to guns. This case was made doubly worse by the fact the birds were present when the guns went off. Now they hate guns and they think the birds did it.

This problem is one of the hardest to fix and many times the damage is irreversible.

These and similar stories are not exceptions. These mistakes are repeated over and over in this country every year.

Just take a six-month-old baby out of her mother's arms and

dump a couple of 12-gauge loads over her head. Heck, she'll be in therapy for 25 years.

Let's be smart here. There is too much at stake. Let's take it easy during this transition so we can get on up the hill.

Here's how I like to introduce puppies to guns: We do some work with them while they are still in the litter, but you probably don't have that luxury.

Gary Ruppel

I don't see any real need to start with a cap gun with a puppy that is a couple of months old. You can start with a blank gun or light shotgun loads if you are careful about how you go about it. I like to take a pup out on a normal field workout where he is romping and playing and getting involved with all of the fun things you have been experiencing out there every day.

Sometimes it's good to have someone help you with your training and this is one

Gary Ruppel and Labrador

of them. While you are playing with the pup and keeping his attention, have your helper shoot the gun from a distance of 100 yards or so. I also like the gunner to point the gun away from the dog so the noise is the softest you can make it.

Blank guns make a sharper report than shotguns, so there is not much of an advantage in using a blank gun over a 20-gauge. I never introduce a pup with a 12-gauge for any reason. There is just no sense in it. A .410 or a 20-gauge are the best shotguns and a .22 blank is not nearly as sharp as a .32 caliber.

If the puppy looks up or seems startled by the noise, tell your helper to stop shooting for that session. If the pup is still excited and doesn't really notice the shot, wave to your helper to come a little closer, say 15 yards, and shoot again.

I like to tell the helper to only shoot when I wave to him. This keeps the shots going off when I decide instead of when the shooter decides.

Anytime the pup gets concerned or worried about the next shot, I stop right there and start again the next day.

Do not use birds while you're working on the gun. You don't want something to go wrong where your pup can associate it with birds.

Over a period of a couple of days, the puppy will go about his business without batting an eye while the gun is being shot at fairly close range.

Once he is OK with this, I like to throw wing-clipped pigeons until he is consumed with chasing and catching them. When he shows you that he throws all caution to the wind when you throw him a wing clip, then start shooting your blank gun as he chases wildly. Point your gun directly away from the pup and be very watchful of any negative reactions.

When a pup is flying after a pigeon I shoot the blank gun. I generally will shoot several shots in succession. I then experiment with shots as he is returning with the bird or carrying it. If all goes well, you can rest assured he probably won't be sensitive to the gun if you take this just a little further by shooting the shotgun over him.

When I first shoot the shotgun over a pup, I like to plant a pigeon, a good flyer, and let the pup flush it. The pup is used to wing-clipped birds and will assume the bird will land in a short distance. Wait until the bird has flown at least 35 yards and is well into the air before you shoot it.

The pup will burn up the ground and roll end over end as he tries to pick it up. Always let the bird fly a good distance before shooting. Never shoot a bird at close range for a young dog.

If things aren't going well with the shot, get off of it for a while, maybe a couple of weeks, while you bold your dog up with the part of training he likes best. Don't go on from here until you fix whatever ails you.

If you get frustrated or scared while adjusting your pup to the gun, call in a pro. Most professional trainers can give you good advice to keep you in the saddle. The main thing is, just don't take it for granted every thing will be OK if it doesn't feel OK.

Well, hopefully you're still with me 'cause we're getting ready to have some real fun with our puppy. I got Camas squared away with the gun and now we're going to hit the fields with a different purpose than we have had until now.

We are still working on our waist cord at the first of the workout, the middle, and at the end. We are still working on influence handling and the fundamentals of control, we are still trying to flush all the birds we can, but now I'm shooting some of them.

Here is a word to the wise you should not forget: try to never shoot the first bird of a workout if you can help it. The pup needs to know that every bird that gets flushed doesn't get shot. If you make the mistake of shooting them all, it will promote a bad chasing habit that is hard to break afterward. Just shoot one every now and then and your pup won't want to run out of the country when you miss one.

If I'm planting pigeons for the pup to flush, I usually plant three—two homers and one bird that I intend to shoot. Sometimes I shoot in the air as the homers fly away just for drill, but I only shoot one.

Always encourage your pup to retrieve the bird naturally and again you can use your influence to help bring the bird all the way back. Puppies commonly run with the bird when they first pick it up and sometimes they run in big circles or off in another direction. The best thing to do is to back away from him to see if you have any influence. If the pup starts back toward you, say "here" once and keep moving backward. As the pup approaches, kneel down and take whatever he gives you. Maybe he will start chewing it, maybe the pup will drop it 20 feet away, maybe he will take off on another spin, maybe he will bring it to you. Just take what you get because you can fix anything about this delivery later on in training. The important thing is the association of the hunt, the bird, the flush, the shot, and the retrieve.

A young bird dog really starts to get intense at this stage of his development. It is always best to work toward the bird into the wind if you can. Try to avoid working your dog downwind.

Here is one of the natural controls we have talked about, so use it to your best advantage. Dogs don't like to run directly into the wind. When you work your pup into the wind, he will start quartering so he won't have to encounter the wind directly.

He will hunt from side to side to avoid the straight-on wind and he will hunt side to side. Because of your influence, before you know it, your pup will be quartering just like a pro with no formal controls whatsoever. If you find yourself working downwind, you will notice your dog casting straight away and then returning straight back. Straight out, straight in, straight out, straight in. This is an awful hunting pattern and it's your fault, not your dog's.

How many times have you seen this scenario:

Out in the Midwest, most upland hunting is done around row crops of some kind—either wheat, corn, milo or whatever you choose. When these crops are harvested there is normally a stubble left behind and many of us have logged plenty of miles walking up and down those grain fields. Sometimes hunters place blockers at the other end of those fields because pheasant in particular like to run to the end before flying.

If you work a flushing dog while you are walking down the rows, you are putting your dog at a serious disadvantage. He will have a tendency to hunt straight out and straight in, instead of quartering the field. If he strikes bird scent while hunting out, you're in real trouble because he will take it on down the row towards the end of the field.

I have seen some amazing screaming fits out in those fields and I'm sure many a good dog has been thrashed after bumping all the pheasant out of a cornfield.

Usually the dogs start to pick up their pace as they realize the bird is running and soon after the hunters figure out they have no control on the dogs. The hunters start walking faster and faster, screaming louder and louder, until everybody is nearly at a dead run when the birds get up two hundred yards out in front.

I have seen red-faced hunters throw loaded shotguns toward their dogs and I've see some nice headers when the hunter tried to run after his dog. This whole situation is the hunter's fault. This is a no-win deal for the dog.

When the hunters quicken their pace in the same direction the dog is going, it gives the dog the slack and the motivation to speed up and run bigger. When the hunters slow down, stop, or better yet back up, the dog feels obligated to come around.

You can take the same dog that just ran the entire length of a half-section of grain and try it again, only this time you hunt him into the wind and across the rows. Because you are crossing the rows instead of going down them, he will naturally quarter and because you are hunting into the wind, he will be less inclined to line out. If the dog starts to break down a row, influence him back by moving away from him.

You can turn failure into success just by anticipating problems and avoiding them. If you give your dog the chance to be successful he will do the same for you.

I'm going to be away for a couple of months while Camas and I work on our pyramid. We are going to attempt to find and flush every game bird in northern Idaho.

We're going to work on it before work, after work, on weekdays and weekends. My pup's getting pretty wild about now, so I will have to pay close attention to my structure. These are foundation bricks I'm placing. I will be sure they are firm and square so she will stand like a single oak when she is mature.

I'm thinking of you today. I wonder how your pup is doing. There is so much to say, so much to write about. I worry if I failed to tell you of something. I want your pup to turn out as good as mine. I will give you this personal promise: You cannot find all of the answers to the problems that may plague you as you read this book and train your dog, but I know where you can find them. I will give you something to think about for a time. I'll see you in a few months. We will compare notes then before we get on with the task at hand. We have a long way to go.

Today Camas and I walked along Lawyer Creek just after sunrise. We jumped a few ducks and shot a couple of drake mallards. I love this country. The elevation is only about 1200 ft. but one surely gets the feeling of being in the mountains. I was thinking of my first trip to this area. The locals told me of the mild winters and moderate temperatures because of the maritime air patterns. I'm from western Colorado, so I've seen some winter, and this sure feels like winter to me. I haven't seen the sun in three weeks now and most mornings reveal a couple of inches of new snow. The air is more humid than I'm used to. It seems odd to feel such dampness in winter. The humidity sure makes for some spectacular mornings as the river and creeks are usually enshrouded in mist.

Lawyer Creek wiggles through a rugged canyon that originates near the Salmon River and cuts deeper and deeper until it eases into the Clearwater River at Kamiah.

Legend has it that this creek is the namesake of a famous Nez Perce chief who lived somewhere near where I am standing this morning. I looked about the canyon. The cliffs above Lawyer Creek are striking. They are significant enough to be noted in the diary of the Lewis and Clark expedition to the West Coast in the early 1800s.

Some of the older locals talk of caves in those cliffs where people actually lived for a time. Could there be some artifacts up there to tell the story, or parts of it?

I gazed across the tops of the cliffs. I heard chukar calling from the grassy knolls on the ridge. Old Chief Lawyer never heard that call, nor of the rooster pheasant. I suppose there have always been eagles and accipiters touring the thermals. Today was no exception.

Yesterday on the news I heard we are having the most snowfall recorded in more than 22 years. Long-needle pines are drooping and side canyons are crowded with whitetail deer. I saw the signs early last fall. I should have known.

Oh, I heard what folks were telling me about the climate, but I also saw signs of more winter than they were used to.

Camas drove up a side hill and disappeared into thick hawthorns. She climbed another 400 feet, bounced up on her back legs and dived off into a sharp ravine.

Wild rose, thimbleberry, hawthorn and some chokecherry had survived by holing up near a small seeping springs in the bottom. This puppy was telling me of things to come so I slid out into an opening and dropped two shells in the tubes of my 20-gauge.

I heard them coming long before I saw them: eight roosters screaming down the draw, sailing, beating, and weaving their way through the brush before five of them came over me. One unlucky soul bounced as he hit behind me, but before he came to a rest, Camas snatched him up, shook him once, and trotted to me.

I took the pheasant and waited while she hustled back up in the ravine and after a time she showed back up, satisfied the birds were gone.

I was trying to poke the pheasant in my bag as we walked up the creek. Camas was leaping and grabbing at my hands until I got him stowed and then she was off to the front, flying.

Along the creek I noticed the rich, natural grass mixture had been gradually degraded by over-grazing livestock, dredge mining, and logging operations. Many species of noxious weeds vied for what nutrition the soil had left to offer. This beautiful canyon was clearly reeling.

The land was anxious about its future. Things had not gone well for this ranch, probably since Chief Lawyer lived here. First, the cattlemen pounded it with more cattle than this harsh environment could provide food for, then the creek bed was destroyed while early western miners high-graded the most valuable soil of the riparian area.

The logging industry showed up in time to clear-cut entire hillsides and to leave stumps and slash piles throughout the bottoms.

Through all this adversity, the resources fought to regain their balance. The land threw up all the stickers and thorns it could to discourage the livestock, the stream frantically tried to find its bed again as the thin layer of topsoil was carried on down the creek and into the river, leaving only rock bars and flats.

Maybe the topsoil was only six inches deep. Maybe it wasn't good for farming, but it took about 10,000 years to accumulate and it was gone in less than fifty. This is very characteristic of what happened to the entire American west. This is a sad story, folks.

All throughout nature there are signs relevant to what has happened, what is happening, and what will happen. As you walk your dog, you can study this great manuscript. You can learn to feel your way and to understand hope and truth. The earth has a spirit, the land has a destiny, the river a reason. There are specific reasons for the marshes, the lakes, the grasses, the rock, and the forested mountains. They are trying to provide for the future, theirs and ours.

I believe the dogs are our window into this natural world. The land has a heartbeat. Look for it. Place your hand flat on the surface of the river and feel for its heartbeat.

"Nice place you have here, Chief. Thanks for having us. Come on, Camas, let's get going. What the heck are you chewing on anyway? Damn, a dog can eat anything."

Chapter Ten:
Formal Obedience

*I*s that pup of yours getting wild yet? Is he tearing up the country, hard to handle, driving your family crazy? Are you cussing me for talking you into putting the burn in your pup without any real controls? Well, could be your pup is ready for formal obedience now. You might be cussing the program right now, but I'm willing to bet you will be grateful for it later.

There are many accepted ways to accomplish what you could consider formal obedience and all of them have their merits. The system I prefer revolves around a device called the Power Obedience Bar, or "Power Bar" for short.

One day I was working dogs at my old kennel near Rifle,

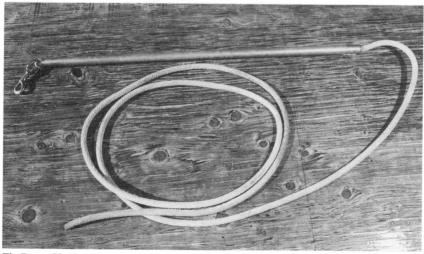

The Power Obedience Bar

Colorado. I was doing some obedience work on a group of young retrievers. I had learned to teach obedience using the loose lead method and watched as other trainers put the good obedience in their dogs with this tried and true philosophy. It occurred to me there could be a better way of achieving solid obedience by better control of the dog while training.

I was walking down a dirt road with a Labrador at heel. I was daydreaming as I thought about proper obedience structure. I wondered how I could develop a system that would be better for me as a trainer and also better for the dogs.

I saw a pile of old lumber under a barn. A broom handle caught my eye, so I drug it out of the mix and broke it in half. I tied my lead around the broom handle, top and bottom, and resumed the workout with my new custom training tool.

The enormous value of the lever was immediately apparent. Over the next few months I tried different types of materials such as PVC pipe, black pipe, oak dowels, cottonwood branches and driftwood.

I finally settled on half-inch electrical conduit and went about studying the principals of leverage and how they could apply to dog training. I'm still finding new uses for the bar, and most of them are worth keeping.

I met Bill Tarrant at the first AKC hunting retriever championship in western America. We talked about dogs and training as well as philosophy and methodology.

During our few days together, I got a brief glimpse of the man I now consider to be the most knowledgeable dog man I know of. Bill is also a treasured friend these days.

Bill is not only a friend of mine, he is the greatest friend the canine world could ever know. He has risked his job and his reputation as he made the public aware of the terrible indiscretions of gun dog trainers.

Bill is a fighter, and I know him, he will not concede. He won't quit trying to take the whip from the dog trainer's hand until they drag him away. He steadily reminds us that dogs have all the traits God said men should have but usually don't:

steadfastness, gentleness, devotion, loyalty, love and total acceptance.

Bill Tarrant was the gun dog editor for *Field and Stream* magazine for more than 23 years. Bill was named twice by the Dog Writers Association as the "Writer of the Year."

He won the Deepwoods award given by the Outdoor Writers of America for the best story of the year in any media.

Bill Tarrant wrote at least eight books featuring many innovative ways to train with your head instead of your hand, and several that none of us have been lucky enough to read yet.

Bill traveled the world to work dogs and talk to dog men. He didn't do this for money. He did it because his true love is dogs.

Gene Hill once said of Bill, "I think he probably turns around three times before he lays down."

He has trained with royalty and run the swap with hillbillies pushing a three-legged wolf as a hound. He was the father of the hunting retriever movement in the United States, a field trial judge, a mayor of a major city, a professor, and a philosopher patterned after Aristotle and Socrates. He was a politician, and a good one, until he was sickened by the whole process and cast his lot to the natural world. Bill was the all-Navy boxing champion at 146 pounds. He has suffered through two hip replacements and years of serious arthritis, and I still wouldn't fight him.

When the circus came to town and the challenge was to stay in the ring with some guy called Brutus of Mongo for three rounds and you win 50 bucks, he not only stayed in there, he always won. One time the outfit wouldn't pay him the money, so he and his friends caused a ruckus so wild they tore down the big top.

Tough? You bet. Determined? You're darned right. Stay with me as I tell you of someone I've come to admire so much.

As you read Bill's stories, they stir you to wonder about yourself and your ideals. As you read on, you long to have been there while the story was taking place. You can visualize the people, the animals, and the attitudes. Bill Tarrant is an amazingly talented painter of story. He has given us all a great gift, a notion to dream and to remember what went before. He writes mostly of others and always gives credit where credit is due. He seems drawn to adversity and offers stability as he scarcely mentions his fierce battle within.

Bill is intelligent and articulate. His words ring with truth and his handshake is honest. One of the main reasons I am standing today is because Bill helped me and inspired me to be courageous and patient.

We have watched the sun come up along the Rockies together. We have counted deer and talked dogs. We have hunted grouse and fished for trout, trained together and sipped iced tea as we evaluated puppies under the sagging boughs of an evergreen tree. Thankfully, we are friends.

Bill has seen and admired all kinds of shooting dogs. He says, "There is only a dog. Oh, yes, they come in different sizes and shapes, but there is only a dog."

He lives with what he calls "What-not dogs" and dotes on them like they were national champs.

I remember one day during a field trial, Bill was the senior judge. He saw a young Labrador had outrun his legs on a very hot day. The dog wouldn't stop hunting for a mark that had been wing clipped and flew out of the normal fall zone. He was frothing and choking for air while his handler stood with his whistle in his hand and hoped for the dog to come up with the bird. Even though it was highly irregular, Bill placed his hand on the handler's shoulder and calmly said, "Son, go get that dog of yours a drink and when you come back we'll finish up here."

The same day he won a first-time handler to dogs forever when he allowed him to run out of contention for the duration of the test even though the dog was clearly out of her working class. He gave the fellow some training tips and a duck to work with and then turned his head while the guy introduced his dog to ducks for the first time. Training at a field trial is forbidden, but not to Bill. He realized the dog wasn't a factor on that day and she never would be without a helping hand. That same dog earned a Grand Hunting Retriever Championship a few years later.

You know how dog trainers are. They like to sit around together after working dogs, have a beer and talk shop. Sooner or later the conversation gets around to electric collars and how beneficial the electric program is, (if the collar is used right).

About that time you will catch the shadow of a short, stocky guy shuttling out of the firelight. That would be Bill Tarrant leaving. You want to talk dogs, fine. You want to talk training, fine. You want to talk intimidation, domination, whips, prods or electricity, he's got better things to do. Don't ask him where he's going. He's trying to be nice. If he turns around you won't want to hear what he has to say.

Bill Tarrant introduced the Power Obedience Bar in the pages of *Field and Stream* in February 1986. Since then he and I have been working on the principle of the bar and have discovered a great many values of this training technique. I think the Power Obedience Bar method of obedience training is the finest, most thorough means of getting the hard obedience in a dog. It's a little clumsy at first, but if you stick with it, the bar will pay great dividends.

You may look to the pages of *"Tarrant Trains Gun Dogs"* by Stackpole Publishing Co., or *"Training the Hunting Retriever"* by Bill Tarrant and the Howell Book House. Bill does a good job of describing the bar and how to make one for yourself. I make my bars out of half-inch rigid electrical conduit. Since I am six feet tall, I cut my bars 29 inches long. If you are shorter or taller than me, you should make the bar to fit yourself. With one end anchored at my solar plexus the other end is about at my wrist when the bar is straight up and down. If you don't feel like making one, look in the back of this book for ordering information, and we'll send you a Power Obedience Bar and video kit.

The Power Obedience Bar system works on the principles of leverage. The bar allows the trainer to apply leverage to the dog to influence the dog to do what he wants. The bar provides incredibly efficient and permanent training.

The applications of the power bar system are broad and unique. The obedience is first mastered at your side and then through a series of increments, and it is transferred into off lead and field obedience.

We commonly call this training "ground work," or "yard work." Pointers, spaniels, and retrievers have to go through a period of obedience before they can go further on to the advanced skills of field work.

I like to run a stout diamond weave nylon cord through the bar and then through a brass snap and back into the bar for at least twelve inches. I fill both ends of the bar with epoxy putty so the rope is secured forever. I think it is important to make sure the snap is held firmly against the end of the bar. I usually leave about 15 feet of rope on the opposite end of the bar and no longer tie a knot in the end.

The thing looks like this: a brass snap snugged to a 29-inch piece of conduit with a 15-foot trail rope.

To make the contraption work right, you need a good collar to snap it to. I have always used a JASA force-training collar, or pinch collar, made by Bud Hulan. I used Bud's collars for 20 years, not only because I liked him personally, but because they were the finest, stoutest, and most consistently well-made collars I've ever seen. Unfortunately, Bud has recently passed away and I've only recently found a quality outlet for equipment. (See ordering information in the back of this book.) I think any well-made collar will do the trick for you. I have always preferred leather.

It is not mandatory that you use a pinch collar. Your regular collar will work OK. Just make sure it's a decent one. Don't go to the pet store to buy a collar for a working dog. Look around for something substantial with good buckles and D-rings.

If you choose to use a pinch collar, use it only for obedience and then put it away. We may need it later on, but probably not. When you are not using the collar make sure you store it straightened out, not in a circle. It is critical the collar retain its stiffness and its spring. When you first buy the collar, it will be very stiff. Don't oil or soften it in any way, it must remain stiff. If it gets limber, throw it in a mud puddle or spray it with the hose until it is soaked and then hang it out in the sun to dry. When you can no longer keep it stiff, throw it away.

If you decide to use the dog's regular collar, make sure to tighten it slightly before you start your training sessions and, of

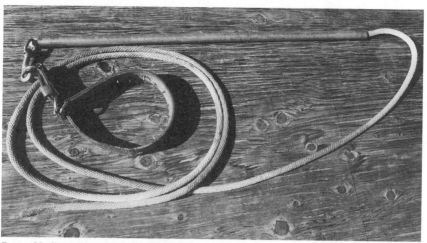

Power Obedience Bar and pinch collar

course, remember to re-adjust it after the workout. You read lots of stuff about how to adjust your dog's collar, but basically it just needs to stay on. Fix it so it won't come over the dog's ears but is not tight enough to choke him.

As we start our Power Bar training, we must remind ourselves, the key word is "power." This bar can provide some dramatic leverage, so be careful with it as you learn how to use it. You don't need to pump it or jerk on it to get results. Just taps and tugs will get you where you need to be in short order.

As you study the Power Obedience Bar you might get the idea the thing is indestructible. Not so. Every now and then I get a dog in for training who bends my bar into a horseshoe. I have seen dogs who could completely dismantle the power bar in one session. I have been thankful, on several occasions, that the bar was as long as it was.

I have protected myself with it and held vicious dogs off until I could get them secured. When you train for the public, you never know what kind of critter is coming down the road. When you get a 170-pound Rottweiler with a reputation as a hard case on the end of your Power Bar, you no longer question the virtue of it.

On the other end of the spectrum, the bar can be gentle enough to train puppies or small dogs without intimidating them. This is a tremendously versatile training aid.

One note before we go on. If you are using a pinch collar, you need to make sure you have it on correctly. The collar needs to be able to let up on its own when there is no pressure on it. The whole idea is to only pinch the dog when it's necessary and then only as long as necessary. The collar must easily slide back to a relaxed position as long as the dog is in the proper place.

I always start by teaching "sit" and "heel" simultaneously. Keep the sessions fairly short. Just remember to put one brick on every day and leave it at that.

As we teach obedience, we are going to condition our dog to a definite sequence of

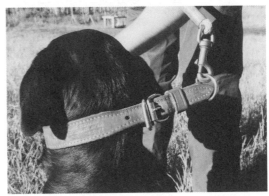

Pinch collar

events each and every time out of the blocks. The dog will learn to cue off of us with at least three of his senses and sometimes four. When we give each command we will make sure to cue the dog with feel, sound and sight.

OK, let's start with heel and sit. I don't care which side you want your dog to heel on, just be consistent.

I like to work off my left side, some out of habit, but there are physical reasons why this side works best for me. The power bar is a lever, and as Bill Tarrant says, it's similar to a canoe paddle. The top hand is the power hand. The lower hand provides the fulcrum. Together they give you the leverage to handle the toughest or the softest dog. Because the top hand provides the power and the directional influence, I like to use my right hand up there.

As we begin our first session, place your collar on the dog and snap the power bar onto it inside the kennel or truck. Establish this control device first off. Walk to your training area with the dog at your side. If he jumps or pulls or tries to get away, just remain calm and supportive and try not to jolt him with the power bar.

When you get to the spot where you want to start the session, you need to apply leverage for him to sit. To do this, the snap end of the bar has to be just above his collar and the top end should be directly in front of the dog. The bar should be in a straight line with the dog's spinal column. The top end of the bar has to be

Tap the bar with your left hand, say "heel," and begin walking.

held slightly lower than the snap end for the leverage to be right. Cup your left hand under the snap end of the bar and reach out with the top end as you lower it into place. Now, simply move the bar toward the rear of the dog being careful to keep it in line with the backbone. Because the front of the bar is lower than the back and because you are providing support to the snap end, the leverage will cause the dog's head to rise and his butt to go down.

Sometimes the dog will initially resist, but soon he will sit when he feels the pressure. This levered force allows you to make the dog come to a sitting position. You also have the ability to move the dog's front end away from you or toward you, depending on where he ended up. We want the dog to be sitting by our side looking straight ahead. We want him to sit up straight and hold his head up. From this point on, we will never let him sit sloppy (over to one side or the other) and we want him to look up and show confidence.

Dogs are just like people. If a person doesn't like what he's told to do he tries to avoid doing it. He will go to any length to get out of it and this is where escape re-

Teaching "sit"

sponses come in. Dogs don't like to be told what to do, either. When you start the formal obedience sessions with your dog, you are going to get a good practical look at escape responses and how to handle them.

"Heel"

Let's say you have given your dog the sit command and he has complied with it for the most part. Is he yawning all of the sudden? Did he put his front foot on your foot when he sat? Did he try to sit sloppy or crooked? Did he stand up and shake like he had just come out of

144

Photos by Gary Hubbell

K.D. McGraw

K.D. McGraw

K.D. McGraw

K.D. McGraw

K.D. McGraw

Gary Hubbell

K.D. McGraw

Gary Hubbell

Gary Hubbell

K.D. McGraw

Gary Hubbell

Gary Hubbell

K.D. McGraw

K.D. McGraw

Gary Hubbell

K.D. McGraw

K.D. McGraw

the water? Did he whine or bark while looking up at you? Did he try to lay down? Did he look away from you and refuse to give you eye contact? Did he grab at the end of the bar? Did he try to talk you into playing with him? Did he growl or act aggressive? Did he try to bounce up on you, especially on your back? Is he leaning against your leg?

Escape response (sloppy "sit")

These are all escape responses. He isn't sleepy, he isn't shaking off dirt or water, and he isn't confused or suddenly aggressive. He is trying to avoid "sit." We aren't asking him to sit, we are telling him to and that brings out the escape response.

When you tell your children to go to bed because it is getting late, one of them will say, "Just a minute," one will say, "I'm going to watch the end of this show," and one might say, "I don't feel well," or "I'm going to get a drink." This is the same stuff, folks. No matter how you cut it, the kids are trying to escape the command. If your kids knew you were serious when you told them to go to bed and if they knew you expected quick reaction, they would all get up and head off to bed. The problems come with inconsistent cues. For instance, how often have you seen this scenario take place: "OK, kids, it's bed time. It's getting late, kids, no kidding now. I really mean it, it's been an hour since I asked you to go to bed. I'm serious and I'm getting mad here. OK, this time I really mean it. Goddammit, go to bed, you little creeps, before I beat you to a pulp." Sound like some dog trainers

"Affection" escape   *"My foot on your foot" escape*

you've been around? I'll be willing to bet it does.

Learn to watch for escapes. You will see many of them as you go through training. I believe it is very easy to deal with all of them if you get started right now while we are doing formal obedience.

When you give your dog a command and you get an escape response, REPEAT the command and apply the appropriate pressure. If you command your dog to "sit" and he puts his front foot on your foot, push him out with the bar until he is lined up correctly and repeat the word "sit." If he stands up and shakes, give him the sit leverage and repeat the word "sit." He is not shaking off water or dirt, he is shaking off "sit." If he yawns after hearing a command, he is yawning off the command. Laugh if you want, but this information is really valuable.

You will have to eliminate each of his escapes individually. Every temperament is different and each one associates escapes differently. Once you go through all of them, the dog will generally respond to you quickly and correctly each time you give him a command. Never take an escape response lightly. Deal with it then and there. If you do this, your dog will respond to your commands and be happy about it. Watch for escapes!

Keep the workouts inside of 20 minutes. Don't be tempted to try and accomplish these skills in two days. You can do several workouts a day if you want, but don't exceed 20 minutes in one session. Brick by brick you can accomplish your goal.

Let's work on "heel." With your dog sitting properly beside you, say the dog's name, then step off with your inside leg, (leg nearest the dog). Tap the snap end of the bar forward, and say "heel" all at the same time. These three things have to happen simultaneously to get the right results.

He feels the tap of your left hand, he hears you say "heel," and he sees your left foot move forward.

As you walk your dog at heel, make sure you set the pace. If the dog wants to walk slow, you walk faster, if he wants to walk fast, you slow down. Show him you get to decide where to walk and at what speed.

As you are walking, keep the power bar fairly straight up and down with the top end anchored at your solar plexus. Grip the bar tightly there but let your left hand tap and bump as need be to adjust the dog. With the top end anchored, you can slap, tap or bump the snap end of the bar to move the dog up or back and from side to side. Throw the loose end of the rope over your right shoulder and let it drag behind you. We will explain what role it plays a little later.

After you have walked your dog at heel for a ways, it's time to stop and practice sit again. Just before you stop walking, lower the top end of the bar to the sit position and begin to lift up on the snap end. When you stop walking, apply the sit leverage and say "sit." The dog feels the leverage, he hears you say "sit," and he sees you stop, all at the same time. Again, three things happen at the same time and they all mean the same thing. This is quality dog training here. When you get your timing right, you won't believe the results you'll see.

If you don't apply your levered pressure directly down the spinal column, you will experience problems with your dog's sitting technique.

If the top end of the bar is closer to you than the snap end when you apply leverage, the dog will sit with his rear end near your leg and his front quarters out away at an angle. If you give the dog sit pressure with the top end of your bar further away from your leg than the snap end, the dog will sit with his rear end away from your leg and his front end very near your leg. Make sure to align your levered pressure directly down the spinal column so the dog learns you want him to sit straight.

Dog training is all about timing, and the more cues you can incorporate at once, the better your chances of success are. Also, later on, you can get the desired response from one cue or a combination of the three. This is multiple-sensory impact and it is layered-up obedience. It is absolutely permanent.

After formal obedience, you can let your dog lay in the backyard for five years without any control whatsoever and five minutes of power bar work will put him back on the beam. No kidding!

OK, back to "heel." Step, command, tap and off we go. Keep him walking straight, head up, looking ahead. We want him to look like a pro, so slouching doesn't get it.

Now, let's sit. Stop, command, leverage.

Work on it, it takes some practice before it starts coming around.

As you feel more comfortable with the heel and sit command, then start walking in a circle. I like to work on circles to the right first.

The circle can be a large one. Don't try to crank the dog in a tight circle the first time you show him one. A nice circle, oh, I'd say about 20 feet in diameter is best. When you walk in a circle to the right, keep the bar anchored at your solar plexus and tap the snap end of the bar toward your left leg. You will find you can keep the dog's head right where you need it to be without much trouble. If the dog veers out to the left, drags or pulls ahead, adjust him accordingly and say "heel" again. Each time he resists, show him some pressure and repeat the command. Don't lean on him about this. Make your adjustments light and firm. He'll get the idea, just give him time.

Now let's walk in a circle to the left. Lower the bar so it is parallel to the ground, right across your lap. I usually hold it right about belt high. The top hand is still power and the lower hand still shows the way. You can move the dog's head in or out, back and forward with unbelievable ease. If the dog is walking too close to you, push the bar across your lap to the left. This will move his head immediately to the left. If he is wandering out away from you, pull the bar to the right and he will again align.

One nice thing about heeling to the left using the power bar technique is that you will notice how the dragging rope helps to keep his rear end in line. The dog feels the rope as it touches his back feet and generally scoots into position. Each time you change directions, tell him what you are going to do. Don't try to trick him into thinking one way and then turn the other. The dog will feel the tap, hear the command, and see you turn. You want your dog to be consistent? Then you be consistent.

Practice your heeling and sitting for awhile as you work on your timing together. Remember to place the collar and bar on the dog before you get him out, go through the workout, and then put the dog back into his kennel before taking it off. You will be surprised how quickly his attitude will change from one of escape to pride in accomplishment. Gradually he will enjoy his obedience because he is successful with it. As soon as you think you have it down, do it for at least a couple more days.

Now, after you have worked on "heel" and "sit," let's introduce the "stay" command into our program. Start your session just like you have been doing with "heel" and "sit" for a few minutes then while the dog is sitting beside you, drop the bar to the ground but keep ahold of the drag rope. The bar is attached to the collar so the snap end will stay up along the dog's neck as the top end of the bar rests on the ground. The bar will rest at an angle from the dog's neck to the ground. I hold the rope in my right hand because the left hand will serve useful in showing the dog "stay." This part of the power bar system takes some practice, but it's very useful once you get the hang of it. Lift the top end of the bar off the ground just slightly and place your left foot on the top end of the bar itself. Keep the top end of the bar just off the ground as you push the bar back along the side of the dog until the dog feels a nudge from the rear.

Boy, this is hard to explain. Luckily, it's a heck of a lot easier to do. Stay with me, I promise it's worth it.

As the dog feels the nudge, say "stay," and show him the flat of your left palm. The dog feels the backward pressure, he hears "stay," and he sees your hand all at the same time. Again, three things, and they all mean "stay."

Come on now, it's not that wild. You don't think I'd go to all the trouble of writing this down if it didn't pay off big time as we go up the pyramid, do you?

"Sit" and "Stay" sequence

Here is where you play a dirty trick on your dog. When you give the dog the backward pressure, push the top end of the bar into the ground with your left foot.

Keep showing the dog your left palm in a gesture resembling a traffic cop as he tells you to wait until it's clear to go. Now, back away from the dog a few feet, say eight or 10, while still holding onto the rope. If the dog tries to follow you, the bar will dig into the ground, and because of the angle, the bar will give him a firm jolt from the back. Say "stay" and re-position the dog. The bar actually disciplines the dog for moving without being told to, and more importantly, without you having anything to do with it. Once the dog accepts the "stay" command and waits while you back away, you will often see some more of the escapes appear. Many dogs will look away and refuse eye contact. Some will lay down or turn sideways. Some will try the old, "sit on the side of the butt," routine. Insist he sit up straight with his head up, but don't reach down to touch him. Drop a little loop from your drag rope and lift his head with it.

A great advantage of training with the power bar method is you never have to actually touch the dog as you adjust him. Dogs love to make you touch them and if you can do obedience without touching them it's greatly humbling to the dog.

Now let's call the dog back to heel. Keep the drag rope in your right hand and gently pull on it so the top end of the bar comes off the ground. Your left hand should still be in the stay position. Pull on the rope until the bar is pointing toward you and reveal the left side of your body to the dog. Say "stay" and slightly pull on the rope so the dog feels pressure to come to you. That sounds weird, doesn't it? Why would you pull on the dog to come and say stay at the same time? Well, because it reinforces stay, that's why. You will find that the dog has to lean against your pressure to come if he is to comply with your command so he will be trying his best to stay even though he feels direct pressure to come to you. Any dog who has a tough time with the stay command can be fixed permanently by pulling on him slightly as you tell him stay, only letting him come to you when you call him.

When you get ready to call the dog back to heel, make sure you have eye contact, then tap on the rope with your left hand and say "heel" at the same time. The dog feels a tug, hears the command "heel," and sees your left hand drop all at the same time. As the dog starts to you, catch the bar in your left hand and bring the dog to heel with the bar in the original position.

We have taught the dog to heel, sit, stay and come back to heel and we have used three cues with every command. I like to work the dog on the power bar for a couple of weeks before moving on.

Keep practicing on all of your timing as you watch that young dog acquire good obedience skills. Walk in circles to the left, then to the right. Do figure-eights and long walks down the road. Get it perfect and as soon as you think you have it down, do it for at least five more days.

We have the power bar drills down by now, so it's time to move on with the transition. We now put the old waist cord to use. Remember when we talked about the waist cord and how important it was that it be just right? Just the right length, just the right material, just the right degree of stiffness, just the right knot? Well, now you'll know why.

The next time you take your dog out for obedience, instead of hooking him up to the power bar, slip your waist cord on him. Make sure the loop is on your dog's neck the same as the pinch collar was. The waist cord has a front and back, so remember to use it right.

Go through your usual obedience workout and use the waist cord just like the bar was in there. The cord is very stiff and retains much of the leverage the bar provided. Keep your hands in the same positions and make the same adjustments as you would with the bar. Everything will be much easier now and your dog's obedience will be coming together. The training is getting fun for both of you because the cord isn't nearly as intimidating to the dog.

Your timing is getting sharp and your understanding of obedience is forever changed. Your dog is gaining confidence every day and is happy to show you his achievements at your slightest prompting.

Quickly the dog will jump to the same level of obedience that

you were seeing while on the power bar and this tells you he is ready to move on. As soon as you think he is perfect, do it for at least five more days.

We have made the transition from absolute obedience on the power bar to super control on the waist cord and now we begin our transition to off-lead obedience.

Always start each session by establishing control with the waist cord. After a short obedience drill, you are ready to cut the tie.

Waist cord transition

If you pull and say "sit," the command sticks.

While your dog is walking at heel, just drop the cord to the ground and keep walking. He may be intimidated by the cord dragging behind him but he shouldn't pay much attention to it. If he drops back or moves away, just pick up the cord and start again. He will soon walk as smartly at heel while the cord drags as he was doing before. Go through all of his obedience steps with the cord dragging and finish up the session with a few minutes of work while handling the cord.

Establish control, go through the drill, and re-establish control before putting him away. You'll see where I'm going with this later.

Now you can start experimenting with off-lead obedience as long as you keep it in the middle of your training sessions. I like to lay the loose end of my waist cord on the dog's outside front

Dragging lead

154

shoulder as I walk him at heel to get a feel for how well he is doing. Most of the time the dog will work his obedience picture-perfect with the cord barely touching his shoulder. It just reminds him of what we have learned together and I might still have complete control.

When the dog is working well while off lead a full 50 percent of the time, I start working on the formal "here" command. I tell the dog to stay and walk further away than usual. I wait for a short time then call the dog with "here." I don't use the command "come." It just doesn't work as well as "here." Here sounds like "heel" and it means the same thing. You can hear the word "here" farther than you can the word "come" and so can your dog. Use "come" if you want, but I use "here."

After the dog will comply with "here," I move farther and farther away from him before I call him in. I like to get to the point where I can leave the dog at stay and walk a couple hundred yards away before I call him to me. Always wait for a time before you call him or he will get in the habit of breaking toward you as soon as you turn around to look at him. I also like to turn back about halfway out and reinforce stay with voice and hand signal.

I also generally walk around some once I get to the distance

Dragging lead and off-lead obedience

I'm going to call him from. I walk back and forth a little so he doesn't get the idea I'm going to call him right off.

Also, moving around some at long distances causes the dog to concentrate on you as he waits for the command. He will stare at you intently and follow your every move. This will pay off major when you start handling him by remote casting. I stagger the time delay so he really never knows when the recall command is coming. This helps to keep his attention.

The Power Obedience Bar obedience system is terrific. I know some trainers who won't even do obedience if they can't find their bar in the morning.

Let's move on to some new stuff. Bring all your hopes and dreams with you, bring your new skills and your brimming confidence. Take your pup to the hilltop and let him look out upon his kingdom. He is on his way up the pyramid. Be thankful you're together, be grateful for what he has taught you.

We are moving from formal obedience on to formal field work. We will be forever afield. We will be adventures and explorers together. I would like to share a tip that will make all of your workouts more enjoyable for you and your dog.

I have made reference to Bob Wehle and his breeding program. I also have told you how much I admire Bill Tarrant and his contribution to dogs. There is significant common ground between these two dog men. Both of these men are intelligent and sensitive. Both are inspirational and culturally sophisticated. Both are tenacious yet compassionate. These are the two greatest dog men I know.

Both of them will tell of the unmeasurable value of a table when working dogs. Bill Tarrant calls it the magic table, Bob Wehle calls it the love table. Call it anything you want, but if you don't include a working table in your program, you are missing what may be the most powerful and useful connection of all.

I use my table for everything. I use it every day, not only for the benefit the dog receives, but for the enormous benefit I receive. I have come to look forward to the time I spend with the dogs on the table more than any other time in the program.

I can jump a dog up on the table and talk to him as I brush him and style him up. I look for ticks or cuts I might have missed during training. I check his toes and his teeth. I make sure his eyes are healthy and clear.

Ears are always a problem if you don't pay attention to them, and the table lets you look at them on eye level so it's easy to notice warning signs.

I rub my hand across the dog's neck and under his abdomen, down the legs and tail, always brushing and talking to him, always being thoughtful and caring. When a dog is up on a table in front of you, it is just natural to become soft and supportive.

The brushing helps in several ways. It encourages the dog to relax on the table as it allows you to relax and dream. Maybe you weren't quite ready to train this morning, maybe you are stressed about money or your family. Maybe a friend is sick or in trouble. As you brush your dog and talk to him, he will settle and relax, and you will drift and reflect.

I have a back problem that has bothered me for twenty years.

Dog on table

I have a place on my table where I can elevate one foot for a time and then switch to the other. I love the feeling of relief. I sometimes sit on the table and talk to the dog with my arm around his neck. We look to the mountains. "There's grouse up there," I tell him, and he seems to understand.

Dog training is not dragging and shocking, barking out commands and expecting absolute compliance. Quality training has to be good for both of you. A good training program allows you both to give and receive. If you want to be accepted and respected, first you have to accept and respect.

As you spend time with your dog on the table, try to talk directly to him when you can. Make eye contact and talk to him.

Even dogs that may resent you for one reason or another will eventually warm to your efforts and look at you when you talk. Bob Wehle says they like to smell your breath. It's bonding, folks, and it's big time training technique. Bill Tarrant calls it magic, and so it is.

Try to include a table in your program. Put it in a comfortable place like under a shade tree and try to locate it on fairly level ground. I put mine right in front of the kennels. Get into the habit of jumping your dog up on the table before you take him to the field. A couple of minutes a day is all it takes.

There will come a time during our training process when the table will represent authority. We will come to the point where we have to sort out who gets to be boss. Every operation has to have a leader. The day will come in which you will have to establish control. Let's worry about that later. We'll come back to it down the road. That's when you will understand why I build my table like I do, and you will see how versatile it really is.

Gary Ruppel and Kodak

Chapter Eleven:
Marking and Field Work

*A*fter we have established some formal obedience and feel fairly comfortable with what we have accomplished, the next step is to develop the dog's marking ability.

Throughout a Labrador shooting dog's life he will encounter many situations in which he must be able to sort out falls and remember where they are. He will sometimes see wounded birds sail for several hundred yards before they pitch in. He will commonly have to keep track of birds that may fall from a covey or flight. He will gradually learn to understand how a bird acts when it is slightly hit or missed completely. The birds that fold up and fall within shotgun range are generally not hard to mark or pick up, but the long sailers and birds in heavy background cover can present real problems.

While we train for marking experience, we also have to remember to work on hunting "dead," or looking for the downed game. A good marking dog who has never really had much work on sifting out problems with wounded and ground-running birds will never be as valuable to the hunter as a dog who is proficient at hunting "dead." Marking the fall is only the first part of picking up birds; finding them is the most important part.

Some of the most brilliant pieces of dog work I've ever witnessed involved searching for a bird who had fallen and then ran to cover. It is quite easy to keep concentrating on the spot where you were sure the bird fell while your dog is telling you the bird has left the vicinity.

On guided hunts many hunters will say things like, "Get your dog in here, the bird fell right here," or "I saw the bird fall, I marked it down right here," or "I know it didn't go that far because it was hit hard and dropped straight down."

OK, maybe it did, maybe it didn't, but if you have worked your dog faithfully on finding wounded birds, you have a good chance of picking it up.

In the first place, I have never seen a hunter who could mark worth beans during an actual hunting situation. He is excited about the flushing and the shooting and marking the bird is many times cut short as his attention is jerked to another bird flushing, or another shooter. What usually ends up happening is the guy has to guess where the bird ended up based on his recollection of the whole scene.

This involves trying to remember just where he was standing at the flush, how many birds there were, how many shots he took, and how many he thinks were successful. Did his hunting buddy beat him to the punch? Did he get the double or was he late on both birds? Did he think to reload in case there were late risers, or did he blow the whole chance and miss all of them?

Often, after it's all over, the hunters end up looking for a downed bird and haven't got an honest clue where it might be.

Here is where the mystery of the ego of men comes into play. "It was just over that bush." "No, it kept going past that knoll and fell into the creek." "I saw it bounce behind that mesquite tree, it's got to be right around there somewhere."

It goes on and on, but the dog is usually the only one in the group who has knowledge and the perseverance necessary to get the bird picked up. What I have always found ironic about this sequence is this: The hunters fully expect the dog to keep track of all this wildness and calmly mark the birds who are shot and forget about the ones who weren't, even though they themselves were totally confused about almost every detail of the event.

If you prepare in training for this situation, your dog will most often come through. Of course, he still won't be able to find the one that you shot eighteen inches behind and two feet over, even though you were sure it was centered and had to be the toughest bird in the country.

Even while hunting from a blind, a good dog won't be just mindlessly sitting still logging in the successful efforts of the shooters. He will be moving all over the place, watching, remembering, trying to make something good happen.

Good marking dogs have to be developed. They don't just come out of the blocks with the knowledge required to pull off complicated marking challenges.

We are going to put the marks in our shooting dog because in the end, good marks will translate to birds in the vest, and the mark training process gives us more steadiness and dependability.

We teach marking by careful structure of our training sessions. I know many programs will have you running double and triple marked retrieves while the dog is still in early training, but I'm going to ask you nicely to again be patient until the mortar is set around the very important building stones of your dog's marking foundation.

We will show your young dog at least a thousand single marks before we go on to bigger and better things. We will build confidence in marking as we explore obstacles in cover, water, terrain, and weather conditions.

I really mean it when I say a thousand. You will come to appreciate the results of this approach when we get nearer to the top of our pyramid.

Let's do a little inventory here before we go on. We have started our dog. We have him buzzing and humming as he goes about his workouts. He loves birds and training and has been introduced to retrieving. He has learned his formal obedience and feels fairly comfortable within his role.

Now, let's start formal singles. We will start with the setup. Always keep things simple at first. These will be handler-thrown dummies for the most part. Before we go on, let's talk about dummies and what kind we want to use. Basically you have several choices when you go to purchase retriever training dummies. Most trainers use

Dummies

either canvas dummies or rubber knobbies throughout the dog's life.

Canvas dummies come in different sizes, from the small puppy size to the large goose model. I have used all of them from time to time and have some interesting observations based upon what I have seen. I like the puppy size canvas dummies for the early stages, say six weeks of age and up to about fourteen weeks. I then move to the medium size, about twelve inches long and three inches in diameter. I used to like the large size when working adult dogs but have changed my mind lately.

The large size dummies are about 15 inches long and exceed three and one half inches in diameter. I have noticed some mouth problems that have occurred from using the large canvas dummies, even with big dogs. I think dogs are prone to carry them by the end or the tip, especially when they are tired. I believe the dummy is uncomfortable in the dog's mouth for an extended period of time. Some of our retriever drills will include retrieving many dummies in a single session so comfort is a key issue. After all, dummies are just a training device–why not use something that the dog prefers? I have seen more than one instance where a dog injured his jaw while picking up or carrying a large dummy.

I remember a great young Labrador who was going through his casting and lining drills with me when he started exhibiting holding problems. He appeared to have trouble holding the dummy tight enough to carry it while he was running. He would occasionally drop it en route back to me and sometimes when he came to heel to deliver.

I decided to send him to a dead chukar because I knew he would not drop a bird. Lo and behold, he dropped the bird twice on the way back. I started to get frustrated with him because he was force broke to retrieve and hadn't shown any retrieving problems in over a year. I put some pressure on him to fetch and heel, but still the problem persisted.

Remember this if you remember nothing else you read in this book: When you run into a problem in training, I don't care what it is, first think about your role. Ask yourself, "Did I do something to cause the problem? Is he just reacting to something I did?" Before you increase pressure or discipline your dog, make sure your read is accurate.

I told the dog to sit and stay and walked away from him a short distance. As I looked back and studied his attitude, I noticed his lower jaw was hanging a little. This dog usually held his mouth closed while sitting, but he continued to hold it open. It was late morning and was warming up some so I thought he might have been a little hot. I let him rest for a few minutes and gave him a drink, but still his mouth was slightly open.

As it turned out, he had sprained his lower jaw picking up the dummy. It took several days before he could resume his retrieving training. Keep your eyes open out there. Not all things are as they first appear.

I have never used those large canvas dummies since that day and never will. The medium size is plenty big and still heavy enough for you to throw a good distance.

Most retriever trainers use the rubber dummies for water work. I use the small ones for puppies and force table work but find little use for them in field training sessions.

They will sometimes be frustrating in water also as they are very heavy and slender. They will go into water like a bullet on occasion, and if you're throwing marks in shallow water, they will stick like glue in the mud at the bottom. I have seen those things stay submerged for weeks before they pop to the surface long after the marking session was over.

I like the large rubber dummies for water work and I think the dogs like them, too. They are about the size of the medium canvas dummies and both the small and the large rubber dummies have rubber knobs on the outside. These knobbies can be helpful in developing good mouths.

Dogs do love to chew them if they are left available between sessions and the benefit of the knobby exterior is lost forever. Put them away between training sessions.

If I could only use one type of dummy, I would use the canvas. Canvas holds scent better and feels more like a bird in the dog's mouth. I think the canvas dummies hold up well enough to use in the water also and most of my water drills and all of my blinds work best for me when I use canvas.

Dummies come in a variety of colors. Some are white, at least when you first buy them, and some are orange, black, camo, or gray. The off-color ones are harder for the dog to see and because of that, I like the white ones. I'm not trying to trick him out there, I want him to see it and see it clearly. When my dummies get dirty and gray, I wash them so the dog can again see them easily. I want our shooting dog to be brimming with confidence on his marks, so white's the color and canvas is the material. You can add scent if you want, but the canvas scent alone will turn a dog's head from 40 yards.

If you buy some tightly woven nylon rope, about the same diameter as your waist cord, it will barely fit through the grommet of your dummy. If you cut the cord in 18-inch lengths, tie an overhand knot in one end, stick the other through the grommet and tie an overhand knot in it. You will end up with a throwing rope twelve inches long. Any shorter and it's hard to throw with accuracy, any longer and the dog will continually be stepping on in when he's running. Don't tie your throwing rope in a loop, because the dog can catch his front foot in there while swimming or running and nothing good can happen after that.

Don't be a cheapskate. Buy at least a dozen or two training dummies. It takes a lot of dummies to get it done. Keep them together and only give the dog access when you're training.

If you want your dog to acquire good marking skills, you have to be patient and work in increments. Don't just go to the field and cut your dog loose and throw dummies for him to retrieve as he tears around. Remember, we are now talking about formal singles so the structure has to start when we get the dog out of the truck.

Common training practice is to let the dog out to stretch and loosen up as he finds the perfect place to go potty and get cranked up. The dog is allowed to run around, jump in the water, or do whatever he wants for a short time before the training session is to begin. I think this is the wrong approach to a training session.

I like to put my waist cord on the dog as he gets out of the truck. I go through about two minutes of heel, sit, stay and here. I heel him for a short distance, I tell him to stay and walk back to where we started. I wait for just a second or two, long enough to get a read on his attitude, then I call him to heel again. During this little exercise, I make sure the dog's obedience is very tight. I don't end this segment until the dog is doing a sharp job and feeling good about it. I then remove the waist cord as I tell him to stay. This tells the dog that just because I am removing the cord, I don't want him to move yet. If he accepts this situation, I release him by tapping him on the back of the head and telling him, "Let's go." I let him loosen up now and take care of his personal business while he stretches and explores.

We have established control here before we started the session rather than cut him loose and then try to establish control afterward.

This is a very important tip in dog training: always estab-

Do your obedience prior to retrieving work

167

lish control going into the session rather than waiting for a time and then trying to get a handle on the dog.

You have programmed the dog to be obedient from the get-go so when you decide it is time to proceed with the session, he will readily comply.

OK, let's start with handler-thrown dummies. From here on we are going to ask our dog to stay for marks, so we can start the process right now. I like to use the loose end of my waist cord to get things moving. I put the cord around the dog's neck and hold the knot between two fingers.

If you pull the slack out, you end up with a firm hold on the dog, much like a collar, but it is very easy to release. Pull up slightly on the cord as you say "stay." Remember, timing is everything, so make sure you say "stay" at the same time the dog feels the tug. With your other hand, swing the dummy out and let it go a few yards. This doesn't have to be much of a toss, just get it out there a ways. The dog will want to go because you have been letting him go at least up until now. Restrain him momentarily and then drop the knot from your fingers and let the cord go. The dog will rush out and snag the dummy and hopefully bring it back to you.

It is very important to call the dog just before he reaches to pick the dummy up. Don't wait until he picks it up and starts a big loop—call him just before he gets it in his mouth. By doing this, you get the dog

Use the waist cord to keep the dog close while marking

thinking of coming back before he makes the pickup so he is less tempted to go for a spin or make a big circle.

Throughout all of his retrieving training, try to call him according to this sequence. This will help to give you quick pickups and prompt returns.

One caution here: when you get to the point where you are training on blind retrieves, or if you are not sure right where the mark is, don't call him prematurely. If you are uncertain where the mark is, don't call him until you are sure he has picked it up.

Another habit I want you to start forming is to concentrate on the dog from the time you initiate the mark until the retrieve is in your hand.

Let me explain: I don't care if the setup is a single retrieve, a double, or a complicated triple, never take your eyes off the dog until the last bird is in your hand. I have seen many disasters occur because the handler turned around to talk to the judges, or his training friends, while the dog was still unfinished with his retrieving tasks.

Remember when we discussed influence handling and its dramatic power? Don't shift your influence while the dog is still in the process of completing what you sent him to do.

Once I watched as a handler sent his retriever for the last bird on a difficult triple during a field trial. The dog entered the vicinity of the fall and the handler was sure the pickup was eminent. He calmly turned to the judges to hobnob and show his confidence while in the distant background his dog blew out and lost his focus.

After the handler finally realized he was in a jam, the damage was done and even after extending handling attempts, he failed to pick up the mark and was disqualified.

I have seen literally hundreds of problems that have happened during the return end of a retrieve because the handler quit paying attention, especially in the water. There is plenty of time to talk to your friends and take the praise for a job well done after the job is done. If you presume success before you have it, you are setting yourself up for problems. Oh, and of course, the dog is always blamed for the misfortune.

Establish control before you start, then concentrate on the goal until it is complete. Your dog learns to cue on you from the very start, so keep it consistent.

Stand the same, talk the same, say the same things, whistle the same, send the dog the same, and finish the same on each session and you will achieve super dog work as you acquire good handling skills.

On your first formal marks, throw the marks into short cover. Don't make the dog wait too long before sending him. Make the marks short and meaningful. We will gradually make the marks longer and harder as we ask our dog to remain longer and longer. After a few days, the dog will stay until sent and there is no sudden stop at the end of a loose lead or heavy pressure to stay the first time out.

Let's take this opportunity to discuss some more of our natural controls and how to handle them initially.

Dogs and people adjust to natural controls as we go about our environment. Don't include roads, creeks, ditches, hillsides, or heavy cover in your early marks. When a dog encounters an obstacle like this, he just naturally tends to make changes in his speed and direction of travel. Keep the marks on fairly level ground for now. We will build in each of these distractions as we go.

Ideally, we want the dog to go straight to the mark, pick it up quickly, and then come straight home. If we leave it up to nature, our dog will be weaving all over the place and learning habits we will have to deal with later.

Straight out and straight back in, that's our goal (even though we must realize how hard this is to achieve).

Sometimes when the dog is asked to stay for the mark he will decide not to pick up the dummy or he might pick it up and then drop it after carrying it a short distance. Don't be too concerned about this. The important thing is that he comes directly back to you with or without it.

If he shows this behavior, just stay fundamental and insist he come quickly to heel after he gets to the dummy. He will soon go back to his happy retrieving self and will accept this change in his routine, but it could be a few uncertain days of frustration before he decides to.

I like to end each session with a short stint of obedience. The concept is simple: Start under control, go through the workout, then finish under control. The dog will stay happy and content with himself while he learns terrific structure in his training sessions. This will translate to the same quality structure in his field work.

We need to talk about sending the dog: How do we do it, what do we say, and what difference does it make?

I like to send retrievers with their names. Many trainers will send their dogs with "fetch", or "back," and some even have whistle cadences that they prefer. I don't think there is any problem with sending on "fetch" or "back." I have really never seen any great troubling situation because of these word commands. So, if you like one of those commands, go ahead.

I have, however, seen many problems occur with the whistle command to retrieve. I think it is a poor concept that wasn't thought through before implementation. I see no benefit in using a two-whistle cadence to send your dog to retrieve.

My preference is to send the dog with his name, or a shortened version of it, and then to back it up with the word "fetch." Let me explain: As long as everything is going well with the dog's retrieving, I send him on his name. When the dog shows reluctance or refusal to retrieve, I say his name and follow with the word "fetch."

At some point here in his development, our dog will be force broke to retrieve and that is when we will install the "fetch muscle." If ever he refuses to retrieve, or go for you, you can simply say his name and tell him to fetch.

Sometimes you need extra muscle, and I like to keep it in reserve, using it only when I need it. It is much like a trainer who screams at his dog constantly. He has no backup. He hasn't layered in the increments of control that we are working toward. He is going for his big gun every time he opens his mouth so his options are very limited.

The timing involved in sending your dog to retrieve is crucial to your success in later training. Observation and patience is as key here as anywhere else in your program. As a handler, you have to concentrate on the attitude of the dog and make sure he is ready before you send him. You need to develop a "sending rhythm" in your training sessions.

It's much like a starter in a sprint race. He says, "Get ready, get set, go." A good starter is so consistent that the sprinters never really hear the word "Go." They have memorized the rhythm of the cadence through training and blast out of the blocks as the starter says "Go," not after he says "Go."

When a dog marks a fall, his ears will break over and he will study the area intently. He will lean forward and every part of his body will tell you he has seen it, marked the fall, and is ready to go.

Don't get in the habit of putting your hand down to send the dog on marks. We will show him how to take a line during our handling and training, but we don't need to line him on marks. If you start giving your young dog a line to his marks he will not gain the full benefit of marking his own falls. As we get more advanced in training and are running blinds and marks, the dog will appreciate your consistency. The dog will think to himself, "If he puts his hand down to line me, it's a blind; if he doesn't, it's a mark."

I guess the best advice I can give you as we go into formal marks is be patient, use the same sequence, and be consistent. Don't make a lot of noise as you're sending the dog and be quiet while the dog is doing the work. Be ready to whistle him in just before he picks up the mark and then be supportive and enthusiastic while he returns. When the dog returns to you with the mark, tell him to come to heel and sit.

A young dog who is not force broke yet will probably drop the dummy somewhere in the process, but again, don't get worried about this. We will encourage him to hold during this initial marking and will lock in all of his line manners and delivery skills when we force break him.

Let's analyze a mark from start to finish and then let's get out there and throw a thousand of them.

- Establish lead control
- Let him loosen up
- Re-establish control
- Bring the dog to heel position
- Make sure the dog is lined up straight
- Show him the mark
- Send him with the proper sequence
- Call him as he reaches the dummy
- Bring him back to the heel position
- Collect the dummy
- Finish under control

Now, while you're out there throwing all of those marks, I will give you some things to think about when you come in at night and in between sessions.

One of the most important skills a handler has to learn is the proper use of wind and scenting conditions. As I go to the field, I am constantly checking the wind direction and strength. The easiest way to do this is to either crumble seed heads in your hand or pick up a small amount of dry dirt and sift it through your fingers so you can watch which direction it goes as it falls to the ground. I like to pull the tops off of dry weed heads because they are light and very sensitive to wind current. If you have a cigarette lighter or matches on you, they will help to determine wind direction.

It doesn't matter if you are working on marking, casting, lining drills, or hunting birds. The wind can either help you or hurt you. Remember, we want to train for confidence, so let's learn how to let it help us in our task.

As you set up your marks, try to set up so your dog is either driving into the wind or crosswind. In other words, you want the wind coming into his face as he runs out for the retrieve or you want it quartering across his face as he runs. This will carry the scent of the mark to him before he gets to it and will help to confirm his memory of the fall. If you throw marks directly downwind, your dog will often go beyond the mark before he winds it and will have to hunt back toward you. If the wind is brisk, he may go very deep before he realizes he went too far and he might become confused or disoriented about the fall. The longer a dog hunts for a mark, the foggier he is about remembering the exact location. When a dog is running downwind for a mark, he can be off just a fraction and totally miss the opportunity.

When you move on to advanced marks and multiples, you will appreciate the value in getting the mark in the dog's mouth as soon as you can so you can go on to the harder memory birds. Long hunts are beautiful to watch, but they will seriously compromise the dog's ability to remember the other marks in the situation.

Ideally, we want the dog to run directly to the area, quickly locate the mark, snatch it up and hustle back to you. This is when all that obedience starts paying off for you in a big way. When the dog returns to you with the mark, insist he come directly to heel whether he delivers the dummy to you or not. Don't let him circle you two or three times before coming to heel. If he gets into the habit of circling, or wetting on a bush, or coming into heel in a crooked position, he will do it for the rest of his life. Make him come directly into heel and sit facing the next mark.

Always check the wind going into a training session and keep checking it throughout the workout. We have established the fact that a dog doesn't particularly like to run straight into the wind so he will naturally try to quarter into it. When he does this, his nose is reaching out 50 yards instead of a few feet. When you run your dog downwind, you are making it very hard for him to wind and work out his objectives until he is either right on them or just past them.

"Lining out" is another problem that comes to the surface when training or hunting with the wind and can be very frustrating. When a dog lines out, he hunts in a pattern that takes him straight out to the front and then straight back to the handler. He will also have the tendency to hunt deep before he starts back.

What you end up with is a dog who is hunting like a yo-yo–out, in, out, in, out, in. If you are hunting in row crops, like corn, the dog can actually run clear out of the field on you and it's your fault.

This kind of hunting pattern also keeps the hunters moving faster than they would like, and in some cases causes them to run.

Your dog will quarter the field when you work him into the wind and he will hunt closer. He will do both of these things without any whistle or verbal commands and he will be much more productive to boot.

Meander

What do you think this word "meander" has to do with dog training?

Continents meander from north to south, from east to west. Mountain ranges meander across continents. Rivers and their tributary systems meander from elevation to the sea. Oceans and seas meander to and fro between and around continents. Drainages and plateaus meander and define.

The next time you get a chance, walk across a field of snow. Try to hold your course by marking a tree or house in the distance and walk directly for it. It doesn't even have to be snow—tomorrow morning while the dew is still heavy on the grass, try the same thing. Do your best to keep your line straight. When you get to your goal, look back at your tracks. Do you call that a straight line? Come on now, you weren't even trying. Do it again, and again.

You can't get it straight no matter what you try, can you? Watch as elk or deer walk across the fields. They can't do it either. Even the single-tracking coyote, fox or bobcat all have trouble coming close to a decent line.

Why then do you suppose the retriever field trial folks spend so much of their training time trying to achieve what no other part of nature can, a straight line? People think in straight lines, but nature doesn't know the meaning of one.

Your shooting dog needs to acquire good handling skills if

we are to reach the top of the pyramid, and that means he must learn to run a reasonably straight line to his marks and blinds.

As you go about your marking practice, take the time to notice what causes the animal to weave and meander. The dog will respond to the same forces that you did as you walked across the field of snow. He will have the same tendency to wander as you did. He will show the same movement in the water, also. Sometimes it seems worse when they're wet.

A training term for this force is "suction." The dog is pulled one way or another by something in his environment. He is responding to the notion that there is an easier way, a faster way to get where he's going.

If you put a road, or a ditch, or a pond, or a river, or a fence, or a hill in the middle of your field of snow, your straight line will become a laugher. You will be lucky to stay in the same field. You think I'm kidding? Just give it a try.

If you are running across a field with one single irrigation ditch angling out across the middle, you will naturally want to stop at the bank, square off, jump straight across the narrowest point of the ditch, and then try to regain your original course. If you are running across the same field and it becomes necessary to cross a road, you will find yourself slipping down the side of the road for a short distance before you blast across to get back on track. If the same field holds a creek or a pond, the natural thing to do is again take it at the narrows and worry about your course after you get to the far shore.

Why, then, do marks and blinds in a retriever trial often contain as many of these distractions as can be accumulated in one test setting?

Take into consideration the dog may also come across an old pheasant scent, or, even worse, a bird, while on his way and it becomes easy to see why field trial dogs have to spend so much of their life learning skills that are, for the most part, useless in a normal day's hunt.

The dog has to learn to turn his head and ignore all of his natural senses, even his most trusted ally, his nose.

You can build good, strong lines in your shooting dog if you are keen to recognize the importance and strength of natural suction. When you are working on your marks, try to stay away from situations that cause your dog to fall off his game.

What I'm trying to say is this: Be careful as you introduce these natural distractions to your dog. If you want lines to be as straight as they can be, there are many things you can do to help yourself out. For instance, always introduce one distraction at a time and always present your marks on 90-degree angles.

If you're dealing with a ditch, throw your marks so the dog will hit the ditch square to the bank. If you are trying to run your marks across the road, be sure to introduce them at a square angle to the road. Don't show your dog water marks that will give him the temptation to run the bank or swim to the other side before retrieving the mark.

As soon as you develop good marking structure then you can start increasing the angles. You can incrementally work into complicated angles without severe pressure or training aids.

Another problem that can occur while learning marking is usually too heavy of cover too fast. Start out in fairly light cover and progress into heavier cover as the dog gains confidence. If you ever see your dog's confidence wavering because of the complexity of the setup, back up and analyze what you're doing and where you're going with it.

Learn to show the dog cover at the end of the mark, at the middle of the mark, and at the beginning of the mark. Show the obstacles at different intervals. Don't let the dog gauge your training sessions. Keep mixing it up so he has to rely on his marking ability. He has to develop a dependency on structure. He will learn that sharp obedience and attention to detail will make the workouts go smoothly.

By the time you throw a few hundred marks for your dog you will see him start to smooth out and relax with the system. I like to show him a lot of remote marks for the remainder of his singles training.

Let's talk about remote singles and how to present them. As much as I enjoy training alone, I definitely recognize the value of

Marking group

training with other trainers. You can get so much more done during your training sessions if you can incorporate other people and other dogs. We have already discussed some of the value of group work concerning the dogs. From the time the dogs are whelped, we give them a daily dose of group work. They learn how to respond to the handler as one. When you want to take your dog up a notch with his workout structure and marking ability, think about how you can build group work into your program.

One of the greatest training aids a dog man has in his grab bag is the chain gang. Pointer trainers have long held the chain gang dear to their respective programs, but it is surprising to see how few retriever trainers even consider it as a useful approach.

A chain gang can be anything from one single tie-out chain to a long chain with several dozen drop chains along the way. I have chain gangs strung all over the place and wouldn't give them up for love nor money. I believe the chain gang is one of the most important features of the program.

You can build them any way you want, but basically you need a tie-out that is, first of all, safe to leave your dog on, and secondly, stout enough to keep him there.

I like to use link-type chain instead of the fancy twisted link because it is easier to keep from tangling. I am always packing these things with me as I go from on training area to another, and I don't want to spend half of my morning untangling my chain gang.

You don't need a chain that will hold a team of horses, but you do need one that will take some heat because a bunch of fired-up Labradors can put some major tension on the chain. Drop your tie chains every six feet so you can achieve good separation. You don't need dogs fighting while they're tied up. Your drop chains need only be 18 inches long. Any longer than that and you will sooner or later see a rear leg injury due to a chain wrap.

When dogs are on the chain and they see other dogs working out to the front, they get very excited. That is part of the value of the chain but it also represents some of the danger. The dogs are in an agitated state so they may act different than they do when they are working alone. Use brass snaps for everything you do with dogs, and use brass snaps with swivels on the end of your drop chains. If the drop chains don't swivel right, the chain will twist and any time you get a chain twisted up you have problems.

The ends of the chain gang have to be secured close to the ground. I like to use heavy metal stakes to secure my ends so I can stretch the chain as tight as I can. The chain gang needs to be as tight as can be accomplished to get the full effect and to keep it safe for the dogs.

Chain gang

When you work one dog while others watch from the chain gang, you get a magnified effect from all of the dogs. The working dog is a little worried about the others getting his mark and the dogs on the chain are doing everything they can to get into the act.

After a dog spends some time on the chain while another dog is being worked, he comes off of there wanting to get something done. You need not worry about his working attitude—he will be spinning and leaning, pulling and whining.

Don't forget to put your waist cord on the dog before you let him off the chain. Go through your usual startup drill. Stay fundamental. Make sure he is coming to heel and his obedience is sharp before you go on with the marking drill.

What difference does it make? Why do I keep repeating myself on this? Let me try to explain. You have instilled this routine over the past few months of first establishing control before you go on with whatever you are doing. You have been doing this within the confines of a training program. The dog may be in a good mood during training. He might have a good, positive attitude, but he has not been exposed to the kind of stimulation the chain gang provides. He will be drunk with excitement, he will be frothing and driving to get out there when it is his turn. He will say, "To hell with the structure, turn me loose." This is the same kind of excitement he will feel when birds are factored into the equation. If he learns to work within his regular structure even when he is frantic with enthusiasm, he will be laying in bricks of dependability and steadiness he can rest on later.

All dogs are steady when nothing is going on. Any dog can do it when nothing's on the line.

Be prepared. Even if your dog has been rock-steady for your marks, he will want to break the first time you get him off the chain gang and throw a mark in front of his peers. Don't get him off the chain and calmly tell him to stay as you signal for the mark. He will blast out of there at first sign of a mark and throw dirt in your face for twenty yards. Use your waist cord, anticipate his not being able to contain himself and help him to be successful.

If you show him you expect him to work the same today as he did yesterday, he will get right on the beam but with added energy that you have never seen before.

I like to set up my group marking drills like this: I send a helper out to the location where we want to show the dogs the mark. He needs to carry every dummy you can pile on him. Look under the training table, out in the garage, in the truck, wherever you have to until you find every dummy that will hold together long enough to get thrown and retrieved.

One handler starts the working dog and then takes him to the area where we have decided to use as a marking line. We usually show the dog several marks thrown to the same location, or as close to it as the thrower can get. While this is going on, another handler starts a dog and makes him sit at heel while he watched the working dog.

You have one dog working, one dog honoring, and all the rest coming out of their skin on the chain gang.

As soon as the first dog is through with his session on the hot seat, move him back to the chain gang and give him a drink. The honor dog now moves up to the line and the first handler starts a new dog off the chain gang and brings him up to honor.

You keep doing this until all of the dogs have been worked. All of the dogs get to work on the marking test, they get to work at honoring while at a handler's side, and they get to work on honoring while on the chain gang with the rest of the pack. If you have a dozen dogs on the chain gang, all 12 of them are getting worked at something every time a mark is shown. You are training 12 dogs at one time instead of one.

Another great spin-off of this training is that your dog doesn't necessarily have to experience a problem for you to learn how to train for it. Your dog might have a problem with steadiness, another might be soft on marking. One might show aggressiveness or surliness, one might be intimidated by the chain, one might be hardheaded, who knows? The important thing is you are learning how to handle all of these problems without having to experience them personally.

Another effective method of group marking practice is for

Trainers throwing marks for each other

the handlers to throw marks for each other. I really like this drill because it allows all of the dogs to work on honoring, marking, and steadiness at the same time. This drill is as fun to do as any of the drills associated with retriever training.

I like to do this marking drill with three or four other handlers. Everybody needs to take at least three dummies with them as they go to the field with their dog.

The handlers split up and walk to different areas of the field. Don't get spread out over several hundred yards. Keep it within the abilities of your dogs. One handler might be 60 yards from you, one might be 90 yards, and then another could be more than 100 yards distant.

When you have another person show your dog marks, make sure they get the dog's attention first, then loft the dummy high into the air in a nice arc. Don't tell them to try to throw the things as far as they can because the quality of the mark is compromised. A nice, high arc is what you want to see so the dog can get a good look at it. If you think the dog doesn't see the mark, throw it for him again. Don't send him unless you are sure he saw it.

One dog works at a time while the others watch. The handler signals for a mark thrown by one of the handlers. If the dog does a good job on that one, he turns his body to address another handler and signals him to throw one. The dog is sent to retrieve a mark thrown by all of the handlers and maybe one thrown by his own handler, but all of them are shown as singles. If he has any problem marking or finding any of them, his handler should call for that one again. Don't just go out there with a set plan of retrieving all the marks and call it good. Always be willing to adjust to the situation. If a dog is having trouble with a certain mark, or a certain type of mark, then show it to him until he feels good about it. Even if you only get to work on that one mark, you will get more done than if you pushed him on when he really didn't understand what he was doing.

The real beauty of this drill is in the fact that you can show your dog several different singles in the same setup. He will see shorter ones, longer ones, and marks in heavier cover or across water. Make it like you want it. Then, when every dog in the drill has been worked, the handlers need only to move around some and you have a whole new marking challenge. This is a great way to study other handlers and other dogs in action. You can do this drill with two people or five and the benefits are the same.

Marking group

Intro Doubles

When your dog is running well on single marks of all types, then you can begin your transition to multiples, beginning with doubles.

Singles teach marking and hone concentration skills, while doubles teach memory. The dog has to mark the single just as always, but now he has to remember it while he watches a second mark go down and is sent to pick the first one up.

This is another very important tip in developing solid marking skills: when training, always show multiples as singles first. Think about that for a minute. Always show multiple marks as singles first. If you are working on advanced doubles or triples, always show them as singles first. When your dog is getting good at multiples, the temptation is to set up something meaty then go get your dog and show it to him as a test. I have seen this happen hundreds of times and almost always it ends up in a battle.

The handler is starting to get cocky about the dog's ability to sort out tough marking tests so he gets lazy with his training structure. Instead of going to the trouble of showing the marks as singles, he just jumps the dog out of the truck and walks to the line and signals for the birds. Many times he doesn't even let the dog loosen up properly. When the dog fails to complete the test, the handler applies pressure and away we go.

Don't think this will not happen to you—it will. We all fall prey to what I call "The John Wayne Syndrome." It's kind of a macho thing and it normally occurs when there is a crowd watching.

I don't care if the President or Governor is watching, stay fundamental.

When the dog is in advanced multiple training, you may get away with only showing him the memory bird–the last one he will have to pick up–as a single, but at least do that for him.

Granted, if you are competing in a retriever trial you won't have the luxury of showing him the marks, but in training you always do.

When working on a complicated double or triple retrieve, I will always show my dog the memory bird as a single first, then run the whole test. Remember, we're not trying to deceive him, we're building confidence.

I mentioned something a bit ago about you getting cocky as a handler. I said it usually happens when people are watching you. You better prepare yourself for this problem because it will come about sooner or later. You will find yourself in a situation where a bunch of folks will be watching you work your dog.

It might be at a trial or a field test or even in the city park. You might be working in a field or a nice stretch of river when you look up to see cars parked along the interstate—they're watching you train. People love to watch dogs work. You will draw a crowd, bet on it. Stay within your structure and you are home free. Try to play gunslinger and you will go slinking home with a bruised ego and lost ground to show for it.

Train for total confidence and you will be training for success;

Train for total compliance and your program will ultimately fail.

Before we go on marking let's think about what we are trying to accomplish. How is this segment of our program going to help us get up the pyramid? We have a goal, you know, to develop the best Labrador shooting dog we can. We set this goal way back when our dog was a baby.

I believe it is important to build good marking into our dog but not for the reasons you might think. We will show our dog long, meaningful singles and complicated multiples not because he will see them regularly when he is afield–in fact, he will rarely see them in a real hunting situation–but to instill and reinforce his ability to concentrate and relax with his job. He is just like us in the sense that he needs to be able to relax and think while doing his job or his performance suffers. Yes, marking teaches a dog to watch and multiples teach him to remember, but more importantly, he is learning to be patient and thoughtful rather

185

than impulsive and spontaneous.

Good marking structure will also strengthen perseverance and courage. He will learn to drive deep and push through. He will learn the value of not giving up when he isn't successful immediately. He will keep trying, keep running, keep swimming, and keep hunting until he comes up with the bird. These are the true treasures we are pursuing as we explore marking together. Our dog must believe in himself and never think of compromise.

Marking training teaches our shooting dog to believe in himself, but casting and lining training teaches him to believe in his handler.

I got off track there for a while but I didn't forget you. We were talking about introducing double marks. I introduce doubles as handler-thrown marks. I show the dog a couple of good singles thrown to the same location. I then throw the same single but instead of sending him, I tap my leg and tell him to heel as I turn my body about half a turn. Because of all his obedience training, he knows to turn with me and align with my body again. I then throw him a short mark so it lands in plain sight. It is important for the marks to be at least 90 degrees apart. It doesn't even hurt to make the first few greater than that.

As he looks to the last mark down, I send him for it and usually the dog will fire out and snatch up the short mark. Call him to heel, but before he gets there be sure to turn your body so when he lines up at heel he will be facing the first mark. As he lines up with you, he will be looking directly at he location of the longer mark.

He will remember it because you threw it for him several times before attempting the double. If he leans forward and breaks his ears over you know he is ready, go ahead and send him. He will probably pick it up with no problem. Make sure he is lined up straight and make sure he is looking at the mark prior to sending him. Because we are now working on memory, let's talk about which bird is the memory bird. The memory bird is the one the dog will pick up last.

In this stage of training you should always send your dog for the last mark of the double first. In other words, the dog will be looking right at the last mark you threw him, so don't try to switch his attention to the first one thrown. He will keep looking over to the one he wants. Don't get into it with him over this. Get in the habit of sending him for the last mark down. Later on in training you can switch him to any of the marks thrown, but for now send him to the last bird down.

When working on double marks always vary the distances. Don't show the dog doubles where both of the marks are the same distance from the dog. Throw one long one and one short one, one short one and one long one. The dog can quickly memorize distances, so don't give him the chance. I can give you an example of what I'm saying here.

I knew a trainer who worked very hard on his dogs but always threw marks himself. He would continually struggle with his dogs because they were conditioned to pick up marks at about 40 yards. That was as far as the handler could throw consistently, so they were accustomed to finding their marks somewhere in that range. The dogs found it difficult to drive deep on longer natural marks.

We have come so far together. We have our dogs moving toward the top. We have established great long-term goals and have seen solid progress. Everything has been positive and supportive. We only care about making our dog, not breaking him.

As we all learn in life, building structure involves some negative training. I usually introduce the word "NO!" to my dog right about here in the training. I tell him NO when he starts for the wrong mark or does something repeatedly that I know he understands to be wrong.

You will read many articles and books that will tell you NO is as important as any other word command. "That dog has to know that the NO command has teeth."

Please be careful with this. I'll tell you why.

I've heard numerous handlers scream "NO!" over and over again until they lose their voice while the dog circled and failed. I have watched them run to their dog screaming, "NO! NO! NO!"

and then beat the tar out of him when they got there. While the handler was beating the dog he would continue to holler, "NO! NO! NO!"

At this time, the dog is seized up with fear and distress and finally succumbs to the pressure and takes his beating like a concentration camp prisoner.

I have seen field trial trainers put their dogs through absolute hell during water blind training. I've seen dogs spinning and panting in the water while they tried to maintain balance as the trainer stood on dry ground shrieking, "NO! NO! NO!"

The dog is frantic and the trainer grits his teeth as he grinds the hot button on his transmitter.

I remember one such dog who endured an unbelievable hardship until he gave up and sought refuge in a small patch of cattails. His entire body was submerged except for the top of his head and his nose. He was motionless and lifeless in the water except for an occasional violent vibration caused by the electric collar. The trainer had to go out and get him so he could escort him back to the truck.

He walked by me smiling and shaking his head. "I don't think he will be ready for the trial next weekend, " he said.

I stopped him and told him he should get a job with the IRS or maybe as a mercenary soldier. I also told him to go on by my place the next time he was looking for training grounds.

That's not training, folks, that's brutality, no matter how you cut it. I'll bet you think I'm exaggerating, huh? I wish I was.

The word "NO!" is important in training, but if you have to say it more than once, FIX the problem. Go back to your structure and fix the weakness. Go to your pyramid and add mortar, replace the brick, fix it where the problem is. That's why we spend so much time making sure the structure is firm.

When you run into a wall while training, go back to the part of the pyramid that deals with the particular fundamental problem and fix it there. Don't try to beat it out of your dog. Don't try to shock it out of him. FIX IT!

Remember, when you run into a problem during training, it

doesn't matter what it is, be sure to first show the dog how to get out of trouble, then let him get out. After he is safely aboard again, show him the same sequence one more time.

For instance, let's say you are working on a double water mark and your dog is having trouble with switching. He is starting for the mark you had in mind but then switches and sets his course for the other mark. You tell him "NO," but he still pushes on until he grabs the wrong mark and heads back. You set it up again and he does the same thing wrong. OK, it's time to show him what you want. Throw him the mark he has been having trouble with as a single. Send him to it and if things go well, do it again. Now, throw the double again just like you did the first time. Look to all of your line manners and make sure you are consistent. When he does the double like you want him to, repeat it one more time so he fully understands what you mean.

Now, you could have leaned on him for switching. You could have blamed him for all the wrong reasons without even knowing it.

What if the wind had changed? Did you check it?

What if you weren't lined up correctly and he thought you meant the other mark?

What if he was actually looking at the wrong mark when you sent him? Did you look down to check?

What if a fish jumped, or a swallow dipped, or a kingfisher splashed?

If, after careful consideration, you think discipline is necessary, then "NO" can be very helpful. Wait until he makes the mistake, wait until he turns toward the wrong mark and strikes out for it, then say "NO" as firmly as you can without screaming or hollering. He has to understand you are not correcting him for going into the water to make a retrieve, you are correcting him for going to the wrong mark. If he doesn't stop and turn back, say it once more. We can never let him get the idea that going was wrong, it was the direction that was wrong.

You know, we haven't had the chance to talk about water much. When I was writing about the water marking problem above, it occurred to me we need to discuss water.

Labradors are retrievers. They should be natural swimmers. A Lab comes into the world expected to be a full-blown water dog. To say this is not always the case would be a giant understatement. Dogs have to learn to handle water and retrievers are no different. Sure, some are super swimmers while still in the litter under the tutelage of their mother, but many have major problems adjusting to the water and some can't swim a lick.

As we work on our marking, our dog will be wet a lot of the time. The dog has to learn to relax in the water. Even dogs who are natural water dogs aren't born with the courage to handle difficult water conditions. You need to be very careful as you introduce your dog to the various dangers present in the water.

First of all, how do you pick a place to do your water work? The most important factor is safety. We are looking for a place where we can achieve our goals in water, but we must be certain it is safe.

Before you start working your dog, always look carefully up and down the bank for broken glass, old fence posts, tangled wire, submerged logs or debris. A broken beer bottle will lay there for 10,000 years waiting to cut an animal's pad or a child's foot.

If you like to train in rivers, which I do, you have other things to consider. Anytime you are near bridge abutments or cement structures there is the chance of re-bar and twisted steel protruding out of old concrete. Look for bent-over steel fence posts. If your dog has a bold entry into the water, you have to inspect the landing area. This might be 12 to 15 feet off shore. Freestone rivers are fun to work your dog in, but you have to be watchful of the shoreline and submerged rocks. Round river rocks are usually slick and it's easy to sprain a foot or carpal joint.

If you are working along a river in winter there are other dangers to consider before casting your dog. I like to work at least a quarter mile upstream from any ice shelves or ice bridges. Don't set up just above an ice shelf or you might be making a terrible mistake. Your dog could get swept under the ice while he is swimming and you will never see him again. I know of several of these incidents involving ice flows and retrievers.

Teach your dog to handle ice by first working him on a shallow river. In winter the ice will form along the riverbanks. The longer it stays cold the greater the ice formation will become.

The ice provides for unstable footing. Some of it will hold the dog and some of it won't. He needs to keep at it until he understands what's going on.

I know lots of folks who won't throw marks in the water when the ice is formed along the sides, but that's a mistake, to my way of thinking.

When does duck season come in? Oh, about the end of September. When does it end? The middle of January. I'm from the mountains, and January means snow and ice. If your dog doesn't know how to handle ice, then shame on you. Go out and throw your dog some marks in the water when the ice is banked up. He will learn to crab up on the ice and get out on his own.

If you practice with him in shallow water, he will start by pushing off the bottom with his back feet and then he will pull himself up by his front feet. When the water is deep, he cannot push off the bottom so he has to change his tactics. He will find he can still crab up on the ice like a shrimp and pull himself out. If he needs help at first, reach out and push down on his head. That will give him the leverage to pop out of the water.

The same holds true in a boat. If you are trying to get your dog into the boat, just wait until his front feet are aboard then push down on his head and he will scrambled into the boat.

Get this stuff worked out. Don't wait until your dog is in a jam before you think about how you're going to handle it. One more thing: Thin ice can cut your dog's neck. If ice is too thin to hold your dog's weight, chances are it is extremely dangerous.

The most dangerous ice you will ever have to deal with is ice that is just thick enough for your dog to get out on but not thick enough to hold him long. He will break through a ways from shore and the struggle is on to get back. He will no longer think about the retrieve, he will be in a state of panic. Thin ice is also fairly clear, so he won't be able to see it.

When water spills up on the ice it looks just like water to him, but when he tries to swim he keeps bumping against an invisible wall. The dog is in danger of drowning out there. The dilemma is made worse by the fact that you cannot get out there to help him. There really isn't much you can do but try to keep coaxing him on toward the nearest bank.

One time after a half an hour of calling and hoping, I ran to a nearby shed and came up with a long electrical extension cord. As I ran back to the lake I fashioned a loop, and on the third try I was able to get a line around the dog's neck. This dog wasn't even working. She had just walked out on the ice to check out some goose droppings and almost lost her life.

Be smart when you set up in water. Deep mud can hide sharp objects. Look closely when you are checking out the banks. Be careful around beaver dams and log jams.

I guess what I'm getting at is just be careful with water. You don't want to contribute to anything that will rob your dog of courage. Fear is something to avoid when dealing with water.

Two more things concerning water that are worth bringing up. Number one, retrievers are prone to ear problems when they are exposed to water extensively. They always shake when leaving water.

When a retriever shakes, his ears take a beating. They flap back and forth with unbelievable force. Sometimes a condition called a hematoma will show up. This is when a blood vessel is ruptured within the interior of the ear and the ear flap fills up with blood. The ear looks like it's full of air. The ear is very heavy and uncomfortable so the dog continually shakes his head. If you don't take care of this situation the ear will suffer permanent damage, and if that isn't enough to worry about, often the other ear will end up in the same shape. If you see any signs of a hematoma get your dog to the vet quickly. This problem is a booger to deal with, so get on it.

The second problem to watch for with wet dogs is ear infections. Always check your dog's ears regularly so you can keep ear infections from getting bad. You will experience them, so just be ready for it. If your dog gets an ear infection he will start digging and shaking his head. This, many times, will lead to the hematoma condition. Ear infections usually begin when your dog has pond water against his eardrum. For dogs that are prone to them, you can stave off ear infections by gently drying your dog's ears with a twist of clean facial tissue after a water workout.

Your dog needs to know that water will not hurt him. He has to know that he can conquer water. Waves cannot hurt him, depth cannot hurt him, and current cannot hurt him. What can hurt him you can control. Take the time to train and hunt where it is safe. Sometimes while hunting you will run into situations where your dog will be working in water you cannot be sure of. Keep your eyes open and use your head. There is too much at stake to scare your dog off water just because you didn't pay attention.

If your dog is afraid of the water or unsure of himself, wait on him. Give him time to overcome his fears. Don't push on with water work or throw him into the lake. Wait for him. Use group work or peer pressure to help him out. He will start swimming and probably like it. Just be patient. Just because you have chosen a Labrador retriever don't assume he will automatically take to the water like a fish. He might need some help. Give it to him.

At this stage of the game I would like to remind you of the importance of conditioning and nutrition. I would also like to revisit working conformation, speed, agility, balance, and endurance.

As you are going through day after day of extended workouts practicing on field and water work, your dog will be changing into an athlete. You will notice the youthful wildness of your puppy turning into a more serious competitive spirit. He will still be the happy enthusiastic worker he always was, but now there is purpose in his stride and determination in his stare.

I have been watching Camas as she has developed. She is seven months old now. Camas is flying. If I never put in another day of serious training in her she would still be a terrific hunting dog. She loves birds. She has seen hundreds of them. She has flushed pheasant and jumped ducks. She has blasted through coveys of quail and burned the canyon rim for partridge. She has learned the meadow lark is not much fun and the magpie, ha!

Child's play!

She has learned to respect horses and vehicles. She is friendly to anyone she sees, but she adores me.

We have our obedience in. We are marking and moving on. Camas is going to be a shooting dog and I'm going to be richer for it.

Get in the habit of measuring the distance your dog covers during a workout. You can approximate—you don't have to get the tape out, but try to get a good feel for the total in yards. I like to keep track of these things because it helps me to do a better job for my dog. These marking drills can really build up the distances, and if you're not careful you may overextend your dog's physical abilities.

Remember when we discussed working conformation and the importance of proper balance? Well, now is when it starts paying off. If your dog isn't built fairly well, he will start fading just when the training session is heating up. Let's think about this for a minute. If you show your dog 10 marks that average about 70 yards per mark, then your dog has to run, or swim about 1400 yards. Many times your marking sessions will exceed 2500 yards.

The dog is running over broken or uneven ground most of the time, pushing through mud, breaking cover or swimming. You also have to factor in the mental strain of the workout, because sometimes it can outweigh the physical. If the dog is stressed out or worried, he will tire much quicker just like you do when you feel like that.

What if he is hurt? A pulled muscle or a broken toenail will shorten his working distance.

If your dog isn't eating good food his endurance will suffer. If you haven't kept up his worming schedule you will see the same symptoms, for different reasons.

When we put our dog up on the table prior to the workout we can discover problems that might shorten our workout. Watch for injuries and be alert to attitude. Remember when I told you to brush your dog? Now you will understand, brushing your dog before a workout will give your dog up to 15 percent more

Group work

Competition gets 'em going

endurance. Especially the black ones.

Look back upon all of those fun walks together when your dog was young. Remember how you learned to study the movement and locomotion of the dog? Remember when I told you of taking numerous dogs to the field to let them run so I could measure their endurance and athletic ability?

When you observed your own puppy as he ran and played, you were laying in your ability to recognize when he was getting tired. Now that information will pay off for you also. When you see his tail flatten out and you have determined he is showing fatigue, adjust your workout. Don't just keep blazing on, oblivious to his situation. Don't fall into the trap of demanding a certain set of marks before you call it quits. Instead, watch and observe. If he is looking good and he can finish up the drill, great, if he can't, button it up.

If you're out training with other people, don't expect all of the dogs to possess the same endurance level. Don't set up a drill and demand all the dogs go through it. The reason I'm so redundant about these critical points is that you may put unnecessary pressure on your dog. You may even wrongly discipline your dog if you are not fully aware of his conformation weaknesses, his conditioning, his attitude, and his endurance.

Send several dogs after one bumper and put the speed—and courage—into them.

Chapter 12:
Using Cover to Enhance Your Field Work

*H*ow do you use cover to enhance your marks?

If you are hunting upland game birds, you are hunting cover. If you are waterfowl hunting, chances are great there is dense cover of some kind just to the edges of the water. If you are hunting in or across water, there is cover and obstacles within the water itself.

The cover is not uniform. Some of it is grass, some is reeds or cattails, some is brush, some of it is grain crops, some of it is trees. You can't really throw a young dog into all phases of cover at the same time. Again, we will introduce these various cover combination incrementally.

Our dog has been running and hunting through all kinds of cover for months now, but hunting is one thing and marking is another.

The dog will have a natural tendency to hunt the cover lines. He might run across a field where he thought he saw the mark fall but a cover barrier could keep him from driving deep enough to find it.

Try to imagine each transition between types of cover as barriers. The dog will naturally slide down a barrier as opposed to crashing right through it. This can take him completely out of the fall area. If he is not determined enough to stay with his hunt, he will come back without the bird.

I like to arrange marking drills so the cover barrier is encountered at all different points of the mark. For example, let's say you are working on a mark of about 100 yards across land. You can set the mark up so the dog has to fire through five yards of heavy cover just as he leaves your side, medium cover as he crosses the field, and then lighter cover in the area of the fall. You can set up where he has to run across 75 yards of light cover before he is faced with a patch of heavy cover while he is still 25 yards short of the mark. You can put the heavy stuff at the front, the middle, or the end of the mark. You should always try to mix it up so the dog develops the ability to trust his memory and keep driving on to where he thinks the mark is, regardless of what kind of cover he runs into.

Do the same thing with water. Some marks, while hunting, require swimming from start to finish, but most of them only call for running through water or swimming for part of the retrieve.

Incorporate water at the first of the mark, at the middle, and then at the end.

One of the most exasperating things that can happen while hunting rivers or lakes is when your dog goes boldly out to retrieve but gets hung up just short of the bird by a cover barrier. Many times when this occurs the bird will float downstream while you watch helplessly. The dog will frantically search for the bird as he hustles back and forth along the barrier and the bird is getting further and further away. Sometimes this bird will even get beyond the reach of a finished retriever who will take hand and whistle signals well.

You should not get the idea that this could only happen in a river hunting situation. Many times I have seen a combination of wind and waves take what was an easy water mark out to sea.

I remember a day when I was running a great young Labrador in an AKC hunting test. He was about two years old at the time. This was one of the best dogs I've seen and had two full seasons of hunting under his belt. He was steady and was working his way to being a super marker. His owner wanted him to complete his master hunter qualification, so I started running him in some of the AKC stakes held in nearby states. He was entered in the junior division at this particular trial.

Junior hunters are only required to pick up a couple of fairly easy land marks and a pair of water marks to earn a passing score. The dog has to be steady and he must retrieve to hand.

The dog I was running was force broke and very steady. He was a flyer and one of the top two athletes I've ever trained. He was already a good marker and was fearless both on land and water. This test was going to be a piece of cake. Two measly little 60-yard marks with live pigeons, no sweat. Two shot ducks to pick up out of a round pond, kid stuff.

About half an hour before my dog was to go, the wind kicked up. It started out fairly brisk, but no big deal. As I looked out to the west I noticed a thunderhead building up and heading our way. That didn't scare me. My dog was ready for anything.

When we went to the line the waves on this harmless little pond were about two feet high and the wind was howling out of the west. My dog picked up both of his land series without even slowing down. We spun around to face the water so we could get the ducks, get our ribbon and get out of there.

The first water mark was thrown to land about 15 feet off shore just beyond a good patch of cattails. The dog sprinted to the bank and tore into the pond. He was a fast swimmer, especially when he had seen a duck fall. He quickly reached the cattails and briefly checked them out as he past through. He drove on away from the bank toward the center of the pond where he saw the bird fall. The trouble was, however, the duck had been blown to the other side of the lake and disappeared down the outlet channel. The duck wasn't there, it wasn't even on the pond any longer.

In a junior test, once the dog is sent on a marked retrieve, you are not allowed to handle him to the bird. After a gallant 20-minute hunt fell short, the judge asked me to call him in. Tough situation, yes, but it will happen to you, so prepare for it as you train.

Some cover the dog can't see through and some of it he can't see out of. His head is only a few feet off the ground when he is sitting so take this into consideration when you show him marks.

Think about this: When you are walking across a field or a hillside and you come upon a very rocky area, what do you do? Let's say it's the rocky edge of a freestone river, a shale slide, volcanic rock, or maybe just a particularly rocky section of a flat field. How do you react? You slow down and look at the ground, you try to judge the easiest way through and then attempt to maneuver. This usually includes weaving or traversing the obstacle. Sometimes the best way is to jump from rock to rock until you are back on firm ground.

You may not have considered rock as cover for game birds, but if you hunt much, you have dealt with rocks. If you plan to hunt ptarmigan with your dog you'd better plan for rocks. If you are considering chukars or huns, rocky benches and slides are in your future. If you are running the rivers for waterfowl, you learn waterfowl definitely consider rocks as cover. If you like to hunt blue grouse, you better prepare your dog for rocky dropoffs and outright cliffs. The truth is, if you don't include rocky areas in your training program, you won't be ready for situations that regularly happen while hunting.

When you cross rocks, you slow down and change your course to suit the terrain. Your dog will do the same thing. Cut him some slack here. Don't insist he shoot through rocks as straight as an arrow. Many times, when hunting benches or cliffs, the retrieve calls for a big loop.

The dog will have to pick his way down an old deer trail and then try to hold onto the hillside as he curls back toward the fall. Sometimes it's possible to send your dog in a different direction until you know he can safely complete the retrieve and then cast him to the bird.

When you are working on marks, don't neglect working some in rocky cover. You don't have to spend weeks with it but you will need it someday.

Another often overlooked factor of cover is terrain. Not very much land is truly flat. Even out in the Midwest, that flat land isn't really flat. Rolling hills, draws, knolls, depressions, potholes, hillsides and ravines are all sprinkled across the countryside. And guess what, that's where the birds hang out. In the mountains you spend most of the day leaning on one leg or the other as you walk. You go from bench to bench, from drainage to drainage.

All of the areas you hunt, the direction you hunt, and the speed you hunt will be determined by the character of the land.

Your dog will flow over his country as he stretches out. He will spin and eddy under a bluff, just like moving water. Long flats will call him to sprint and reach. Sidehills will cause him to run up for a time and then loop toward the swell just like kids riding dirt bikes.

All animals are drawn to water, especially fast-moving water.

He might want to see what's just over the horizon. I know I did when I was young. He might resent pressure to come back before he gets to satisfy his curiosity. It's like a youngster leading his parents from one carnival ride to the next, excited about the choices, thrilled with life. Your dog is not being rebellious or defiant, he isn't disobedient or discouraged. He is dreaming of success as he searches for it.

If you read somewhere that the only good dog work is straight dog work, you have been terribly misled. Sure, the idea of marking practice is to develop quick, efficient collection of dead or wounded birds, but if you overlook the unbelievable effect of natural influence, you are robbing yourself of one of the greatest treasures of life. The universal truth of the matter is that you are being pulled and pushed, just as your dog is. You are being gently guided from one rise to the next. When you are trying to slab a hillside you will have to fight the urge to go downhill.

I can remember numerous grouse hunts when I spent 15 minutes in the morning telling the hunters to fight off the urge to go downhill. "Keep your position," I would tell them, but the combination of the sidehill and the grouse's propensity to fly downhill would suck the hunters down until they all ended up together at the bottom. We would all get a grin out of it before we struck back out to regain our original course.

It's just natural to respond to the wishes of nature without even knowing it. When you get a chance, walk quickly to a river's edge and close your eyes. What is your first impression? Do you feel like going upstream or downstream? When you open your eyes, you will likely look out to the middle and your head will turn downstream. If you start walking without giving it much thought, you will be walking downstream.

I'll bet you're starting to wonder why you ever got yourself into this. What the heck does all of this have to do with training a bird dog?

Remember I promised you a new look? I'm not dreaming anything up here. I'm telling you of things I've seen and studied that had everything to do with completing our task. I'm trying to explain how ridiculous it is to go about training an animal without considering the environment and the controls within it.

If the mountain and the river have to play by these rules, if the wind and the fire have to play by these rules, if the elk and the groundhog have to play by these rules, if the pheasant and grouse have to play by these rules, then why should you or your shooting dog be any different? The truth is, this is the real game. Field trials are an aberration.

I challenge you to take an electric collar in your hand and go to the canyons. Look until you see an eagle drifting on the thermals. Study the eagle for a time, now look in your hand. Ask yourself, which one of these represents true power and substance? Which one has lasting value, and which one is temporary? Which can enrich your life and give you hope for the future? Which one is positive, which is negative?

I am not asking you to compromise the quality or substance of your training program, I'm encouraging you to enhance it. You always have the option to throw this book into the fire and get on board with every other retriever trainer out there.

Before we go on with marking, I would like to share a true story with you. This is a story that dramatically illuminates the danger and the cruelty field trial competition spawns.

I know a trainer who is very talented, he was raised in the gun dog business and has worked his entire life on shooting estates overseas and big ranches here in America. He was taught about breeding and training by one of the best in the business. While still a young man, he possessed the knowledge to pick good prospects and train them to win. He knew field trials and how to show the judges what they wanted to see.

He was hired by a wealthy rancher who wanted to make a

mark in the trial game. The sole goal of the program was to make field champion, then high point open dog, then National Open Champion. The trainer had two dogs on the string that were of the caliber to achieve the owner's goal. Both dogs were campaigned throughout the country, and expenses were of no concern. Both dogs quickly achieved field champion status, and both were considered great breeding prospects.

The next stage of the goal was to make high point open dog of the year. The trainer drove from one end of the nation to the other in his quest. He wanted desperately to show his boss he could bring home the prize. The next year he did just that. One of the dogs was crowned the high point open dog and the next year he won the National. Great success story? Maybe, maybe not.

One day the trainer and I were sitting on the tailgate of his dog truck talking dogs. He shared with me the amazing journey to the top of his game. You see, one of his dogs was very hard to train and was either on top of his game or on the bottom. He would either win the trial or be eliminated in the first series.

"If I could keep him in the trial, he would usually win," the trainer told me.

As the dog got older, he got harder to handle. The trainer found it necessary to put more and more pressure on him before the trial so he would be capable of winning. Before it was over, the trainer would put the electric collar on his dog before he even got to the trial grounds and would shock him in his kennel while driving to the grounds. This seemed to give the trainer the upper hand long enough to make a good show at the field trial.

After the dog's trial career had been deemed a huge success by the dog game folks, the dog was retired to stud. He was also considered a good candidate to run guided hunts. After all, he was a National Field Champion, right!

The problems first occurred with his breeding potency. He was rendered nearly sterile and was very hard to breed. He had a pretty nasty nature to begin with and nothing had happened throughout the course of his life to change it for the better.

The second problem was that no one could handle him on

guided hunts. He seemed oblivious to handlers' attempts to control him and did whatever he felt like when taken to the field.

This trainer and I are friends. He is a good guy and a hard worker. He didn't know what to do with this dog and he asked me if I was interested in buying him. "I think you could handle him, Mike," he told me. "He could still be fairly useful on your hunts, don't you think?"

"What do you want for him," I offered.

"How's $500 sound?"

"Let me think it over. You know I never have any money."

The trainer had to get back to his work so he left me there to think about the dog and he headed down the road. A few weeks later the price was $300. Two months after that the ranch where the dog was being kept offered me three dogs, including the old champion, for $300.

"I can't use them, " I told him, "I have enough dogs to feed and I have some good young bird dogs to bring up. Good luck."

The next summer I had the chance to spend a little time with the trainer. We talked about the dog and his unfortunate end. We also talked about what brought him to that point. The trainer said, "Damn the game, damn those trials, it just isn't worth it."

He doesn't trial anymore, he tells me he never will again. Instead, he runs shooting dogs and I'll bet he is doing a hell of a job at it. He's a great trainer, he knows dogs, and he knows wildlife.

If you think this story is an exception, I invite you to look around. Ask some of the dog game folks if you can take a look at their old champions. It's against the rules to train at a trial, but just take a little walk out behind some of those dog rigs. Drive down the road for a piece and watch some of these trainers warm up.

I've heard trainers say, "You know, it's not like it's brutal or anything." To that I say, "The hell it ain't."

The next time you're talking to a trainer who tells you how necessary the collar is and how it really isn't brutal if it's used right, you might think about all of the times it's not used right. Think about the dogs who have paid the price so trainers could learn how to use it right. Think about the results, the end of the story.

The field trial game is the culprit, not the electric collar. The field trial game directly causes brutality in training and the game itself can turn a caring, intelligent, hardworking trainer into a close-minded, hard-rock miner in a quest for silver.

Triples and Quads

Well, after throwing all of those singles and some good doubles, I'll bet you're aching to get to the triples. I remember training my first retriever. I loved those triples and set them up every chance I got. I used to bang away day after day on triples and quadruples. You see, once you get a good feel for triple marks, then you can start putting the lines in the dog. Now you can get to retriever heaven, long triples with blinds down the middle.

Before we get into this triple stuff, let's evaluate the significance of it.

I would never assume that I've seen it all out there. Labs are used for so many things, I could never experience all of the scenarios that take place while bird hunting. I have, however, been in the field with several thousand Labradors and I've seen birds in the air over most of them. Some of my Labrador hunting partners have been lucky enough to witness a few thousand birds of their own. I know Web had seen thousands and retrieved a few hundred before he was six months old.

How many times do you suppose, while hunting or guiding, I've seen the opportunity for a dog to pick up a triple marked retrieve, let alone a couple of blinds through the middle of them? How many times have I seen a dog get the chance to calmly mark three falls and pick them up one at a time based solely on his trained marking ability?

Almost never! I wanted to say never, but there have been times while waterfowl hunting when I saw the value of triple work. If you take out waterfowl hunting, I can definitely say, "Never."

When you get into a situation where numerous birds are falling, it is a chaotic scene. The hunters are moving all over, many times there are more birds coming in or flushing, everyone's talking, and everyone's very excited.

When there are enough birds present for the hunters to shoot three or more birds, then there will be a lot of missing going on out there also.

We are not talking about a guy in a white jacket throwing a bird out in front of two other white-jacketed shooters, a nice pause, then another bird presented, a nice pause, then the final bird.

A real good wing shooter will be successful about 50 percent of the time. I've not seen one who could sustain an average above 65 percent. Most shooters will fall into the 20 to 35 percent range.

You think you're a better shooter than that, don't you? You're saying to yourself, "What's this guy talking about, 20 percent?" Try this: next hunting season keep track of your shots and your birds to bag. No excuses, now, only birds in the bag count. Most of the time, when more than one hunter is present at the flush, there are several shots taken at the same bird.

OK, you and your hunting buddy are duck hunting and have just dropped three birds in front of your Labrador. I'll give you guys the benefit of the doubt and say you did this without reloading. You were both shooting auto loaders or pumpers, he got two and you got one. You probably shot all of your shells and he did, too. This means your dog had to keep track of all the birds, at least six shots, and all the falls.

There is nothing sequential about what just happened. The birds are there, the shots are fired, and it all seems to happen at the same time.

Your dog doesn't have the luxury of the birds falling in any order. Most of the time they all fall at nearly the same time. His attention is usually drawn to the closest fall or the one that may land in the water. A big splash can wipe a retriever's memory slate clean, I don't care how accomplished he is. He will leap into the water to retrieve the bird that caused the splash and if a few more birds come over while he's making that retrieve, you can kiss any semblance to a triple marked retrieve goodbye.

What I'm describing here isn't something I dreamed up to illustrate confusion. This is the way it really happens, in a real field trial. Lots of times it's way more complicated out there than what I've just outlined.

When upland game bird hunting, triples mean coveys and coveys mean confusion. You will find yourself moving great distances before you get the birds all picked up.

We haven't even talked about cripples. We haven't even addressed the bird who isn't where he fell. Heck, he might not even be in the same field.

He might be in the water, hooking it for the opposite bank. He might be in a tree. He might be in a gopher hole. If he's still alive, you can bet on one thing, he intends to stay that way.

When your dog gets to the area of the fall, he could be facing a trailing chore that can eat up most of a half an hour. Let me ask you this. What are you going to do while he is searching for the wounded bird? Are you going to patiently wait for him back at the place where you were doing the shooting so he can pick up the remaining marks? I don't think so.

Remember the old saying, "Patience is a virtue seldom seen in women, never in a man." I think you are going to be trying to help out, maybe even by picking up the last of the marks yourself so you can get over there and help him with the cripple. What if the cripple is a strong runner, or a diver? You might have to shoot him again.

Let me give you an example: Gary Ruppel, Ken McGraw and I were working our dogs in an apple orchard one day because rooster pheasants love apples. Orchards always have decent grass in them and during the fall, apples are strung all over the ground. A nice drainage ditch circled the perimeter of this orchard, and it provided super holding cover for the birds.

Deer like apples too, and because of that, orchard owners construct fences of woven wire to keep the deer out. These fences are usually about eight feet tall. An eight-foot woven fence is deer proof all right, but it is retriever proof as well.

We were hunting the edge of the orchard, and Web and I were working next to the fence. I saw a rooster duck through the fence and flush away from the orchard.

When you're hunting with your friends, you tend to be more

aggressive—you know, peer pressure and all. Without considering the situation, I spun and dumped a load into the pheasant. The old fence rattled, the bird flinched, drifted in and hit the ground running.

A rock wall angled out of sight down through some shrubbery into the next orchard. The pheasant quickly reached the wall, scurried over it and disappeared into the thicket. He was about 125 yards from me the last time I saw him, showing no sign of slowing down.

OK, here's the problem. Web saw the whole thing, but he also saw there was no visible way to retrieve the bird even though he had as good mark on him as I did. Web took off down the fence while I stood there trying to figure out why I shot at the bird in the first place. He ran 100 yards to the corner of the orchard, over a huge dirt pile, down into the brushy ditch bottom and found a hole in the fence. He scooted through the fence and climbed back out in the field. Web set sail for the rock wall, jumped into the cover and was gone.

Gary walked over and said, "What are you doing, Gould?"

"Well, I'm not really sure. I dusted a rooster, but he's a strong runner. Web's working on him now."

We stood there for a long while. I was tempted to call the dog back because the bird had some serious legs under him when I saw him last.

That aggravated me. I hadn't been shooting well for a couple of years now.

"I don't know why I shot that bird,"I muttered. About that time, Web came trotting over the rock wall carrying the bird.

"You lucked out, buddy," Gary laughed.

Web retraced his route, slipped under the fence at the ditch and brought the bird back to me like it was no big deal.

Kenny caught up to us while we were analyzing the retrieve. We always admired good dog work whether it was theirs or mine. It was a great retrieve, a great mark, and a great trailing job— after a crummy shot.

Remember when I said your shooting dog needs to be innovative? A straight line to that mark was flat impossible. The fence was too high for the dog to jump or climb over. The running bird took the dog completely out of the area. We could only guess how far the chase went.

This was only a single. What if there were other birds who dropped at the same time? It would have been foolish to leave them on the ground until Web came back with the cripple.

You can only control so much out there. Most of the time you find yourself shucking and jiving, spinning and reeling, reacting to birds like a fly fisherman reacts to rising trout. Use what's working. The fisherman who only throws one pattern all day will not be nearly as effective as one who is willing to adjust his approach.

Don't get locked into a preconceived notion of how marking should be done. Don't fool yourself into believing that everything happens by the book out in the field because almost nothing does.

Why do you think the judges at a field trial want the bird blasted at close range by two gunners? So the dog won't ever be confronted with a real mark on a running bird.

Why do you think judges shy away from fast-moving rivers when they set up their marking tests? If you've ever hunted the river, you know some of those marked falls will take you and your dog a half mile downstream before you can get it done. Picking the birds up is the main thing. If you can do it pretty, great, but as they say, "Pretty is as pretty does."

Where I come from, the ranchers all cut hay in the summer so they can feed their livestock through the winter. They usually start their first cutting somewhere around the Fourth of July. I don't care how nice the weather is prior to the cutting, it invariably rains when the freshly-cut hay is laying in the field. When hay gets rained on for any length of time it can be ruined. It doesn't matter if you have done a great job of irrigating and the hay was taller than it had ever been. It doesn't matter how nice a job you did cutting or how quickly you did it.

It's not hay until it's in a stack or in the barn.

Same thing's true with these marks. A mark isn't hay yet. It has all the potential of being a bird in the bag. You may have made a nice shot and the bird may have fallen in a good location, but it's not hay until it's in your hand. Pick 'em up, that's the name of the game.

Let's look at another marking challenge. This one took place at a sanctioned field event. It gives us comparative information regarding marking and how different people perceive it. You decide which kind of dog you want. You decide what you want to train for.

One day we were running one of our dogs in the seasoned division of the HRC in eastern Colorado. I always like the people who ran that club. They trained at my place some and I always enjoyed attending their hunting tests. Let me tell you how warped some of these tests can get within the guidelines of the parent body.

You can take a regular guy, a nice friendly person who loves his fellow man and loves to train dogs and turn him into a monster overnight.

You want to know how? Tell him he will be the judge at the next field trial. The guy will swell up like a frog—he's all business now. He might have been fun to be with during the last trial. You may have had a few beers together and cussed the setup and the judging. Things are different now. The same congenial old buddy now looks more like one of these white supremacists who vows to change the world.

This is what happened to the poor soul who was chosen to judge the seasoned test. A seasoned dog is defined as one still in training—a middle-of-the-road dog who has some practical experience under his belt but a long way to go. The seasoned dog must remain steady for his marks, he must be able to handle doubles on the land and water, and should be able to pick up a 40-yard blind without too much problem. Most seasoned tests require the working dog to handle at least one diversion bird.

We were ready to go, our dog was almost steady. She was a young Labrador named Jem. She was a decent marker, and her handling was adequate to get the blinds picked up. We thought our chances were good of coming up with a ribbon for the dog's owner.

We made it through the water test and were excited about the prospects of pulling it off. When we were called to get ready for the land series, we loosened Jem up. She seemed to be hitting on all eight. I had a short talk with the handler and took up a position on the top of the dog truck so I could watch the action.

I should have known there was trouble ahead when I saw the handler who had just run the test walk away from the line and into the parking lot. He was a great big guy who looked a little like Rambo. He hadn't shaved in about a week and was wearing a camo headband. He was so mad he was shaking. His dog was shivering and sulking along beside him.

I'll pick this up and tell you what happened next after I tell you of what the test consisted of.

It was a double land mark with a diversion and a short blind across a ditch filled with cattails.

After the dog was shown the double, a wing-clipped pigeon was thrown to fall less than five feet in front of the dog with everybody shooting. This was a young dog who was still in training and his judgeship throws a live bird in her face and puts the hard eye on her for breaking.

My handler couldn't believe Jem was still sitting there when the smoke cleared. He sent her for the marks and lined her to the blind. After 20 minutes of handling, the judge decided to pick her up. She had been in the area of the fall numerous times without finding the bird. The judge asked the bird boy to check the blind for the next dog up. When he got out there he realized he had neglected to place a blind for Jem.

I'm not telling this story to emphasize what was obviously a poorly conceived test. I was sitting with the president of the retriever club while all of this was taking place and we talked about it. I told him I thought his judge was in way over his head and he agreed. Two water marks, two land marks, and one diversion bird were put before the dog that day. Three of the marks landed inside of 15 yards and the diversion bird was inside five feet. The land blind wasn't even there. The judges should have been disqualified instead of the dog.

Anyone could easily understand there wasn't the slightest resemblance of a natural hunting test given at the trial. The whole day was a colossal waste of time. Training for that kind of testing is a waste of valuable time.

I brought up this story because of what happened to the dog who ran just before Jem. I saw that dog take the worst beating of any I've witnessed before or since. Ol' Rambo nearly killed his dog and then threw him into his kennel so hard I swear he moved his truck a few feet forward. That dog took a horrible beating right in the parking lot during a field test and my handler and I were the only ones who saw. I felt like tearing into Rambo myself, but the fear of getting the same beating and then thrown into the dog box kept me quiet.

The point is, the judges were responsible for that beating. The breaking test was so severe it caused Rambo's dog to jump the gun. The test was so absurd a dog was probably scarred for life trying to run it.

This story represents one end of the spectrum, and the open all-age retriever stakes represents the other. From five feet to five hundred yards, these are weekend judges testing the marking ability of retrievers.

Do we want our Labrador shooting dog to know multiple marks? Well, of course we do. What I don't want you to do is spend most of your training time during the prime years of your dog's life working on situations that never occur while hunting.

The object is to get the damn birds picked up and get on with the hunt. Are you and your duck hunting buddy going to wait for a half an hour for the dog to finally come up with the cripple, then go back to the line and try to finish up the marking test? For crying out loud, pick 'em up and get going.

If you decide to train your dog to fully understand all-age triples and quads, you have to also decide to compromise the most productive time of his life in an endeavor to learn skills he will never use hunting birds.

Well, in that case, what good are triples anyway? They are

factors in good quality structures but maybe not for the same reasons you might think. Let's talk about training for multiple marks and how it fits into our program.

As I said, I like to train with triples because I believe it adds a strengthening effect to our pyramid. I think triples teach a dog to relax and concentrate.

Again, triples will extend the dog's memory. This is positive from a fundamental standpoint. In other words, the dog needs to know he is not finished until all of the birds are picked up.

I don't care what kind of work you do for a living, whether you are a doctor, lawyer, plumber, welder, it doesn't matter, if you're any good at it, you make sure each job is finished before you go on to the next.

It's just normal to want to go on to the next opportunity as soon as you can, but the guys you can really depend on stay until they are sure everything's done as well as it can be.

Your shooting dog needs to operate on the same level of integrity. Triples teach a dog to finish up right, stay in there and make sure before you go home.

Multiple marks help to keep his mind in the game and keep him working. The idea that there are other birds still out there keeps him willing to fire out again when sent. I think this helps greatly when you are training for handling.

If a dog gets used to picking up a number of birds in different locations, he will readily go. He will always want to run.

When you start working on lining, if the dog really has the desire to go, it will help tremendously. You need all of that working for you, especially when you go to the water.

Chapter Thirteen:
Table Work and Force Breaking

"**W**hy should I have my dog force broke? Is it absolutely necessary for my dog to be forced? He already likes to retrieve." "Mike, doesn't this force retrieving sort of fall at an angle to the rest of your program? Can I get the consistency I need without hurting my dog?"

Good questions. I have heard them many times. I will try to tell you of my philosophy on forced retrieving and how it's changed dramatically over the years.

Most retriever training books will include a section on force retrieving and someone's particular method of doing it. Each one will start with a disclaimer about the end being worth the means. Each will tell you of how the benefits far outweigh the downside.

Force breaking is unfortunately another spin-off of retriever trial training. To get the kind of dependability you need for the tough situations, force breaking seemed like a natural price to pay.

I have gone through the whole process. I started out believing what I read: "If you're going to be successful in the retriever trials and tests, your dog has to be force broke." It made sense to me when I studied the principle of the work. "If your dog is force broke, he will never quit you, he will always go, he will jump off the highest bank or struggle through the deepest mud just to do what you told him—'fetch.'"

For years I have followed along with the rest of the "wanna-be's," force breaking dogs and hating every minute of it. I started with the ear pinch method and used it for several years.

It sounds easy—you just pinch the end of the dog's ear as you say "fetch." He feels the pinch, opens his mouth and receives the dummy. You steady the dummy properly in his mouth and encourage him to hold it. You simply keep at it until the dog snatches the dummy out of your hand when you say "fetch" and holds it until you tell him to give it to you. From there you go to the ground and then to short tosses. Pretty soon your dog is considered force broke and he will never refuse you again. You have done it, you force broke your own dog. Well, maybe, maybe not.

Let me tell you how it really happens. I have seen many good trainers do force breaking work and I have done a hundred or so myself.

It doesn't usually go according to Hoyle. Sure, some dogs go through the process with little or no serious problems. You are making a mistake if you think you're going to sail right into force breaking and drift out the other side without weathering at least one lengthy storm at sea.

If you get the job done you will have to sooner or later touch the dog's soul. You will have to communicate to him that you aren't asking him to pick up the dummy, you are telling him to.

Dogs are no different than people when it comes to being told what to do. They react just like people would. Some dogs want to run, some want to fight you, some will put up with your requests while they bide their time and depend on your giving up. Occasionally a dog will try to bite you. Some will act like they are getting it just so you will leave them alone.

What about method? Generally, most trainers either use the ear pinch or the force table.

I used the ear pinch until I learned what I consider to be a superior method in the table. What's the problem, you just need to pinch the dog's ear until he feels uncomfortable, then you place the dummy in his mouth as he reaches for it?

Dogs are different. Some dogs will scream like you've shot them if you give them the slightest pinch. Others will look at you with a smirk on their face as you grind the ear until your fingernails touch together. Trainers commonly use the rim of a shotgun shell to apply more pain at the point of contact. I have seen guys use beer openers and any other thing they can grab.

Why do I know this? Because I've done it also. I hated it, but I did it. The real stinking truth is in the fact that the shotgun shell makes it more comfortable for the trainer at the same time as it makes it more uncomfortable for the dog.

On hot days, or days when the trainer is stressed out about something, he leans on his force training and often actually injures the dog's ear. When a man gets mad, his first reaction is always to add more force, more pain.

I like the table method a lot better than the ear pinch for several reasons but don't think you can't cause unbelievable damage if you're not careful.

The idea of the table is to place the dog at your level so you don't have to bend over during your sessions. Also you can fasten the dog to the cable above the table and restrict his movement. You use a nerve hitch to provide the discomfort. Other than that, it's force breaking, pure and simple.

The real benefit of the table has nothing to do with retrieving.

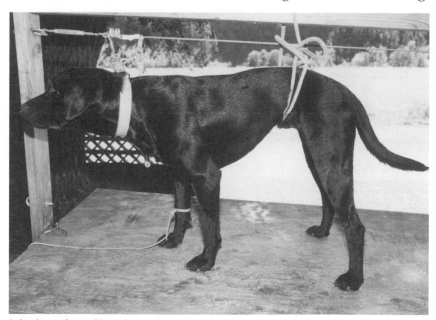

Labrador on force table with waist hitch and nerve cord

The table is one of the most important parts of my program. While we were discussing marking I promised to tell you more about it.

I've already told you I use my table for everything. I like to jump my dog up there to check for injuries, or mites, or ticks. I like to check out his legs and feet, his eyes and ears. It's a lot easier to spot wounds or hot spots. He is compliant while on the table so if you have to give him medicine or doctor him you can do a better job.

I like to brush him and talk to him. I rub the smuck out of his eyes and look for that extra-special eye contact. I look for affection or disgust. I can read his moods and get a good feel for his general health. If you have a female, you can use this opportunity to chart heat cycles.

I like to style the dog up and tell him how wonderful he is and how great a bird dog he will be. I pose the dog to stand up straight and square. I want him to look his best for me and for himself, for you see, self-confidence is important to a dog also. From here on out I want him to be proud and erect.

I often hop up on the table and sit beside the dog. I put my arm around his neck and shoulders. I love to dream with my dog, to look to our future together and tell him he can count on me. They seem to understand your mindset. This is an integral part of the force breaking process.

It's like the relationship we have as parents with our teenagers. They must rely on the trust built over years of fair treatment and honesty, but they must also learn the sting of responsibility and reality.

The dog must know that no matter how deep he goes you will go deeper, no matter how long he stays at it, you will stay longer. A dog respects you for being consistent. You've built your respect brick by brick, day by day.

Force breaking can come down to live-or-die, gut-it-out, man-to-man stuff. Sometimes you have to get to the fatigue factor before he breaks through for you.

Show him you care about him and be fair. Don't get fired up and frustrated and ruin a splendid relationship, maybe the truest friendship you'll ever know. Stay in there day by day and gauge your success carefully. Inch by inch, resolve to go the distance, because the ever-present danger with force breaking is quitting when you're just about out of the woods.

I have talked to trainers who were force breaking the first dogs of their careers and were caving in to the pressure. "I can't do it, for some reason I just can't get him through it," they would often say.

I always say the same thing, "Stay in there, stay fundamental, don't rush, keep trying. When dawn first shows there is no proof the night ever existed, I promise this will end soon."

Many times, when a trainer is ready to give up on his dog, the light is shining through. Just one more time, one more day and he may be out of the dark for good.

I have finished a lot of dogs who were started by their owners. A frequent explanation is, "He was going good for the first week or so, then as soon as we went to the ground, he shut down on me. I'm just too busy to finish up, would you mind helping me out, it probably won't take long, I have to get going, I'll see you later, Mike."

I'm left there with a spinning, panting retriever tugging at my waist cord as a cloud of dust winds its way off the ranch.

The truth is, I will have to start over with this dog. I will try to pick up where he left off, but in the end I will have to go back to square one and start from scratch.

OK, here's the way I see it. It isn't absolutely paramount that you force break your dog. It is, however, necessary to establish the pecking order. He needs to fully understand who gets to decide what gets done. He must know beyond the shadow of a doubt that he is important, high on the list, but I am the last word.

I have seen some terrific Labs who were capable of doing any all-age test who were never formally force broke. I also have seen trial dogs who were forced for their whole life who refused to retrieve when the going got tough.

This force thing, is it really worth it? Well, it all depends. We have to refresh our memories concerning the goals here.

We want our dog to have clean line manners and good bird-handling skills. We want our dog to carry his birds from the middle of the bird instead of by the feet or the neck. We want our dog to have a nice mouth. We want him to hand us the bird so we don't have any last-minute chases with a wounded bird.

We want him to know to come to heel because there might be other birds in the sequence. We want him to pick up anything we send him for (sometimes even drifting decoys). We want to be able to take the bird from him before he shakes water and rocks the boat.

All of these and more are positive results of force breaking. There is luckily much more to glean from a thoughtful breaking process. I always end up with the dog's obedience getting extremely sharp and his working attitude teeming with confidence. All of our work to this point gets locked in and dovetailed so it won't slip on us.

I won't try to make your mind up for you. I'm here to say, you don't have to do this. You can get to where you want to be without it. I hate force breaking and I've always been frustrated because I couldn't come up with a better, more sensible way to get the retrieving problems all lined out.

You can hire a pro to work your dog on force retrieving. That's a good way to accomplish the ends, but when you do that, you can't guarantee the means. The trainer might put your dog through a trauma that he will never recover from. Your dog's trust in you might forever be compromised.

One thing for sure, force breaking is one of those decisions where there is no going back. If you decide to include force retrieving in your program, then make sure you go all the way. If you set out to force break your dog and find the going too rough, you might settle for less than what you had before you started, and more importantly, the dog will always know he outlasted you. He will never forget beating you and it's likely he will try to do it gain somewhere down the line.

The one and only reason I force break most of my personal dogs is the gains far outweigh the losses if I'm diligent and respectful in the process.

If I ever see a wound appear at the point of contact, I am

careful to protect it and keep it healing. When I first started force breaking, I welcomed the onset of a sore spot so I could exploit it to my advantage. Some dogs are so tough that you feel the need for a sore spot to appear so you can finally get the upper hand. I can remember saying to the dog, "I've got you now, you scumbag, you're history, give it up, it's all over."

Don't make the dog pay for your ignorance. Use your head and be patient, stay fundamental and wait on him, he will come around.

You and I have been bringing our dog along, building our pyramid, from the time he was puppy. You will probably not experience an extended struggle with force breaking if you choose to give it a go.

If you want to force break, I'm going to recommend the table method. If you have chosen to ear pinch, or another system, then I will get back together with you after you're finished. Make sure you attend to detail and do a good job.

What kind of table do I use?

I've used lots of different styles. One fall I broke several dogs on the tailgate of my truck. Sometimes I would scrounge old lumber and cobble a table of scraps. I've used log slabs, flat rocks, and dog houses. You can get the job done using just about anything, but I can give you some ideas on how to build a table that will work well and last.

I like a table that is multifaceted. I don't particularly like the tables with the ramps coming up from the ground on both ends. I build my tables 16 feet long, 32 inches wide, and 36 inches tall. I build a shorter table of the same width and attach it to either end of the big table. I like my dogs to jump up on the short table as part of the transition up on the force table and then again on the way back down to the ground.

I secure a cable about 29 inches above the force table so I can keep 'em moving free and easy up and down the table.

I build mine out of 2x4s and ½-inch exterior plywood. I also cross brace between the legs and around the perimeter.

Put your table under a tree if you can. A little shade can make things go a lot easier for you and your dog.

"In the shade" sounds like such a trivial detail, doesn't it?

Let me explain why the comfort of a shady tree can make things smooth out for you.

Tempers always flare more easily in the heat. Some training sessions start out fine but deteriorate into a battle of wills. When this happens a little shade can save the day. Also early morning or evening can help keep attitudes in the groove.

As you go through a session on the table, the dog will take the dummy numerous times in his mouth. If you are using only one or two dummies they will get very slick and slimy. If you are working out in the sun this problem will be greatly exaggerated. The dog's hold will suffer, and as you put more pressures on him to keep his grip, he will want to escape. If you let yourself get into this situation, you will be biting off a lot to chew. You can do significant damage in the heat of the moment.

Here's how I keep from falling into that trap. I have several dummies at my retrieving table. I use the small, rubber knobbies instead of wooden dowels or canvas to start my dogs. I don't see where wooden dowels or bucks work better than the dummies. I keep a gunny sack or an old towel wired to the end of my table so I can rub the dummies clean and dry. If you wash your dummies every now and then the dog will appreciate your effort and repay you with better performance.

I think it's worthwhile to set the table on level ground. I used to spend so much time at my table that I laid rubber belting on the ground to walk on. This belting makes a nice mat. It will cushion your steps and help to keep your attitude positive.

I oil the table at least twice a year with linseed oil. The oil will soften the wood and make it more durable. When wood is soft, it is pliable and will be less likely to splinter or crack. If your table develops a splinter, cut it out. Don't run your dog up and down the table if he can hurt himself. Astroturf works good for the top surface, but I kind of like the slick top. If the table is slightly slick it is much like the table in the vet's office.

You won't have near the trouble keeping a dog where you want him if the table is slick. They hate to skid around and will

Force table collar hook-up

dig into the plywood and hold tight if they can.

Use a good leather collar and brass snaps to hook the dog to the cable. I like to use a leather pinch collar without the spikes so I can adjust it to any dog. I leave it on the table so it hopefully never gets lost.

We've got our table built and picked out some dummies. We had all our friends come over and help carry it to the perfect spot. It's all level and looking good—now what?

As is true with all force breaking systems, you need a device to cause the dog some grief so you can condition him to fetch when he's told. We're going to use a nerve hitch, the same one Bill Tarrant's been writing about for 20 years.

When you're picking out a string to use, you had better keep a couple of things in mind. A light, narrow string like baling twine will fray and a twisted cord will untwist.

Go downtown and find some braided nylon cord about one-quarter inch in diameter. Look for something similar to the diamond weave of your waist cord. Come on now, buy the good stuff, we didn't come all this way to shortchange our dog by yanking on his foot with some discount clothesline. Five feet is plenty, but you better make a few of them because you're going to lose a couple. People will take your cord and use it to hang a hummingbird feeder or whatever and never bring it back. Burn the ends and tie an overhand knot in one end.

Bring a water bucket over near the table so you can reach it without leaving the table for long.

Let's see now, we have built a decent table and we're all set up so we might as well get started. Wait, there's one more thing I like to do before I go get my dog.

I go in the house and dig around until I find a couple of 3x5 cards, you know, the kind you use to keep pertinent notes or recipes on. I always jump the dog up on the short table first so down at that end of the table I tack up two cards. On one of them I write: "If you train for total confidence your program will be successful; if you train for total compliance, your program will ultimately fail." The other reminds me, "Brick by brick, day by day, you can build an entire city, but you can't build it today."

I'm going to grab my waist cord and a big glass of tea right quick. I'll let you know why later.

Camas knows something is a little different today. As I slipped my waist cord on her she looked up and wondered.

The most important thing I'm going to tell you about force breaking is that it doesn't start, or end, on the table. It took a long time to figure this out, so trust me on this one. Start your session the same way we've been doing all along, with obedience.

Just a couple of minutes of obedience is all it takes, but make sure it's sharp. Do it on lead and include at least a few of each of the obedience commands (except lay down). Remember, we're establishing control going in.

Tap the short table and tell the dog to "Get up there." If the dog doesn't hop right up, give some up pressure with the waist cord and keep it constant until the dog makes it all the way up. After a few days, the dog will come directly to the table and jump up without any help.

While the dog is on the short table, style him up like always and talk to him. Keep everything the same as it was the day before. Don't allow yourself to let down on the infrastructure you've come to depend on. Brush him a little and make sure he feels at ease.

Now jump him the rest of the way up to the force table and escort him back and forth from one end of the table to the other. I like to act enthusiastic and supportive as the dog moves up and down the table. Normally, the dog won't relax right away. He will be tentative and anxious. Keep encouraging him to hustle up and down the table until you feel good about it.

Now snap the dog's collar to the cable at one end of the table and snap him short enough so his head is held near the cable. Sometimes it's necessary to fasten another snap from the first one to the end of the cable so the dog can't move down the cable.

The old waist cord comes in handy to snug the dog's body and further immobilize him. Put the loop around the dog's waist and throw the loose end over the cable brace. Now tie the loose end of your waist cord to the cable with a couple of half hitches and back away.

The dog may struggle some, but unless he is in danger of hurting himself, don't go to his assistance. If he gets tangled, calmly go over and re-adjust your hookup and back away again.

The dog will quickly realize he is stuck and will usually stand still. Some will blow up, eyes bugged out, whining and trying to bite the snap or the cable. Some will decide to lay down, but when they try to, the waist cord and the snap will hold them up. Do not stand by the table while this is going on. This has nothing to do with you, so keep it that way. Stand off at a safe distance and watch. This little fit can go all the way from one jerk of the head to a full-fledged tantrum.

The table is heavy, it took at least four guys to carry it, but nevertheless, I've seen more than one dog turn it over while tied to the cable.

As soon as the dog relaxes and accepts the fact he cannot change his predicament, I like to leave him there for a while. I will usually grab another dog and work on obedience somewhere fairly near the table so if something comes up I can get to the table fast.

I leave the dog for at least 10 to 15 minutes before going back to re-establish my presence. I try to talk in soothing tones as I walk up to the table. I'm trying to show him I have come to help. "How's it going, buddy? Let me see here, how about a drink?"

We are going to start unplugging the dog from the table now, so I think the ideal way to do that is start with the waist cord and go in reverse of the procedure we brought him up here with. In other words, first take off the waist cord and slip it over his head. then unsnap his collar and give him a drink. See if you can get him to go up and down the table some with you and then snap his collar back to the cable.

This time take a drink yourself. Relax, you probably are thinking you've made a mistake here. This isn't making much sense. While you're trying to flick the bug out of your iced tea, reassure yourself.

We all need structure in our lives, we all need held in place at some point in our life. When we are faced with unpleasant circumstances, the first thing we want to do is to bolt. Get out of there, to heck with this, I'm outta here. Sometimes holding still is best when we are unsure of our future.

Put him on your waist cord and then unsnap his collar again. This time try to get him all fired up and happy as you urge him back and forth. When he is having fun again, take him right off the end of the table, to the short table, and onto the ground.

Bring him to heel and do another short stint of obedience on the way back to the kennel and put him away happy.

OK, here's what we did:

We started with control on the ground, we jumped to the short table, then to the force table. We led him up and down the table and then hooked him up by the collar. We attached the waist cord and moved away. We gave him some slack before doing the whole routine in reverse. Again we are using small increments to accomplish our task.

If you work your dog two to four times daily, the force breaking will progress quickly for you. If you work him only once daily, it can stretch out.

Oh, by the way, don't ever do any other kind of training while you're working on this. You have got your hands full for at least five weeks.

Go ahead and finish your tea, we'll work on this a little later.

I like to repeat the introduction process until the dog relaxes with it. Sometimes I don't really get into force work until the third or fourth day.

When you feel the dog is ready to go on, you will start applying pressure to influence the dog to reach for the dummy.

When you get your dog to the point in the workout where he is snapped to the cable and tied at the waist, it is time to introduce the nerve hitch.

Using the knotted end of your training cord, tie a clove hitch just above the dog's carpal joint on the dog's front leg nearest you. Always use the leg nearest you so the dog doesn't lose his balance during training. If your dog heels on the left, the leg you will be working on will be his right front.

A clove hitch is basically two half hitches facing each other. The knot in the end of the cord helps to keep the hitch from coming undone.

I position the clove hitch so the long, loose end of my cord is hanging straight down to the center of the dog's foot. Now take another half hitch around the two center toes. You can go either way, in or out, on this half hitch but I seem to favor the inside wrap. This allows me to pull in a straight line from the clove hitch

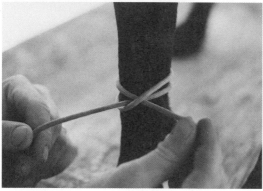

Cord and clove hitch on the carpal joint

on down through the toe hitch.

This contraption really bothers a dog at first. Let him get used to it, even while he runs up and down the table before you try to put any pressure on it.

Don't start pulling on the dog's toes until you've shown him what you're getting ready to ask of him. Squeeze the thumb and second finger of your left hand on both sides of the rear of the dog's mouth until he opens up. Position the dummy so he is holding it by the center. Don't ever let him think you will settle for anything except he middle. Make sure his lips and tongue aren't pinched or hurting. You will need to use your right hand to hold the dummy in place while you secure the hold by tucking your left thumb up into the "V" of the dog's lower jaw. Don't say anything if you can help it, but if you want you can gently tell him to "hold." Once he relaxes and holds the dummy you can remove your right hand from his head and pet him on the neck. Make sure he holds it until you decide to take it from him. When you do take it, say "give" and twist the dummy out and up.

How'd it go? Did he fight you or did he settle down with it? Well, if he had some trouble, do it again and keep doing it until he gets it. "Hold" doesn't mean you're mad at him or anything, it just means hold the dummy until you tell him to give it to you.

OK, now we're going to work on the first fetch. Hold the cord in your left hand and the dummy in your right. Hold the dummy by the end. Take up slack in the cord until it starts to pull on the dog's toes. Don't jerk on it or put instant pressure by pulling quickly. Gradually increase the pull until you see the dog start to react. He may look down at his toes, he may look up and away, or he may show you any one of many different es-capes. Don't say "fetch" until you see the first sign of escape.

When you say "fetch," say it firmly and say it once. Don't

Tension on the nerve hitch makes the dog fetch

get into the habit of saying fetch five, six, seven or more times. Say it once and increase pressure on the dog's toes until you can slip the dummy into his mouth.

Release the pressure immediately when the dog takes the dummy. Work on his hold and encourage him to relax. Be patient, don't get into a big hurry. After a time, tell him to give it to you.

One extremely important tip here is to insist the dog look at you. Don't let the dog get into the habit of looking away before or after he fetches the dummy. Take my word for it, don't go another step until the dog is looking at you. Make him turn to look at you, and don't move your body so he has to look your way.

Start again and work to get your timing right. Don't pull on the cord any harder than you have to and always release as soon as the dog completes the pickup.

This stuff takes practice. You're not going to be very good at it at first. Change dummies and step back for a minute. Think about what you're doing.

Remember to keep checking the clove hitch frequently so the circulation is not cut off to the dog's foot. That clove hitch can get plenty tight if you don't watch out. I have seen injuries occur because of not paying attention to the knots.

After a half dozen fetches, get out of it. First, take the training cord off, then the waist cord, then the collar, then the happy time, then the obedience, then out.

Let me help you identify the areas where you will run into trouble. These areas are what I call "Transition."

There is a transition from the kennel to the table, and then from the table back to the kennel. Transition problems will generally occur when you first go on the table, when you first apply pressure, and when you teach the dog to hold.

A major transition struggle can happen when you are asking the dog to pick the dummy up off the table for the first time. As you leave the table, you will experience a touchy transition zone when the dog's feet hit the ground. Sometimes they will want to forget everything they've learned once they're back on the ground.

There is a transition between fetches right in front of you and ones where the dog has to run out to the mark. There is transition when you go from dummies to birds. Basically every time you introduce something new to the dog, there is a period of resistance.

During transitions, it is especially important that you stay fundamental and stay consistent. It is normal for the trainer to start fearing transition areas and subconsciously try to avoid them. Sometimes trainers will let their force breaking stagnate. They will get stuck in a certain phase and just hope the dog will take them to the next level.

This is a mistake. You will have to push the dog from one phase to the next, being careful all the while not to accelerate out of fear.

It's just like eating a fish. You know there are going to be some bones in there, so you have your choice. You can pick away with the end of your fork until you have destroyed the whole fish without ever working up the courage to take a bite.

My wife's sister is like that. She drives me crazy as she stabs and pokes and drags and separates for half an hour, and when the dishes are being done, her fish gets thrown away.

The other choice is to get in a hurry and take big bites of the fish without checking for bones, hoping they won't come back to haunt you.

Neither of these plans work very well, for fish or for dogs. If you want to eat the fish or train the dog you must eliminate the obstacles by attention to detail.

Be watchful of the transitions. You can beat them all by keeping your cool, being patient, staying within your estab-

Force table escape responses

lished structure, and most of all, measure your success, or failure, by the week instead of by the session.

Keep doing this session after session, day after day until the dog is snatching the dummy from your hand with little or no pressure from the cord. Somewhere along the way you won't have to restrain him with the waist cord and you will be able to give him a lot more slack on the collar snap. He will eventually need to reach down to the tabletop.

Start holding the dummy farther and farther away from the dog until he is taking it out of your hand right at the tabletop.

You will probably suffer a small setback when you tell him to pick the dummy off the table for the first time. Many times the dog will retrieve it enthusiastically while you're holding it, but as soon as you set it on the table and tell him to fetch, he will balk. I've noticed tapping the dummy on the table will help him overcome this problem. I tap the dummy and increase the pressure until he really starts reaching before I let him have it.

Sometimes I will pull for a few seconds before I even show him the dummy so as soon as he sees it, he is inclined to reach for it quickly.

If he is to develop a pickup problem, like trying to hold the dummy by the end, it will happen here. Make him pick it up by the middle. He knows the difference. If he insists on picking it up by the end, increase the pressure and say "fetch" as you adjust it in his mouth. Pretty soon all you will have to do is to repeat the fetch command and he will adjust it himself and hold it correctly.

Once he is picking the dummy off the table, I like to start rolling it ahead of him so he gets excited with the chase. I tap the dummy a couple of times and then roll it a short way down the table. Dogs seem to like this part of the training, and I truly believe that when the dog will chase a rolling dummy without any pressure from you, the worst is over and it's all downhill from here on out.

When the dog is enjoying chasing the dummy down the table, I subtly loosen the clove hitch. Before you know it the string drops off and he is doing it without any pressure from the cord.

The transition I like to see concerning the cord is as follows: First hook up the clove hitch and toe hitch, then drop the toe hitch, then loosen the clove hitch and let it drop off naturally.

Now, our dog is hustling up and down the table to pick up the dummy and bringing it back to heel. He holds it until told to give it up.

Here is where I start the final transition to the ground. When the retrieving session is nearly over, I run him right off the end of

Transitions from the force table to the ground

235

the table while he is holding the dummy. I remind him to hold it as he bounces off the short table and then I call him to heel. From now on I do my ending obedience session with the dog holding the dummy. If he drops it, I squeeze his toes together with my hand and tell him to pick it back up.

By now you can probably tell him to fetch while he's on the ground and he'll comply.

You're getting there, just hang tough for a little longer. Work on it until you no longer need to use the table. Now you go through the whole session while on the ground. He is making short retrieves and bringing them to heel. The old happy attitude is back and confidence has never been this high. Watch out! He's got one more test left in him. If he gives you any trouble, don't worry about it, just jump back to the

236

table for a minute and the lights will go on.

You may also have to go back to the table when you reintroduce birds. Again, break it down: first dummies, then cold pigeons, then on to shot birds.

Some trainers take the force breaking on to the field where they use the whip and then electric collar to force the dog to piles of dummies. I can't think of one sane reason to include this into your program. Of all the stupid training practices I've ever seen, this one is the worst.

Use the waist cord to strengthen "hold" (Bruce Keep)

If you do a good job while you're force breaking your dog, you can't gain anything by humiliating him in this fashion. Some of these trainers have completely lost it.

What happened over the past month or so? What happened to your obedience? What happened to your dog's confidence? What have you accomplished?

Your dog's obedience is tack sharp, he is hitting on all eight and feels like he can lick the world. You have cleaned up all of your dog's retrieving manners and given him the tools to take his game to the top. You're moving, you can see the end of the rainbow now and with renewed spirit you're going for it.

What happens if he refuses you in the field?

First you try to evaluate the problem. When did it happen and where? Give him an easy one. How did he do on that one? Is he balking or sulking on you? Is he still refusing to pick up even the short retrieve?

This is why we train in small increments. First reach down and squeeze his foot while you show him the dummy. If he grabs it quickly, you're all right, just work your way through it. If he still balks, don't mess around, go right back to the table.

Slip the cord on him and give him several fetches. Have him come down the table to heel and hold it correctly before telling him to give. Take the cord off of him and give him a couple more fetches. This should go easy. If it does, bounce him right down to the ground and do it again. Still OK?

Take him back to the field, back to the same location where you got the refusal and show him the same retrieve. He should give you a clean pick up and delivery. If that happens, give him one more and get out of it.

Remember what we've always tried to do if he gets into trouble—first show him how to get out, then let him get out.

We're all getting back together now. Some of you used other methods of force breaking and some decided not to do it at all. No problem either way. I'm excited we are getting up the pyramid together.

I could have spent another 50 pages telling of all the pitfalls of force breaking and how I try to deal with them individually, but what the heck, let's look to the horizon. We're going to learn some about handling and advanced field work, then we can uncork the champagne and toast to the best shooting dog in the country.

This has been like a marathon race. We started out running on adrenaline, sustained for a long time by it, then we went into the long, middle of the race, where many racers are lost to lack of resolve, condition, or courage.

We are now closing in on the final leg where again we will be drawn ahead by the thrill of completing the course and ultimately being successful. It won't be long until we will dance at the top of the pyramid.

Chapter Fourteen:
Handling

*I*f your dog can't be directed to a distant fall, on many occasions he won't be able to finish the job. Birds that fall over the hill or across the lake, down in the draw or out in the cattails are hard to pick up if your dog won't take direction.

This section of the book is dedicated to casting and lining. We are going to teach our dog to run confidently and take adjustments without sulking or copping an attitude.

Remember when I told you, "Marking teaches your dog to believe in himself, handling teaches your dog to believe in you?"

Well, here we go. We have a gassed-up, cranked-up hunting dog who needs refinement and we're going to give it to him. He's hitting on all eight, doing his work and running confidently. By now he is marking well and has his line manners all worked out. We can depend on his steadiness and his working attitude. His retrieving is clean and he is focused, so let's have some fun.

Handling is fun, it's addicting. Heck, I'd just about rather experiment with casting and lining than hunt birds. You can do it in the city park and impress all the girls, heck, you can set up so it looks harder than it is so all your friends think you're the greatest trainer who ever lived.

A retriever who will handle well is one of the most sophisticated trained animals in the world. At the trade shows in the major convention centers it's the handling work that brings the crowd to their feet.

One time Web and I were doing demonstrations at a sport

show in Denver. He was always good at those kinds of things because he was so dependable. We had to do a demonstration every other hour for five days. It's pretty hard to come up with something to keep the interest after the first eight or ten shows.

I sent him to blinds from one side of the convention center to the other even though he had to maintain his course, without my help, while he zigged and zagged through 5,000 people: between the snowmobiles, over the ATVs, past the fly fishermen and the fake river, down the alley past the elk buglers and the goose callers, pausing briefly at the hamburger stand, before driving deep to pick up the dummy in front of the taxidermy competition.

He would have to head back toward me while dodging the crowd and occasionally stopping for a pat on the head from a well-wisher. One time the crowd was so dense he couldn't get back to me without climbing over a couple pallets of Science Diet dog food and scrambling through a curtain.

This kind of control is pretty impressive, to say the least. No shocking or intimidation, just trust—his in me and mine in him.

On the morning of the third day of the show I was cleaning up around my booth space and getting ready for the gates to open. Those shows usually don't open until 10 or so in the morning so it gives you a little time to prepare.

I saw a distinguished-looking character in a three-piece suit enter the hall and head toward my booth. He was carrying a smooth black leather briefcase and looked very important.

For some reason, I could tell he was coming to my booth. He was walking quickly and seemed to have something on his mind. I wondered if I had broken some kind of rule or neglected to pay part of my space rent. He looked like an IRS bandit on a mission to ruin a life. I pretended not to see him, hoping he would bypass my booth and go on to bigger and better things. He walked directly to my booth and stuck his hand out.

"I'm representing the company who hosts this Sports Show."

"Nice to meet you, I'm Mike Gould." I hoped I wasn't taking too much of a chance by telling him my name.

"I just wanted to tell you that you and that dog of yours are bringing more people into this sport show than any other one exhibit."

One fall we were guiding some grouse hunters back on the Roan Plateau of Northwestern Colorado. We were clear at the back of an 18,000-acre pasture where we had seen lots of blue and sage grouse in the previous weeks.

I had dropped the hunters to walk a long ridge and planned to pick them up at the other end. My brother Bob was with the hunters and one of the dog handlers came with me to drive the trucks around.

We decided to road a couple of pointers while we were traveling so we could locate a covey or two if they were near the road. The sage hens usually were hanging just at the furthermost corner of the property and we had been seeing a nice covey of blues in a chokecherry thicket just under the rim.

As we topped the last hill we saw one of the pointers locked down on about a dozen sage hens just inside the boundary fence. When they saw us they flushed and flew about 175 yards up the hill and settled down in some serviceberries and sagebrush on the neighbor's land.

We logged in the location and went about our business of picking up the hunters. When we told the hunters of the birds we had seen, they wanted to quickly jump the fence and thin them out some.

"What's the problem," one of them said. "The chances of getting caught up there are about nil."

"That's probably true," I said, "but I have a policy of not trespassing on any land we don't have permission to use."

"We sure would like to get a shot at those birds," the hunters were all kicking the ground and whining.

"Maybe we can, " I said. "OK, let's try this. Line up along the fence and I'll send Web up there to help us out." The hunters didn't like my plan but Bob and one of the dog handlers decided to give it a try. Finally one of the hunters went with them but his heart wasn't in it.

I told Web to hop over the fence and sit on the other side. I crawled up on the second strand of barbed wire and leaned over to give him a line. Everyone was laughing and seriously doubted whether or not I was all there, but what happened next was one of the greatest pieces of dog work I've ever seen.

I sent him with my firmest tone and he disappeared into the sagebrush. The sagebrush was typical for that part of the country, about three or four feet high and very dense.

I could see a small opening in the brush about 80 yards out or so. I was hoping he would cross there so I could see him in case I needed to handle. I was lucky, partly because he held his line as far out as the opening, and partly because I was still standing on the fence so I could see better.

I stopped him as soon as I saw him and gave him a big "back" in the direction the covey had landed.

I had my hands full just balancing on the fence, especially when you take into consideration the wire was probably older than I was and most of the cedar posts were long past being solid. I think the wire was holding the posts up instead of the other way around. Anyway, while I was weaving and hanging on to the top of a post, the shooters were rubbing their safeties and looking up the hill. After at least three full minutes had passed, I saw the covey half-heartedly flush and fly farther up the hill before easing back into the brush.

I don't really know what everyone else was thinking but at that instant I knew those birds were in trouble. I knew that dog and I told the guys to get ready cause things were going to heat up.

It took him a couple of minutes to get 'em going but here they came, down the ridge in singles and braces. Every one of those sage hens sailed within gun range of our skirmish line but only one of them succumbed to the dark swarms of shot that puffed and rattled them like ground fire around fighter planes.

"Nice shootin', Bob," I kidded by brother as I tried to unsnag my chaps from the barb wire. "I wouldn't have gone to all that trouble if I would've known you guys were going to let them get away that easy."

"I woofed one of them. Boy, they were hookin' it."

Bob was right. If you have ever tried to shoot grouse once

they have a couple hundred yards headstart on you, you're up against it. They are flying low and almost always downhill, combine this with amazing speed and you're in for some humble pie. Sage grouse are faster fliers than quail, believe it or not.

When the dust cleared we all started walking back to the trucks. Right in there somewhere we all realized what a superb piece of dog work we had just witnessed.

This was a bona fide blind, not only for Web but for me also. I saw him at the fence and then briefly in the opening of sagebrush. Other than that, he was on his own.

I've seen hundreds of them over the years, on land and across water, but none any finer. Everything was in the bird's favor—lots of distance, a steep hill, thick brush, no visuals, and a fading afternoon sun that only gave us a hazy look at bullet-shaped grouse.

From convention halls to the Roan Plateau, from roaring rivers to cattail swamps, from sectioned-off farms to cactus-filled ranches—do you want to learn to run blinds? Grab your shooting dog and your dummies. Camas and I will meet you in the field.

I'm not going to attempt to tell you everything about handling. If I did, this section of the book alone would exceed three hundred pages. I am, instead, going to try to tell you important aspects of handling and how you can make it go easier for you and your dog.

Take my word for it, if you put a good handle on your dog, it's going to take a long time and you will have to work to keep it sharp throughout the dog's life.

Trainers who depend on electricity to teach handling are working on intimidation to get the dog to comply. We are developing trust. Be patient. When your dog finally trusts your judgment it will be worth it. You won't have to threaten him with anything, just how him the way and he will go.

I encourage you to read everything you can get your hands on concerning casting and lining. Every trainer has some good ideas, glean what you can from them all. Ask pros how they accomplish good handling structure. Some videos will give you good direction, especially those about spaniels.

Take in stock dog competition if you want to see handling. Sheepherders wrote the book on handling dogs at a distance. They were also the first to use a whistle to assist them. There are some very good videos out on training stock dogs.

Don't just grab an electric collar and set out to teach your dog to handle. Learn how to train him to do it. Use your head, think about what you're doing. Relax at your task. Don't put any timetable on your handling training. It might take a season or two before you can pick up the tough stuff.

Don't worry about it if hunting season interrupts your handling training. Go hunting! You can always work on handling from February through August, but you can't hunt then.

Enjoy what you're doing. Don't ruin what trust you and your dog have accomplished by pushing him too fast into advanced handling situations.

We are running strong with a super pyramid base under us as we set out to develop the fundamentals of casting and lining.

Before we can actually cast a dog, we have to get his attention. He has to be willing to stop and look to us for direction, and then adjust his course as he fires out again.

Most retriever trainers use a single blast on the whistle to stop their dogs. I think this works well and it's hard for the dog to confuse it with other whistle commands.

Introduce the stop whistle while you're working your dog on a leash. Remember when I talked about several different cues happening at the same time that meant the same thing? This is called "Multiple Sensory Impact."

We taught our dog to sit as he heard the word "sit," he felt the levered pressure to sit, and he saw our leg stop. Now we will substitute the whistle command for the word "sit."

He will get the idea immediately and will comply without any reservation. Make sure he drops his butt quickly at the whistle command.

As soon as he is doing a good job while at heel, start experimenting with off-lead stopping.

Let the slack out in increments. Just like we have done with everything else, gradually give him more and more space before commanding him to sit.

I like to leave him at sit for a while after stopping him so he gets into the habit of waiting for the next move. Don't stop your dog and then give him a cast or a command immediately afterward. Always remem-

Kodak sitting

ber to be patient with handling. Many problems are totally related to handling too quickly—not giving the dog enough time to mentally shut down before the next cast.

As soon as the dog is stopping well at your side and at a short distance, you can start working on remote stopping.

I walk the dog to the training field while doing a short stint of obedience. Make sure the dog is clean with his obedience before starting with the whistle-stop drill.

While walking with the dog at heel, occasionally stop and give him the stop whistle so he knows what you're going to be working on. Don't try to trick him. Show him what you want.

When you get to the training field, leave him with a stop whistle and walk at least 70 yards away from him. Turn and face him for a short time before you attempt to move him.

Lower your hand to your side and call him in with a series of short whistles like, "Teet teet teet teet." Let him come all the way to you and bring him around to heel.

Now leave him there and walk back to where he was sitting at the start of the drill. This time as you call him to you, try to

245

stop him at different intervals along the way. Sometimes you will have to reinforce before he gets the idea fully.

When he gets back to you, bring him to heel and tell him to stay again. Walk again to the opposite end of the drill and call him all the way to you without stopping him. Bring him to heel, walk to the other side and call him all the way to you again without attempting to stop him.

On the next trip, whistle him to stop a few times on his way to you. Always insist on quick, sharp sits. Don't let him get into the habit of stopping in four or five strides or sliding off to one side or the other. You want him to sit quickly, facing you straight on.

Be especially careful with this. "Stop" has to mean "red light," not "yellow light." We don't want him to get the idea he can slow down and look both ways and then blast off again.

If you can't stop him, you can't handle him!

Remember to call him all the way to you twice for every time you tell him to stop along the way. If your dog stops easily, you won't have to do it as much as with one who doesn't like to stop.

You be the judge. Don't let him anticipate the stop whistle. Keep him running boldly back and forth.

When the dog is stopping well during this drill, you can move on. Remember to always finish the drill with a short round of obedience. Start under control and finish under control. That's still our structure.

There are lots of drills we can use to teach handling. Variations of the Baseball Drill, T's and Twin T's, Wagon Wheels, Three Leg or Five Leg Drills, Mowed Strips, Star Drills, I don't care, take your pick. All of these drills are fun to do and beneficial for you and your dog. Some are casting drills and some are what I call "line identification drills."

A common question that comes up frequently is, "Which do you start first, casting or lining?"

From the time our dog was a puppy, we have been preparing him for this day. He doesn't know it, but he can already handle. He doesn't yet know why you want him to stop. All he knows is he wants to do whatever you ask of him.

I like to start with casting because it's a natural extension of our influence handling. I like the old Baseball Drill for an introduction to casting and I usually do it for a few weeks.

During handling training, I try to use the whistle as much as I can to talk to the dog. "Teeeet!" means stop. "Teet, teet, teet, teet" means come in. "Teet, teet" means attention or turn. I like to accompany all of these with corresponding hand gestures, dropping my hand to my side for come in, holding my hand high for stop, etc.

Every retriever training book I've ever read tells the reader how to set up and run casting drills so I think it would be pretty redundant to go through them again. I would rather tell you of what I perceive to be the values of the various drills and what I have learned by doing them.

Before we get to the drills themselves, let's talk about where we are going to do this training. Should we do it in the water or on land? Should we show them cover or not? Should we use obstacles or a cleaner look?

I believe the dog needs to get a good look at the entire field when teaching handling. I think he should learn these skills on a field that resembles a football field or the outfield of a baseball park. City parks would be OK and hayfields right after mowing work great. No water, no ditches, no heavy cover. Just smooth grass and lots of it.

You can accomplish a good start right in your backyard. I like to do it in front of the chain gang if I can so all the dogs can watch each other.

Before we take another step, we need to remind ourselves of the mysteries of nature that we have found all along the way. We learned about natural influence and how powerful it is. We learned about meander and suction. We already know we're not going to be operating in the same sterile conditions field trials are run in.

In order to be successful, we must constantly be aware of changing wind conditions, humidity, terrain, heat, water, cover variations, and the ever presence of the other animals and birds in our training field.

While we were working on our marks we learned the dogs don't like running directly into the wind. They don't like running side hills, up or down. We learned how difficult angles were. We learned the impossibilities of straight travel.

When we teach handling, we come face to face with the most powerful force we'll have to deal with: Nature!

Don't bull up here and push your way through. Make sense of it. Be a teacher.

Here is where one of our mottoes means more than all the rest:

"Train for total confidence and your program will be successful;

Train for total compliance and your program will ultimately fail."

OK, let's look at some drills, starting with casting. No matter what drill you are working on, try to estimate the total distance your dog will be traveling or swimming. Don't get so carried away with the schematics of the drill that you forget about your dog's physical needs. Make sure you don't overextend his ability to complete the drill. You have to be sensitive to his conditioning. If he gets tired or worried, you have to shut it down.

Baseball

Baseball is the drill most trainers use to identify right, left and back casts. This drill gets everything going and is fun for both of you. The idea is basically to teach your dog to cast from an imaginary pitching mound to first, second, and third base.

You should walk your dog to the mound and turn him around before you whistle him to sit. Walk back to the area home plate would be and turn to face your dog.

A good tip is to back away from the dog for the first two or three times so you don't have a problem with him moving after you turn around.

You don't need a dozen dummies to do this drill. You can

teach baseball effectively using only two dummies.

Keep it simple and keep it fun!

I read about the Walking Baseball Drill in D.L. Wolters' book *"Training Retrievers to Handle."* This is my favorite casting drill. I have talked to many trainers who have a hard time understanding the drill initially and have decided against using it because of that.

You should take a longer look at Walking Baseball. This drill teaches your dog to take casts in all types of situations, through all types of cover, at all different distances.

You can have your dog casting accurately and boldly in very short order by using Walking Baseball. Once you practice the drill for a time, it's really pretty simple. You can bend Walking Baseball to work on any particular casting problem as you go through your daily workout.

As you already know, I like to introduce changes incrementally and Walking Baseball allows me to do that better than any casting drill I know of.

If everything is going well, I like to run my Walking Baseball according to a certain sequence. The sequence is simple. It goes like this: Right over, right back, left over, left back, right back, left back, right back, left back.

If I go through the sequence twice, I show my dog two right overs, two left overs, six right backs, and six left backs. I think this is especially helpful because it shows the dog lots of backs.

Try to cast your dog back at least twice for every over cast. The dog needs to understand "back." Your worst problem with running blinds in the hunting field will come from your dog's inability to get far enough back. If his right and left handling isn't real sharp, he can still eventually pick up the birds, but if he won't drive deep enough you're in real trouble.

As you set up your casting drills you will notice the dog leaning toward certain dummies. He will want one of them more than the rest. I think it is a good idea to cast him for anything other than the one he wants. Don't give him the one he favors.

Before the dog will handle well, you will have to be able to change his mind. Keep him guessing. Make him wait for your cast before he strikes out for the dummy.

I believe it is truly beneficial to cast your dog with well-rounded handling techniques. I practice in the mirror at home until I know what casts I'm actually giving. Sometimes you will be casting away, confident of what you're trying to tell the dog, but the dog isn't getting the same message. Make sure your casts are clear.

Your hand should be straight above your head, as far as you can reach on back casts. Overs should start from the heart. Start with your hands well inside your body silhouette, then cast straight out while holding your thumb down.

I don't think it's a good idea to just stand in one place and cast with your arms alone. I like to walk in the direction I want my dog to go as I give him the corresponding cast. Remember, we're not trying to trick him or trip him up here, we want to show him where the bird is, that's all.

I think it is very worthwhile to teach your dog to turn right and left on his back casts. If you want him to go back but he's caught up in a bird to his side, you need to be able to spin him away from the temptation and send him on back.

I like to work on left and right backs while teaching Simple Baseball and then galvanize it during Walking Baseball. Your dog should know when you move to the right as you cast, the bird may be anywhere else in the world, but it's not to your left (or his right).

I don't think angle casts are worth worrying about. You can easily influence your dog into angles while using straight backs and overs. Don't confuse and lengthen the process by introducing complications that won't benefit the end result.

Back casts, over casts, and in casts will get he job done. Stay focused there.

Stay with your casting drills until your dog will take nice clean casts and hold them for a long distance. Always start the same way by establishing control and working on your whistle stops. Always end your sessions the same: a happy attitude, a smiling face, and a short jag of obedience.

Lining drills teach your dog to run as straight as he can until he either finds the dummy or you stop him. I use the Three-Legged Drill to introduce lining. I also like the Wagon Wheel, or Star Drill. I set the lining drills up so the dog runs into the wind. I prefer a gentle crosswind rather than an "in your face" wind.

I am careful to start drills from the same place each day, if I can, so the dog can gain confidence with repetition.

When working your dog on lining, it's critical you set your dog up the same way each time and send him with the same sequence. Make sure he is looking at the dummy you are sending him for before you send him. Make sure he gets the picture or he won't go straight. You will get the hang of watching his eyes after a time and will notice even the slightest glance if he changes his focus.

Bring your dog to heel and make sure of his attention to detail. When he is sitting up nice and looking at the dummy, tell him to stay and concentrate on the dummy yourself. Now follow your line of sight from the dummy back to your dog and reach out to meet this line with your extended hand.

I hold my hand vertical and well out in front of the dog's head. Don't cover the dog's head with your sending hand and expect the dog to get a good look at the dummy. Reach way out there and give him the line so he can still see his field.

Some trainers give their dogs a line from directly over his head, or from beside it. I prefer reaching out and providing the front sight while the dog's eyes furnish the back sight.

It's just like a rifle barrel. When you lengthen the distance between the rear sight and the front sight, you add stability to the flight of the bullet. It's a lot easier to identify the target, and eventually hit it, if the sighting plane is longer.

Practice your sending sequence until you get it wired. Your dog's accuracy depends on your consistency, so make sure your timing is correct.

I send my dogs with a sequence that goes like this: I make sure the dog is sitting facing the dummy. I focus on the dummy and draw an imaginary line back to his head. I tell him stay as I give him the line and then send him with his name. The timing is important, so be sure it's consistent.

If the dog won't look where you want, don't send him. Re-adjust his position or bring him around again, but don't send him if he isn't looking. It's often helpful to look toward the dummy until your dog locks in on it and then go through the blind sequence from there.

I think it is important to keep the lining drills short until the dog fully understands what you want him to do. Forty or 50 yards is plenty for the Three-Legged Drill and the Wagon Wheel is even shorter. I have found it easiest to set the wagon wheel around my dog in about a 30-foot radius. I sit my dog in the middle and leave him there while I walk around him dropping dummies in the appropriate locations.

The star drill is similar to the wagon wheel but I think it's more beneficial in the long run.

I start my dogs on the Star Drill by leaving them in the middle and placing dummies at the four corners of the compass. One East, one West, one North, and one South. The dog will quickly understand the differences and have no problems going from on to another.

You should tell your dog "No" when he looks to the wrong dummy so he understands the only one he can go to is the one you are lining him for. If you are careful with "No" training, it won't negatively affect his attitude.

When you add dummies between the four corners of the Star Drill, it resembles the Wagon Wheel. After the dog is picking up all eight of the dummies as you send him, then you introduce eight more lines that split the difference between each of the original eight.

The added dummies are placed between the first group and about five yards deeper. This drill ends up looking like a star when you connect all the lines. Your dog should work on this drill until he can pick up the outer ring first and the inner ring second.

The Star Drill provides pretty good suction as the dog goes

through the inner ring and once again when he returns to you.

My favorite line identification drill is the Looking Glass. I think the Looking Glass is as good for lining as the Walking Baseball drill is for casting.

This drill is extremely versatile and can be used to introduce angles on land or water. It can help you accomplish great accuracy with your lines without any adverse pressure. The dogs seem to love the Looking Glass and will shoot through the "channel" from very long range.

One of the extra-nice spinoffs of the drill is that the dogs feel obligated to come back the same way they went out, thus the name, Looking Glass.

Bill Tarrant covers the Looking Glass in detail in his books, *"Training the Hunting Retriever"* by Howell Book House, and *"Problem Gun Dogs"* and *"Tarrant Trains Gun Dogs"* by Stackpole Publishing Co.

The idea is to simply introduce suction gradually until the dog will shoot through the Looking Glass from a great distance without even glancing at the rows of dummies he is passing just a few feet away.

You can combine the Looking Glass with the Three-Legged Drill and achieve pinpoint lines from as far as you like. On long lines where the call is for an angle entry into cover or water on the far end of the blind, I use the Looking Glass to give the dog a focal point. He is used to seeing the Looking Glass so he forgets about the obstacles around him and charges through the middle without reservation.

Combination drills (Casting and Lining)

The T, Twin T, and the Five-Legged Drill are examples of drills that allow you to work on casting and lining in combination.

This is where you integrate the drills and start lining your dog, stopping him and casting him on again. Your dog will stop on the whistle and look for direction. He will gladly take direction, and he will tear off as you cast him.

Now you're handling. Now you can practice and work out weaknesses. Now you can send him on a line and let him complete it or you can stop him and change his mind totally.

This is fun, and as I said before, it's addicting. You will want to show everyone what you've accomplished.

You did it, you taught your dog to pick up blind retrieves. Put 'em anywhere you want, he can pick 'em up. You'll walk around like a banty rooster looking for trouble.

Before you get too carried away, you should remind yourself that there is much more to come—some good, some not so good. You need to think about this one very important fact.

The idea is to not have to handle! We only taught handling so we could pick up those impossible falls. Don't get so caught up in handling that you forget our mission here. Handling is important, but not the whole picture. We're adding these very great skills to an already successful shooting dog. This knowledge can help take him to the top of the pyramid.

The key element in his ability to pick up the difficult blinds will be the willingness to drive deep enough. When you set up your lining drills, make sure you allow for sufficient depth. It is true, most birds will fall inside 50 yards but if you want to pick up those 150 yard sailers, you will have to train at 200.

The same cover barriers that plagued us in our marking training will rise up again. You have to be able to drive your dog off, or through, a cover barrier to pick up the long birds. Practice with your dog until he learns to push deep. You can always move him from side to side, but if he won't go deep enough, you're in real trouble.

Let me give you an example of an unbelievable cold blind that could never have been picked up if my dog hadn't been thoroughly schooled to handle at extreme distances.

In the late '80s a new outfitting company opened its doors in the Aspen/Snowmass Village area of Western Colorado. The idea was to have something for everyone who was visiting these two well-known resorts. They had fly fishing, shooting schools, bird hunting, some big game hunting, and a top-end sporting goods store in Aspen and Snowmass.

What they really needed was a Canada goose mount for their

marketing display. Bart Chandler, their head guide, came down to my place to see if he could shoot one.

It was the end of December and we still had two weeks remaining of the waterfowl season. There aren't a lot of geese in that area, but what there were normally hung out around my lakes and along the river bottom.

We looked out across the lakes. "I count 69, how about you?" I asked.

"Do you think we could sneak on them?" Bart asked. He was hunkered down near the corner of the cabin.

"I've noticed one thing about those geese, Bart. All this week they've been flying toward the river in the morning. Why don't you sneak around the lower lake and hide down in those red willows next to the river? When you get down there, give me a wave. I'll go get Web and we will try to flush them over you."

Bart took off. I love these plans. Some work, some don't, but it's great fun to try to outsmart waterfowl. I watched until I saw him drop down off the hill at the lower end of the lakes and disappear into the dense willows at the river's edge.

Web was still sleeping in my bedroom when I stuck my head through the door and hollered for his help. We snuck around the end of the cabin. The geese were still there. The lakes were only about half open water. The ice had crept to the warm springs that fed the system.

I decided to send Web to the far side so when the geese jumped, chances were good at least some of them would fly over Bart. Web dashed to the far side of the lake and sprinted down a long dike. He slid across a few feet of thin ice before he reached the open water and started stroking toward the resting geese.

Geese aren't all that afraid of dogs. They honked and cackled, but weren't impressed enough to try to escape. While their attention was fixed on Web, I hustled around the lake and stood up on the dike. They were all eyes now, their necks started to get longer and they quickened their calls. They were ready to go. I waved my arms and the geese splashed into the air.

It was working. They were flying low and they were flying right at Bart.

I saw the geese dodging and separating long before I heard the gunshots. One big gander twisted and tumbled from the flight. I could tell, even from a distance, he was still alive. I lost sight of him as he fell beyond the old cottonwood trees that define an oxbow of the Roaring Fork River.

I called Web, "Bart's going to need some help over there."

He scrambled out of the lake and ran with me as we looped over past the cabin and climbed a hill so we could get a better look toward the river.

From our vantage point we could see Bart looking out in the river and we saw him shoot again. I saw the goose. It was wounded, but held its head up as it entered a strong riffle and bobbed into the main river channel.

We would have never made the river in time to drag the goose out before he made the next bend. Instead, we moved to where we could see the river as it bent to the north, hoping to get a glimpse of the goose.

I saw him again, still well out in the river as he went around the far corner and past a small island. His neck was low in the water and it looked like he was swimming toward the far bank.

Geese will do that when they are hurt badly. They will lay their neck and head out along the water and try to slip out on the bank to hide. When they hold still among the rocks of a riverbank they are just about impossible to see.

I could no longer see the goose. I saw Bart making his way back to me. He probably figured the bird was lost, and it may well have been if I didn't have one of the baddest bird dogs in the history of the game.

"I guess we're going to have to try it from here, Web. I'll never be able to see you out there if I get down by the river."

I lined him up so he would hit the river well upstream and sent him on. We were standing on top of a bank covered with thick brush and vines. The first 50 feet or so was nearly straight down. At the bottom he had to swim across a spring creek and climb over the containment dike of the lower lake. He crossed the dike and jumped into the last remaining open water on his way to the river.

I wondered if we might have bit off more than either of us could handle as I watched him struggle onto the ice shelf at the other side of the pond and streak into the willows. I lost him for a short while until he reached the river's edge. I was ready to handle him back but he crashed into the water and leaned toward the far shore.

Ice floes pushed their way past him as he adjusted and re-adjusted his course until he felt the bottom and lunged out of the water. He was well down the river from our intended line. I stopped him. He looked for me but couldn't see me at first, partly because I was up on that hill, and partly because I was so far away.

I had two choices here. I could send him down river and hope he would hunt it up after he rounded the bend, or I could try to handle him across an old hay field to intersect the river where I judged the goose to have landed.

I sent him over to regain our original line. I felt the field was the better way to go because I could see him most of the time and probably could handle him. I stopped him once more and sent him back with all I had. He was getting near the point where I questioned his ability to hear my whistle. Three-quarters of the way across the field I had to cast him back again. He finally disappeared into the trees and brush near the river.

Bart and I stood there. I held my worthless whistle just on the edge of my lower lip. We both stared out into the mist.

I've led a great life. I am married to the only girl who could ever put up with me and I adore her beyond words. I was present when each of my four children were born and even delivered my oldest daughter. I have lived and worked within the splendor of the Rocky Mountains all my life but never have I experienced a feeling quite like the one I felt when I first saw a dark image emerging from the woods that morning, carrying a goose.

Most wonderful moments in life are just that: moments. They are here to enjoy but ever so briefly. This moment I could savor. I don't know how far Web had to go for this blind but I guessed it to be in excess of half a mile.

I watched him come back across the field and the river. I could have gone down and met him at the river's edge, but that would have cheated him. He was coming back to me and I was going to wait right there until he handed me the goose.

He pushed the goose across the lake like a down pillow. I often wonder if he knows how much I respect and admire him. He climbed up the hill, and we made eye contact as he jogged the last few feet.

"I'll never forget what I just saw," Bart said in a low tone.

I reached down and touched Web between his eyes and as he looked up at me, I said "You're the greatest, buddy. You'll always be the greatest."

Web didn't get to see the goose fall into the river. He heard gunshots and knew we were into something wild. He gladly ran to the top of the hill with me but as I was frantically scanning the waves for a wounded bird, he was concentrating on all the ducks who were cruising the river.

Birds were flying, Bart was walking along the river, Bart and I were talking back and forth as we tried to keep track of the goose.

All of these factors complicated what was already a major-league blind. This wasn't the controlled environment of a field trial. I didn't actually know if the goose came all the way to the bank or not. He might have kicked back into the current and headed for Mexico.

Web had to deal with a steep slope, a frozen lake, shelf ice and the Roaring Fork River. He had to drive off the river and cross the field before again entering the brush line of the river bank. When he got out to where I lost sight of him, he had to work the rest out on his own.

Granted, this kind of blind doesn't come along every day, but it did that day and Web made it look routine. Why? Because of attention to detail! Because of the Baseball Drill and Walking Baseball. Because of the lining drills and the Looking Glass. Because I took the time to make sure the stops were quick and the casts precise. Because I taught him to keep going, keep trusting.

If you want your dog to pick up the tough ones, you have to train him to go deep. Do yourself a favor, be picky. Ask him to do it right. We didn't come all this way to compromise the integrity of our pyramid when we're so near the peak. That's about like setting out to climb a mountain, and after three years of struggle, calling it good when the summit is in view.

Success: Danny Watson and hunters

Chapter Fifteen:
Dancing Labradors

*A*s in every journey, one must keep in mind the place where he started. Think back to the day you and I started our trek together. Remember how worried you were about picking the right dog? Remember how you hoped you could do it yourself?

Somewhere along the way you have realized that the true glory of hunting is the pursuit. Pointer men have known for a long time that the wonder of shooting dogs lies in the race, application of hundreds of years of inherited skills, and the eventual location of game.

The Labs have long been picking up after the party. They have been on the maintenance staff, wearing coveralls and cleaning up after the gala was over. They saw that the ball was wonderful, they could hear the orchestra, and they watched the dancing. They weren't invited or included on the guest list. They were on hand to clean up and make everything glisten again.

When the first retriever men were brought to America to handle large wing shoots for the wealthy, they were treated the same way. They had to eat in the kitchen, or beyond, while the elite stuffed themselves and toasted each other. The handlers were only brought out to work the dogs and make the owners look good. You see, the retriever movement was fatally flawed from the get-go.

Still, today on some ranches, the dog handlers eat lunch by themselves or with the house staff. To tell you the truth, I always kind of liked it. I loved to sit with my chair turned around backward as the cooks and I sopped up the leftover gravy with homemade tortillas. Sometimes I couldn't understand the lingo, but I always understood the laughter.

Dear Sir:

Please consider this your formal invitation to the Labrador shooting dog coming-out festival. Wear something comfortable, and, oh yes, bring your dancing shoes because we're going to cut a rug. We're going to provide our own music, we're going to dance into the night and we will still do the picking up.

Labradors are some of the most intelligent of the sporting dogs and I can prove it.

Labradors have some of the best bird-finding talent in the gun dog world and I can prove it.

Labradors have some of the best noses in the gun dog world and I can prove it.

Labradors can run a shooting dog race, find the birds, put them before the gun, mark the falls, retrieve, hunt dead, and do it all with style without any verbal, whistle, or hand commands and I can prove it.

Do you know how I can say this? Because I tested. I ran Labs, goldens, chessies, pointing dogs and spaniels. I ran 'em on birds and I was the judge. I ran 'em together so I could see who made it happen and who was along for the ride. I ran 'em in the morning, in the afternoon, in the rain, the heat, and in the snow. I ran 'em in the woods and lowlands. I ran 'em on the prairie and along the Continental Divide. I watched 'em swim for miles as I studied and learned.

I got up early and stayed late, then got up and did it again the next day. I did it the next week, the next month, and the next year.

I wasn't alone out there. Many training friends and clients saw the results for themselves. Ask any one of them which breed was the most productive. Ask any one of them which dogs put the majority of the birds in the air. The Labs did it, almost every time.

Take it or leave it, I don't really care. I don't care what the standards say. I don't care how a trial committee sets up or why. What I have seen is an honest-to-goodness field trial, my friend, and the Labs won it. I'm just giving credit where credit is due.

Come on out of the haze, but before you do, you had better take a little slack out of those laces in your dancing shoes. You might check to make sure your clothes won't pick up stick-tights or burrs. I hope you don't mind getting those shoes wet.

Let's start enjoying some of the success you've worked so hard for. Get out there and suit yourself, make yourself happy and don't worry about what the folks in the white jackets think.

I'm going to talk some about field work and how you can combine the various skills to help you accomplish your goals. I will try to outline some pertinent values as we take to the hunting fields.

Always establish control before and after the hunt!

Learn to lean on your structure. When you feel the wheels are coming off, go back to your structure. When you feel the fire coming up in your stomach, don't fight fire with fire, fight it with structure.

Boy, I'll bet you're getting pretty tired of me telling you to remember to do obedience before and after your sessions. I'll bet you quit doing that a long time ago. I'm going to give you a few examples of how this practice will serve you well throughout the life of your dog.

It sounds so simple: "Just do a few minutes of obedience before and after your workout."

How can that help me all that much when I'm working on advanced field and handling skills? Isn't this going a little far? You've only read this about 18 times in this book.

A while back I trained one of our Lab puppies for a friend of mine. She was a barn burner!

What a dog! She was born pretty and got better every day. Her name was Powell, after the lake. She belonged to Doug Boyles, a serious hunter who hadn't had any prior experience with Labs. He owned one setter when he bought Powell and loved the setter's specific style of hunting.

Powell broke every accepted rule for a flushing dog. She was a splendid athlete and one of the quickest females I've ever worked with. Powell was bird crazy, and because of her speed, she could be beyond gun range in a split second. Such a beautiful dog to watch. Man, could she run. She had as good a build as any female I've ever seen, so she could sustain her race with the best of them.

While all of these traits were good, it concerned Doug because he wanted to shoot some of those birds she was flushing and he wasn't getting the chance.

Powell was young and a little bit of a rebel, so she kept at it, flying after her birds while Doug growled and wished he would have bought another setter.

Doug lived just up the road from me so we got the opportunity to talk about his dog quite a lot. She was brought to me for starting when she was a year old. I did her formal obedience and worked on her retrieving some before Doug took her home the first time. I stressed the need to get a handle on her before cutting her loose, but somehow I failed to convince Doug of the importance of it.

Her first hunts were disasters, for the most part, with an occasional flash of brilliance mixed in (just enough to keep her from getting killed).

One day Doug brought her down, clearly frustrated with his dog. "I know you can control her on lead, or here in the training field, Mike, but there is no way God himself could get her attention when she flushes a bird."

"Why don't you leave her with me today, Doug? I'd like you to come down to the kennel tomorrow evening after work, and bring your wife."

Sure enough, Doug and Joan showed up the next day. I asked them to meet Powell and me up at the bird pen. I also asked them not to say or do anything to distract her. I wanted them to simply observe the experiment.

I slipped my waist cord on Powell and headed for the bird pen. I guess it was about half a mile up there, so I had a nice chance to work on her obedience along the way. I'm not talking beating and shocking here, just good, sharp obedience.

When I reached the pen, I asked the Boyles to stay outside

while I unlatched the door and took Powell inside. Doug was laughing, "You better not let her off that lead, Gould."

I walked Powell to the center of a 50x50 square pen where I was keeping about 250 pheasant. I told her to stay as I slipped the waist cord off of her neck. She was staring at me, hardly even noticing the pheasants, who were by now hugging the outside edge of the pen. I walked around the pen until the pheasants started running and flushing. Powell sat right there with 250 pheasants flying in front of and behind her, some within a few feet. The biggest reaction I saw from her was when she spun around as one rooster nearly hit her in the back.

I walked back to Powell and told her to heel. We walked toward the gate together and just before we went outside, I put my cord back on her. We finished under control, then I turned her loose to run.

"I never would've believed that if I hadn't seen it," Doug said. "She didn't even look at those birds."

"Structure," I replied. "She will mind you, too, as soon as you get your structure worked out."

A year later Doug returned from a pheasant hunt out in Kansas and he dropped by the house.

"She's still pretty wild. We were out there with a bunch of guys and some other dogs and she outran them all," Doug said.

"How many birds did you get?" I asked.

"We did really good this year, that CRP program has done a lot to improve the pheasant habitat and we saw a few quail also."

"You say Powell was running pretty big, huh?"

"Yeah, but if it weren't for her, we wouldn't have ended up with anywhere near the birds we did. She produced most of them."

That didn't surprise me much. She was a great athlete with a build that allowed her to stretch it out, a more experienced nose, and a handler who has the wisdom to let her run. How could she fail?

One client of mine skidded up to the kennel one day to complain how he couldn't control his dog while hunting.

"You got your dog with you?" I asked.

"Sure I do," he fired back, "I'd like to see you keep her close enough to hunt over."

His dog blasted out of his pickup and started screaming around the kennel buildings. On the second pass, I flipped a loop out in front of her and brought her to heel. I had done her formal obedience a year or so before and I really liked this dog.

"Let's go," I said. "Grab that shotgun laying over on the force table, will you?"

As we walked toward the riverbottom, I worked on the dog's obedience. She was rough for the first little while, but sure enough, by the time we circled the lakes she was tuning in.

I turned to the owner and asked him if he would do me a favor.

"Would you please put your whistle in your pocket and I wish you wouldn't say anything to her, either, while she's hunting."

"No problem, she wouldn't mind me anyway."

I told the dog to stay as I slipped the waist cord off, and let her sit there for a while. I saw her face and I studied her as she looked up at me. She was no renegade, she was a bird dog and this guy was so caught up in his own criteria for her to work within 20 yards that he was blinded to her enormous talent.

I cast her into the wind and she dashed to the front.

"Just do what I do," I told him as I gently pulled her from side to side. She tore up that riverbottom and the flabbergasted dog owner managed to scratch down three of the five roosters she sailed past him in a short half an hour. I didn't use my whistle during the hunt. The only thing I said to her was to compliment her on a retrieve or particularly pretty cast.

The guy was a jerk. He left upset because he missed two easy birds. By the way, he missed both of them twice!

The poor dog was, unfortunately, stuck with a stiff.

I've included these two examples for a very good reason. The one biggest complaint a flushing dog trainer hears is: "My dog flushes the birds too far out in front, how can I get my dog to hunt closer?"

Second place goes to: "How can I keep my dog from chasing

after birds, like hen pheasants, or birds I've missed? He will run clear out of the country on me if he sees a bird fly."

Hunting closer is not the answer! Hunting smarter is.

If you explain these faults to most trainers and ask them to help you with it, out will come the electricity and the shot pistols. "I'll stop that son-of-a-bitch from chasing. He'll think twice before he chases another bird."

I have seen too many dogs who endured amazing pressure for their one great sin: "Birdiness."

Yes, you can stop your dog from chasing a bird with an electric collar. Yes, you can take him down a notch or two, you can take some of the steam out of him. You can flirt with disaster and crush his desire to chase while he's intoxicated with his game. You can show him who's boss and shoot him in the butt with a shotgun or a shot pistol. That'll teach him.

There is one more thing you could try.

Go back to your structure and fix the problem. Remember, when we were talking about the bricks of our pyramid and I asked you to always be willing to go back to the fundamental that deals with the problem and fix it there. Get out your trowel and mix some mortar. It's like a recipe. You have to keep your confidence, so throw in plenty of it as you add obedience and practice with your steadiness.

Show him what you want and then let him show you he understands. Put a brick in and make it stick. Break it down into increments of ingredients. When you see some success, try to show him some birds again and expect the best from him. Anytime you feel you cannot control your dog, I call this "Coming off the hook." He's not being hard to deal with—he's off the hook. All you need to do is put him back on the hook. Don't shock him or shoot him. Bring him to heel and do a little obedience.

Now cast him off. When he is 30 yards out, say his name firmly. If he looks at you, call him to heel and he will attend. If he doesn't look at you, that tells you that you didn't do enough obedience. Get him back as quickly as you can and give him a couple more minutes of good obedience on your waist cord.

Now, cast him off again, and again call his name when he is

about 30 yards out. Did he look this time? I'll bet he did, but if he didn't, go through the sequence again.

Do you want to know why this works? Because you have influenced him back and forth, in and out ever since he was a kid. You have called him to you on group walks and asked him to sit by you when he was full of energy and excitement. You weren't mad, you just wanted him to sit by you for a while. After a short wait, you let him fly again and he learned that your controls weren't cramping his style. You steadied him on marks and you adjusted his brakes with his handling practice. You demonstrated at the force table how you cared enough to make him do it right every time. You never disciplined him unfairly, you gave him someone to trust and believe in. You now are telling him that you don't want him to chase wildly and he says OK.

When you handle your training problems with this mindset, you are building your dog, not breaking him. Any fool can go for his gun in the heat of the battle. The smart guy prefers to end the conflict by fixing the problem instead of winning a single gunfight.

OK, what if you are lucky enough to own a dog who likes to run the big race. Yes, I truly consider you lucky because you can take a little of that out if you want, but you'll never put any in.

Let's say your dog wants to fly and he has the wheels to get it done. You can be more of a help to your dog by trying to hold up your end of the bargain instead of standing around ordering him over, or in, or out, or heel, or whatever.

I hope we have established some facts since we got together: Number one, you can only hit a few birds he finds anyway. Number two, he was born with more knowledge of the natural world than you will die with. Number three, he's a pro. The birds hold all the secrets and he knows how to break the code.

Get on board here, play your position. Don't complain about the other players on the team. Get it together. Instead of putting the hard eye on his performance, put your energy into making sure you don't blow it. When the birds come up, they are going somewhere. Be there. Sound strange? Come with me as we go grouse hunting again to illustrate my point.

One fall I was training along the rim of the Deep Creek Canyon with training friends Butch Goodwin and Terry Hayes. Butch runs Chesapeakes and Terry was working a yellow Lab. We were accompanied by some of the best clients I ever knew. Loy and Virginia Waddell were visiting and Loy brought his dad along.

These are the good kind of clients who end up being very close friends in the process. The Waddells have bought a couple of dogs through us and I trained for them for quite some time. They were life members at Upland Mesa Wildlife Park and enjoyed fly fishing as well as the wing sports.

Loy brought his young yellow Labrador, Cosmo, to get some practical experience with grouse. He was really coming on, all he needed was some quality bird contact.

Grouse can be tricky to get the hang of. It's always best if a guy can use an experienced dog to give the younger dogs a good look at the way it's supposed to be done. Hound men use this system to perfection. They run the young dogs with old cagey veterans until they know their way with track, trail, and tree.

We were running Cosmo with Web along the bottom of one of the greatest grouse hunting parks I've ever known. This park lazily slipped into the canyon occasionally as it swept along the granite cliffs overlooking Deep Creek.

Each time the park would dip into the canyon, a small patch of quakies would come up to meet it. The quakies would extend into the park for a short distance, giving the grouse perfect coordinates for an escape from any pressure. The grouse have been using those escape routes forever, I guess. I know they have for my lifetime.

Loy, Virginia and I were walking near the rim as we discussed the dogs and admired the early morning. Cosmo and Web were hunting far up the hill, concerned with the interior of the park.

"How does this work?" Loy asked.

"Well, when the grouse are flushed, they will seek their normal escape. If they are pushed wide for some reason, they will still usually correct their course so they hit the rim at the same place each time. They don't vary too much, I guess they figure the plan has worked for generations before them, so why change it.

"Take this little quakie thicket we're coming to, for instance.

This is the primary escape route for birds coming off this side of the park."

We weren't hunting, we were just having some fun as we worked dogs. We stopped in the shade of the quakie trees and watched the dogs as they cut up the park a couple hundred yards above us. Butch and Terry were working the top of the park with their dogs.

Cos and Web started getting birdy, and before long one single blue grouse flushed and flew directly toward us. Maybe we were concealed by the shade or maybe he hadn't got the bugs quite worked out of his flight gear, I don't know.

He was coming right for us about five feet off the ground. We all stood motionless as this daredevil grouse bore down on us.

He might have been a grouse playing chicken, who knows? He might of thought we would hit the dirt at the last minute so he could cruise into the trees and laugh himself to sleep.

We'll never know what he thought, but I caught him just like a football. He didn't even wiggle. It felt like a hot pass from John Elway. We checked his age and decided he was a sixteen-week-old cock blue grouse. We laughed and bid him well as I threw him back into the air.

"How many times have you done that?" Loy grinned.

"I've foul-tipped a few, but that's the first one I actually caught. My brother-in-law hit one with his hat one afternoon, but this was tops."

If we had been worried about the dog's range, and were handling them all over the place, we probably would have missed the most astonishing event I've seen while training dogs.

If you get a chance to see a covey of birds settle into cover, you can come up with a plan to pinch them or flush them overhead. If you see a rooster pheasant drop into a drainage ditch, you can use your blind handling skills to collect him. If you sneak down to the riverbank to see a bunch of mallards huddled in a spring creek back eddy, you can leave your dog there while you try to get around them. If you see upland birds running, streaking toward escape cover, have fun with it. Don't put your dog out and quarter him 20 yards in front of you in hopes of getting anywhere near those birds.

Dogs love this stuff. I have seen them crawl up to a slough, crash into briars, and hit wire fences so hard I could hear staples squeak for a hundred yards. Some plans don't work. Sometimes it's your fault, sometimes it's the dog's fault. Who cares?

We're not playing by any rules here. We're just having fun hunting. I thought that was the reason we came out, to enjoy our friends and boost some birds. It's just bird hunting, folks. It's just bird hunting.

Don't worry about his range when he's hunting uphill. Think about that for a minute. If your dog is driving up the hill, let him go as far as he wants. Chances are pretty good the birds will come down off there when they flush. I like to teach my dogs to drive uphill and loop out to the front. Once you get him interested in going up, don't check him at all. Let him go. Some of the sportiest shooting you can get is when you're confronted with slopes and birds.

Sure I catch some flak about my philosophy on running flushing dogs. I have been asked, "What good does it do for your dog to be flushing birds out of gun range? Why do you let your dogs run so big?"

Simple. I love to shoot at birds as they fly toward me. I have found if you let your dog roll a little, many of your shots will be closing shots rather than going-away shots. There's not a finer wing shot, in my opinion, than pheasant streaming over your head. Why do you think all those rich Americans travel to Europe to shoot driven birds? I could never afford the England trip, so I taught my dogs to drive birds to me.

I will concede one thing: you can't just stumble along through the fields whistling and hollering at your dog. You can't go about bird hunting with the same old plan. You have to be willing to try something new and possibly fail. You will definitely fail, on many occasions, to bring the bird into gun range.

I hope you're not going to tell me that never happened before. I hope you aren't so far gone that you really believe you were more productive before.

Have you ever considered hunting your Labrador shooting dog off horseback? You thought I forgot about that, didn't you? Way back in the front of the book I told you how productive it could be and I meant it. Obviously you probably wouldn't hunt all species of birds from a horse, but you can hunt partridge, grouse, and quail very successfully while riding.

It's really quite simple. It's no different than running pointers off horseback. Once your dog will sit reliably to your whistle, you can stop him as soon as he makes game, dismount, walk within shooting range and cast him in.

Sure, go ahead and laugh. Come to think of it, that's a good one all right. I can just imagine how the field trial judges would try to simulate that one. Probably every handler would have to ride the same horse so all of the tests would be equal. Why do you think I waited until the last of the book before I told you about it? You would have thrown the book in the fire for sure. There's only one thing better than spending a day afield with a dog and that's spending one with a dog and a horse. Go on, give it a try.

Chapter Sixteen:
Holding Up Your End of the Stick

W e have spent a great deal of time together discussing the dogs and training. We have talked some of habitat and natural controls. We have continually graded our dogs' performance and tried to structure him to be the best he could be.

We have not, however, adequately analyzed the other important position on our team, the hunter. In my experience, men are very hard to talk to regarding their gun handling and safety practices. I know it is common thinking to consider most hunters as passively safe and knowledgeable about firearms. The National Rifle Association cries out, "It's just a few bad apples out there who are ruining it for all hunters."

Folks, we are on the verge of losing our hunting privileges. As sportsmen, we have to initiate more educational opportunities for the general public. The vast majority (about 88 percent) are not anti-hunting, they are simply non-hunters.

I believe the assumption that "most hunters are pretty safe," is an unreal misunderstanding of the true situation. When you expose yourself to literally thousands of hunters, as I have, you get educated quickly. Most shooters are not entirely safe and many are outright dangerous. We need to seriously upgrade our hunter safety and sportsmen etiquette programs if we are to have a chance in preserving our sport for the future.

You don't believe me?

Consider this: I know many dog handlers who regularly guide bird hunts for the public. I don't know one who hasn't been shot or at least stung while guiding. It's hard to find one who has only been shot once.

I have one friend who has been shot twice by the same guy. Another took a whole load while still in the vehicle. I've seen quail guides get their hat blown off from the rear and numerous close calls where the shooters never did realize the near tragedy.

A handler has a unique vantage point while guiding. He sees the action from a ringside seat, hopefully from behind the hunters. It can get pretty chilling and re-defines the term preparation, or self-defense. The hunters calmly go from one covey to the next without even knowing what almost happened.

Everyone knows at least one person who has been stung by stray pellets while blocking for pheasant hunters.

I remember one pheasant hunt I was guiding for a bunch of businessmen. We had been in the thick of it for a few minutes and I was trying to get a couple of downed birds picked up before we went on. I was behind the group, working a dog into some cover where I thought the last bird had fallen. I heard a pheasant flush between me and the hunters. I looked their way in time to see all the guns come up so I spun to the ground and turned my back to them in the same motion. I heard five shots before a dead pheasant hit me in the middle of the back. I was still resting on my knees as I reached around, picked the bird up and stowed it in my game vest.

Unusual? I wish! There is very little a guide can do in a spot like I was in. You can scream, you can cuss, you can throw a fit, but the fact is the hunters were unsafe and they will continue to be until they get educated.

I've noticed if you ask a man if he is familiar with a particular gun, he will automatically say, "Yes." Even if he had never laid eyes on a gun like this he will usually claim he had. If you ask him in front of his cronies it will galvanize the problem. A man will never admit to being ignorant about such a macho thing as hunting while in the company of his peers, especially if they work together.

Hand this guy a shotgun and keep an eye on him for a time. He will tell you of his experience without even knowing it. When

I see the need, I will generally sidle up to him while he is walking so we can talk about proper gun-handling safety. No sense in embarrassing him anymore than he already is, and he will thank you for it by paying closer attention.

The corporate executive is the worst of these offenders. This is a person who is used to making decisions. He can hire and fire, he can make people's lives miserable under the heading of doing a good job. He doesn't need advice, he doesn't need help with anything. What makes matters worse is that often times this problem child is the leader of hunting party. For him to admit to being ignorant about firearms is beyond our expectations. I think it's the feeling of being informed somewhat about everything. Corporate executives are used to being self-imposed experts on everything.

For eight years I worked on the Upland Wildlife Park project in Western Colorado. The park laid along the Roaring Fork River, a gold medal trout stream. The Fork and the nearby Frying Pan are favorites of fly fishermen from around the world. The Crystal River came into the Roaring Fork at the upstream boundary of Upland Mesa.

One day the Chief Executive Officer of Unocal, who just happened to own the property the project was based on, reserved a fishing date on the river.

We planned to show him a great time, so we booked the best fishing guide we knew of. We provided for top-quality equipment and supplies. We arranged for a wonderful lunch catered by a local favorite. We were all available to help make his trip the most memorable ever.

This guy got out of a rental car with the look of a man of wisdom and understanding. I greeted him and excitedly told him of our preparations on his behalf. It was important to us that he have a good time.

"I've been fishing all my life and I won't need any assistance," he announced.

"We would sure like to help in any way we could," I said, trying to soften him up.

"Look, I said I don't need any help," the man bristled.

He walked around the car and started dragging fishing gear out of the trunk. It was clear that all of the gear was borrowed and unfamiliar to him and he proudly showed us his fly box. It was a starter's box containing some common dry-fly patterns they sell down at the Wal-mart store.

An experienced fly fisherman wouldn't even let another fisherman see it, much less show it off.

"You are welcome to fish alone if that's what you want, but we are all here if there is anything we can do for you."

He said he wouldn't be eating lunch with us—you know, an important meeting with the mayor and all. He only had a few hours to fish.

He reached out and let his hand drop on my shoulder, squeezed a little and said, "There is one thing you could get me."

"Name it," I said, no longer trying to conceal feelings of disgust.

"I could use some waders."

I turned around and walked into the cabin to pick out some chest waders for his highness. I brought them out to him and again politely asked if there was anything else. He didn't answer me, he just looked my way for a moment and then went back to what he was doing.

This man, this CEO, this man of obvious power and influence, this man who needed no help, this man who had been fishing all of his life put my waders on inside out and backwards and stood out in the Roaring Fork River for two hours for all the world to see.

Several guides stopped by to ask who the dork was flailing the water without a clue. One even beached his dory boat to openly wonder, "Who dressed that guy?"

I proudly declared to all who inquired, "He is the CEO of Union Oil of California and he's been fishing all his life. He doesn't need any help."

This poor fellow was bound up with self-inflated pride. He couldn't say thank you for thinking of him because he considered that a weakness. He didn't feel a fish on his slack line that afternoon and he drove away with the words, "and they call that a gold medal river," fading with the dust. He didn't present much of a danger to anyone other than himself with a fly rod, but put a shotgun in his hands and you have the potential for disaster.

Oddly, women and youngsters are not likely to lie about their experience. Women who are unfamiliar with firearms will blurt out their concerns without prompting. Sometimes they require several run-throughs to finally feel comfortable enough to carry the gun, much less load it. I think women are also less likely to shoot until they've relieved their fears. I have seen many who didn't shoot at all for the first hunt. I always tell them how I respect this attitude and I would lots rather see them hold back instead of just wading in like a man would do.

Sometimes a woman is intimidated into unsafe practice by her male escort. I had to completely stop one pheasant hunt until I convinced a very affluent, experienced man that I would not allow him or his new wife to release the safety in anticipation of the flush.

We were hunting with a pointing dog and he ordered her to take her safety off while still some 50 yards distant from where the dog was pointing. I repeatedly reminded him of the severity of this habit. I explained how easily an accident could occur while walking with a loaded gun off safe.

I asked to hold her gun for a minute as I demonstrated how to release the safety as part of the mounting process. The man turned away while I was talking to his wife and pretended to be interested in other things even though I was doing it more for his benefit than hers.

In a short time the dog was pointing again. We changed directions to walk to the dog. He said in a very firm tone, "Take your safety off now, Joan." She didn't feel right in doing so, but she complied because she was afraid of upsetting her husband. When I heard both safeties click, I stopped the hunt right there.

This man was a very successful businessman who had shot at some of the most prestigious hunting estates in America. He was a member of a fine hunting club on New York's Long Island. I guessed him to be about 65 years old, long beyond being flexible.

We learn these skills from the person we hunt with first. We teach these skills to those who hunt with us first.

Talk to any bird-hunting guide you choose and I'll bet he has his own version of hunting horror stories. I know most hunters think I'm talking about other shooters, certainly not them. Not true. I've seen sudden gun handling miscues from some of the surest hands around. I continually work to improve my overall gun handling, but still occasionally see the opportunity for accident. Finished gun safety skills are never acquired. We all have to check, recheck, and recheck our habits.

I'll bet you think I'm exaggerating some, but I'm not kidding. If you saw, first hand, the average gun handling skills of shotgun shooters, you would shudder.

I've lost substantial hearing in my left ear and some of my right because I exposed my ears to gun blasts for most of my life. Young people don't think about long-term damage—it's permanent! I take care of my hearing these days and even with my loss I can hear a safety come off from 50 yards. Stay awake out there. Protect yourself and become informed.

The saying, "Guns don't kill people, people kill people," is wrong. Guns definitely kill people, and ignorance of proper gun safety kills more people than anything else.

I used to be pretty passive about hard-core safety. I didn't want to get on the shooters too much. I would single out someone who was trouble and stick to them like their sunscreen. I was never caught out of position when the birds jumped into the air. I was diplomatic and low-key as I tried to focus on key elements of safety. I cared about "not hurting people's feelings" or "embarrassing them in front of their friends."

I genuinely wanted them to enjoy the hunt without a lot of negative connotation about safety—that is, until one day I felt the heat from the fire I had been playing with.

While guiding a quail hunt in south Texas I went to the front momentarily to water a dog. I heard a late-rising quail buzz to my left. I instinctively turned to look and what I saw nearly stopped my heart. A shooter was swinging on the quail, concentrating only on the shot. I was looking right at him when he shot.

I saw the puff of smoke as the charge left the barrel. I was jolted backward by what felt like most of the some 500 pellets in a load of 7½'s.

I was lucky for two reasons: One, it was cold and I was wearing two polar-fleece jackets, my snake boots, and my normal working chaps. Secondly, all of the pellets hit me from the neck down. Three of them hit me in the neck about at the Adam's apple. Damn, that hurt.

I quickly assessed the damage.

"I'm all right," I kept thinking to myself. The three that hit me in the neck were the only ones to keep hurting once all those "bee stings" calmed down. Those three glanced off the right side of my neck instead of penetrating and left long, red marks.

As I was rubbing my neck, I looked back toward the shooter. He was hurt worse than I was by the uncertainty of the situation. He asked if I was OK, his voice cracked and wavered.

I'll never forget the look on his face. He was so scared, I felt bad for him.

"I'm OK, Gene," I responded with my best brave tone. Everyone let out the breath they had been holding and rushed over to where I was standing. There wasn't much to say, we had all learned the lesson at hand. I guided the group for the rest of that day and the next. The lingering thoughts of what nearly happened kept us all uneasy.

I always wear eye protection in the field, always. I wear sunglasses or shooting glasses anytime I am guiding or hunting, but the day I got shot was unique.

I had lost my shooting glasses just before dark the previous day, and because I had to get up at 5 a.m. the next morning, I hadn't yet replaced them. For the first time in years, I wasn't wearing eye protection when I saw that gun go off. Lucky? Naw, we're talking the grace of God here.

The accident happened on my last hunt of the winter. I had a 19-hour drive home to think about my approach to safety. I still felt bad for Gene, and reasoned I was out of position and got caught. Even after I explained to my family that everything was OK, I felt bad for him.

Almost a year later, when I arrived back at the camp to guide some hunts, I learned I was to help with a special bank hunt the next morning. This bank is very influential in that part of the country. They host hunters in an effort to say thank you to significant clientele. The hunt I was to take was celebrating a beer distribution company. We started at sunrise and the hunters started drinking the namesake beer shortly afterward.

Less than an hour into the hunt, I was nearly shot off the dog truck by the leader of the group, the boss. He was already getting drunk. I was standing on the tailgate of the hunt truck. This was out-and-out stupidity. The bank representative said nothing, the hunters said nothing, not even the one who shot at me.

In this day and age of the lawyer and liability lawsuits, I can't imagine an institution like a bank who would knowingly encourage drinking and shooting on a hunt they outfitted. I'll never know how that shot charge missed me, but this one affected me much more than the first.

I'm not diplomatic anymore and you shouldn't be either. There are plenty of hunters out there who are just plain idiots. They need told in no uncertain terms of the danger they represent. They are not just bad apples. They are bad news for all hunters.

Whether you are in a duck blind, walking the fields, or blocking for pheasants, protect yourself. Arm yourself with good hunting and shooting skills. Any hunter education course is good. Seek out professional instructors for your family and yourself.

We have spent all this time developing a first-class shooting dog. Don't expose him to unsafe hunters and dangerous scenarios. I haven't told you of stories dogs getting shot, even though it happens frequently.

How do we learn gun safety? Where can we go? Who can we call? How can we upgrade our present skills while we give our kids the benefit of a good program? Let's think about these questions as we relate them to our goal here. We're trying to do the best job we can. Let's not send our Labrador shooting dog out with hunting slobs.

We're trying to understand more about nature. We want to appreciate our environment more. We need our hunting habits to reflect a true desire to protect our privileges, and our quality of sport.

If a fellow hunter reminds you to open your gun or points to a safety problem that you may not have noticed, please resist the temptation to flare your nostrils and puff up. Tell him how much you appreciate his concern. We're all in this together.

Chapter Seventeen:
Living the Vision

*I*n the opening of this book I invited you to seek a vision. I challenged you to take your dog to the heights of the pyramid. I wanted so much to tell you of a place where few trainers have been. I am not only glad for you and your dog, I am happy for every dog you train for the rest of your life. I know you will never look at shooting dogs again through the same eyes.

I know you will wonder about natural controls and influences. You will consider your own life and wonder how far up the pyramid you have come. You will go to the river and look for the vision. When no one is watching you will feel for its heartbeat.

I have told you many stories about training and watching shooting dogs, but I know you have related them to your struggle.

I'm proud to have come from a country background where if a person wants to be treated like somebody, first he has to be somebody. A person isn't judged by what he says as much as what he does. I didn't decide to love the dogs, the dogs decided to love me. I didn't choose the mountains, the mountains chose me. I am so thankful for the trail I've walked and I hope some of it inspires others as well.

My dad was a dreamer. He, his brother, and a couple of friends drove an old stock truck to Alaska in the early forties. He always dreamed of going back. He lived for hunting big mule deer bucks and fly fishing for brown trout.

Because we were a ranching family, he perfected the fine art of poaching bucks—he always had a deer hanging somewhere.

He set up hunting camps and guided hunters long before we knew there was any money in it. Hunting camp was a labor of passion, for all of us. Oh, he did get paid, a Stetson hat or a down vest occasionally. Once, after his first heart attack, a Texan family who had been hunting with him for several years brought a new jeep with them so it would be easier for him to get around.

The guides were paid with thank-you's and pats on the back, sometimes kicks in the butt. For you see, the guides were my brothers and uncles and cousins.

Dad said to do it, so we did it.

They say the older a brown trout gets, the more nocturnal his feeding habits become. I don't know if that's true or not, but I do know you can catch them late at night by drifting big, wet flies in and out of the shadow of the moonlight.

Dad called them Lochs. He liked to catch any kind of fish, but the Lochs were special.

Even though fishing was illegal after 9 p.m., he stalked up and down Colorado's world famous Frying Pan River almost every night of each summer and fall. When I was a kid, the only way I could tell where my dad was, when he was fishing, was by the little red glow of his cigarette.

I learned to love the darkness and the uncertainty of fishing, or trying to fish where you couldn't see the riffle or pools. I perfected casting into the blackness, trusting my ears and the touch of the fly line to teach me the character of the river, believing the fly was always where I thought it was.

I would look up to the canyon rim and the stars beyond, because this told me where I was on the river. I was sometimes frightened until I finally saw Dad's cigarette or made out his silhouette in the darkness.

Still today, when I feel especially pressured about life, I look to the darkness. I still search for the canyon rim, the stars, and the burning ember.

We hadn't heard of insect repellent. He taught us to break off short pieces of wood vine and smoke it. We called it "Smoke

Weed." It kept the mosquitoes away most of the time. I can still remember the harsh smoke as it burned my throat and made me cough. Dad said to do it, so I did it.

We broke gobs of "pitch" (dried pine sap) off of trees as a substitute for chewing gum. You just scrape the pine needles and dust off, pop it in your mouth and start chewing. The first few minutes after you put it in your mouth it's awful. Gradually the bitterness dissipates and it ends up being pretty darn good gum. It took some practice before you could decide on a really good piece of pitch.

You had to be educated as to how dry was dry enough and how soft was soft enough. Some pitch was so bitter it would never come around. I learned not to waste time with a piece of it. Just throw it away and get another one.

Boy, that stuff can stick to your teeth. If I tried chewing pitch today, every filling I have would be rolled up in it within five minutes. Oh well, you have good teeth when you're a kid, and Dad said to do it, so I did it.

Somewhere around 1959, Dad decided to branch out into bird hunting. Jump shootin' ducks and cornfield pheasants naturally came first. He soon learned of a different kind of bird that hung out down in the canyons of Escalante and Dominguez. I can still remember asking him, "What do they look like, Dad?"

"Hell, I don't know," he said. "All I know is they're called chukars and there's s'post to be some down here somewhere."

After a half an hour of looking for a dead chukar on a canyon wall, I came to the realization that "Dogs are the only way to go." Oh, we had a dog along, half German shorthair and half something else. He was a pup and hadn't had any training or bird introduction. We got a couple of birds and left, like the Spaniards, victorious.

My life and destiny were forever cast.

Dad started building a pen out in back of the house, over by the horse pasture, using old posts and hog wire. "What the heck's he up to?" I thought.

We had an old family dog. He looked like all the rest of the dogs around there. You know, collie, shepherd, bulldog, farm dog, etc. He didn't need a pen, or a dog house for that matter. He had the run of the place.

I remember walking by the pen to get a bucket of coal and asking my dad, "What ya' building?"

"A daaa hennno," he said.

"What?"

He took 15 or 20 bent-up rusty nails out of his mouth and said, "A dog kennel."

"I thought that's what you said. Sounds good to me."

Later that week he put a young German shorthaired pointer in the kennel and wired a bucket to the fence. He came in the house and said to me, "Get out there and feed that dog."

Dad said to do it, and I've been doing it ever since.

I watched my dad die on the morning of Dec. 19, 1964, just after my 15th birthday. I've been keeping vigil over his dreams as well as his dog, and he was right, those chukars are really something.

My dad was always dreaming and wondering what was over the next hill, but the real strength and steel of our family was my mom. In 1964 she was forced to re-focus because me and my two sisters were still at home.

Mom was still a young woman when Dad died, but she had worked her whole adult life in an effort to take care of the family. She didn't have a trade or a career other than a starry-eyed husband and five kids. This was before the women's lib movement, when being a good mother was considered to be more important than being fashionable.

She went to work for a stockbroker even though the only real office skills she had were beautiful penmanship and a sharp mind. She worked until she understood the business and without the help of a high school or college degree, she passed the test and became a stockbroker herself. She finally graduated from high school when she was 67 years old, long after she had retired from her broker job.

My mom is the most decent person I've ever known. She

doesn't drink, she doesn't smoke, she doesn't cuss, and she loves her family. She taught me the value of staying in there when things get tough. She taught me to believe the best—always.

What does all this have to do with dogs? Maybe nothing...but then again...

I'm a child of the mountains, my dad inspired me to look beyond what is obvious. I was cursed by his propensity to wander and dream. I grew up learning to pay attention and to remember my lessons.

I learned from my mother to be dependable and honest. She was worthy of respect and honor. I learned to be respectful and honorable.

My dad taught me to build a fire and my mother taught me to withstand heat.

My dad allowed me to shoot a deer and cast a fly. My mother gave me cause to be satisfied with seeing the deer and admiring the rising trout.

My dad said, "He who perseveres is strong."
My mom says, "He who loves is all powerful."

When I am discouraged I am called back to the river to build the fire. As I sit by my fire I stare at excitement. I am aware of my problems as the fire lifts and illuminates them. The wind brings me the secrets of success and the rushing water soothes and heals my spirit.

My beloved friend Bill Tarrant reminds all of us, "Dogs have all the qualities God said men should have but don't: Faithfulness, steadfastness, dependability, loyalty, forgiveness, devotion, hope and love."

Reach high for your answers and be grateful they are there at your reach. Take your dog with you always, for I don't know anything that can beat a dog. I don't think anyone else does either.

Nice talking to you. I'll see you down the road!